THE **EDUCATIONAL MINISTRY OF THE CHU**RCH

THE EDUCATIONAL MINISTRY
OF THE CHURCH

A PERSPECTIVE

THE CRAIG PRESS

1968

To Marcia

THE AUTHOR

Mr. De Graaff is a man of three countries. He was born in 1933 in The Netherlands, where he received his early schooling. In the early 1950's he accompanied his family to western Canada, where he found employment in experimentation and banking. In 1953, after resettling in Michigan, De Graaff resumed his academic life at Calvin College, earning his AB degree in 1957. The next three years he pursued theology at Calvin Seminary, graduating with his BD degree in 1960.

Going full circle, De Graaff with his wife and family returned to his native country in 1960 to carry on his post-graduate studies at the Free Reformed University of Amsterdam. In his doctoral program he concentrated on pastoral care, catechetics, psychology, and philosophy. In 1966 he received his doctor's degree in theology, based upon this book, his doctoral dissertation, which was begun under the tutelage of Dr. J. H. Bavinck and completed under the sponsorship of Dr. J. T. Bakker.

Upon returning to the United States De Graaff began his teaching career at Trinity Christian College, near Chicago. There at present he is bringing his inter-disciplinary training in theology and psychology to bear upon his courses in Biblical Theology, Introduction to Psychology, and Developmental Psychology.

Along the way De Graaff has gained valuable practical experience as counsellor at a summer youth camp, as member of a Workshop in Catechetics, and as teacher in catechism classroom situations.

*"We will ... tell to the coming
generation the glorious deeds
of the Lord, and his might, and
the wonders which he has wrought.*

*He established a testimony in
Jacob, and appointed a law in
Israel, which he commanded our
fathers to teach to their children;*

*that the next generation might
know them, the children yet
unborn, and arise and tell them
to their children, so that they
should set their hope in God, and
not forget the works of God, but
keep his commandments; ..."*

Psalm 78

INTRODUCTION

As a tree is known by the fruit it bears, so an author is known by the books he writes. The book at hand is an excellent piece of work from the pen of a promising young scholar. I count it a great pleasure to introduce to the reading public both this book and the man who stands behind it — a personal friend, fellow Christian, and colleague in scholarship and teaching.

Education of all kinds is getting to be big business these days, almost everybody's business, it seems. Our contemporaries by the millions are staking their hopes for the survival of modern civilization on more and better education. Our feverish process of educational escalation is carrying the church along with it. Large claims are being made for "religious education" as a way of rescuing Christianity from oblivion and recapturing its relevance. The more "religious education" is dropped in our schools and fails to hold its own in our homes, the more urgently many people look to the church to fill the gaps.

The past couple of decades have witnessed a growing concern for the educational ministry of the church. Traditional methods of teaching are losing ground. Everything pedagogical is up for review. The church is finding it increasingly difficult to keep pace with our changing times. It feels the strong pressures of sharp competition from other educating agencies with their slick handbooks, programmed methods, streamlined curricula, computerized techniques, sophisticated equipment. Facing these pressures, the church often falls into the trap of uncritically imitating secular programs of education, taking over unthinkingly current trends in psychology and pedagogy, without trying seriously to develop an educational program uniquely suited to its Biblically prescribed mandate.

The book at hand can contribute significantly to setting the educational ministery of the church in clearer focus. The author makes a good case for greater clarity in defining the church's teaching task in serving the younger members of the congregation. His analysis also points the way toward a better division of labors among the various teaching centers in the Christian community. Only in this way can we ward off expansionistic tendencies by which the church is tempted, educationally speaking, to become all things Christian to all Christian men.

In broader context, the author breaks through the unrewarding polarities which have developed in European and American "religious education" by offering a more integrally unified Christian perspective on the educational ministry of the church. Taking its stand solidly within the Reformed Christian tradition, this book reminds us that we must seek our startingpoint in a renewed understanding of the calling of the church in promoting a full-orbed Christian life within the Christian community and in society at large. Only by reaching greater consensus on what the church is called to be can we arrive at greater clarity on what the church is called to do educationally. For its nurture must be expressive of its nature. A meaningful rethinking of the church's teaching mission can therefore be achieved only by faithfully applying the principle of sphere sovereignty to the life of the church, directed and illumined by the Word of God.

This timely book is more than a critique on current practices. It also offers promising guidelines for capitalizing on our present prospects for good teaching and on the pedagogical potentials at our disposal. The author makes no pretense to speaking the last word on the question at hand. The somewhat clipped ending leaves the impression of open-endedness and stands as an open invitation to further exploration. But the author lays good foundations. The direction is clear, and is certainly worth pursuing.

Closing on a personal note, let me say that I welcome the republication of this important book. It merits a hearty recommendation to every serious reader. As for the future, I hope Dr. De Graaff will find it possible to push his studies forward in the service of the educational ministry of the church by spelling out more fully the pedagogical principles implicit in this book.

Gordon J. Spykman

CONTENTS

page

Chapter I. Orientation   1

A. Some American Studies   3
B. The German Dilemma   16
C. Developments in the Netherlands . . .   24
D. A Preliminary Question   37

Chapter II. The Church and its Ministry   56

A. The Central Issue   57
B. The Structure and the Functions of the
Church   79

Chapter III. The Nature of Education   89

A. Some Christian Theories of Education . .   94
B. Anthropological Presuppositions 108
C. The Norms for Education 113
D. The Structure of Education 118

Chapter IV. The Church's Instruction in the Faith . . . 138

A. The Knowledge of Faith . . . . . .
B. Instruction in the Faith . . . . . .
1. The Scope of the Curriculum . . . .
2. Methodological Considerations . . .
C. Perspective . . . .

Bibliography . . . .

Index . . . .

CHAPTER I

ORIENTATION

The words "religious education" cover a great variety of activities. Sometimes they have reference to the regular day school operated by a particular denomination, the so-called church school; sometimes they may be used to describe a one or two hour course in "religion" given by a local pastor in a public school, as is quite common in Europe; and at other times this term may merely designate the educational programs carried on by the churches themselves. "Religious education", therefore, may refer to such widely different enterprises as instruction in world religions, Sunday school, confirmation classes, catechetical instruction, or the church school for the entire family.

Not only does the concept "religious education" **cover** a wide range of activities, but, to complicate matters, the term itself is confusing, since all education can be characterized by the word "religious". Education is always of a religious nature, that is, driven and motivated by a religious conviction, whether that be a Humanistic ideal, the Mohammedan religion, the neutrality postulate, or a Christian view of life. But what is usually meant by "religious education" is the instruction (of the church) in the Christian faith. The use of the word "religious" in this context can only be misleading, for it suggests that religion is limited to a small area of life, while in reality, whether it is realized or not, it gives meaning and direction to all of life.

This lack of clarity with regard to the term "religious education" and the variety of activities indicated by these words immediately confronts us with a fundamental problem. It forces us to reflect upon the proper place of instruction in the Christian faith. No doubt the primary responsibility for the "religious" upbringing of the child lies with the parents. Furthermore, it is generally recognized that next to the family the church has an important task with respect to "religious" education. But as soon as we mention the school, or other organizations, opinions and practices begin to vary. The first question we face, therefore, is the question concerning the peculiar place given to and occupied by ecclesiastical instruction amid all the other institutions and organizations also engaged in "religious" training.

"Religious" education is commonly conceived of as a form of *instruction,* but, strangely enough, this is often taken for granted or considered to be a formal matter. Consequently there has been very little reflection on the nature of "religious" education. The uniqueness of the church's instruction *and* its relation to education in general is seldom subjected to a critical analysis.

The notion that the teaching process can be treated as a secondary or formal aspect has resulted in two divergent approaches toward "religious" education. On the one hand there is a tendency to minimize the educational aspect, but no matter how much the faith-aspect of "religious" education is emphasized, it remains a form of instruction which requires certain methods. When this state of affairs is not recognized, the church usually takes recourse, sometimes quite unawares, to antiquated methods of teaching.[1] Many so-called catechism booklets, especially the older ones, give ample evidence of this tendency. On the other hand there is a tendency to become so preoccupied with educational principles and psychology that the distinctive nature of "religious" education is completely overlooked. In practice this often means an uncritical adaptation of current educational theories and practices. Especially American writings on "religious" educaton suffer from this one-sided emphasis. But however divergent these two approaches may ultimately prove to be, they are based upon a similar view of the teaching process as a more or less autonomous and external aspect of "religious" education.

The *nature* of the church's instruction, therefore, constitutes a second major difficulty. We shall have to consider whether the methods used in the church's teaching are identical to the methods used in general education and whether the educational aspect of the church's teaching-ministry can be treated independently, apart from the *content* of its instruction.

With these two sets of questions in mind, concerning the *nature*

---

[1] Cf. P. ten Have, *Een Methode van Bijbelse Catechese,* Groningen: J. B. Wolters, 1946, p. 129: "En juist de catechese die zich het meest wilde distantiëren van de schoolmethodiek, verviel maar al te licht nolens volens in een schoolmethode, maar dan een verouderde".

and *place* of the church's instruction in the Christian faith, we shall examine, by way of orientation, a number of characteristic or representative studies. Even though the outward circumstances vary from country to country and the traditions of the various denominations differ, nevertheless the basic issues remain the same, as will become apparent in the course of this chapter.

A. SOME AMERICAN STUDIES

During the last decades there has been a renewed interest in "religious" education in North-America.[2] As a result many reports and studies have been published, exploring new approaches to the church's educational ministry. A few of these publications are of special interest to our present inquiry. At the same time these reports will introduce us to the general nature and problems of "religious" education in America.

In 1959 three denominations, the Presbyterian Church in the U.S., the Reformed Church in America, and the Moravian Church in America, adopted a number of basic presuppositions and guiding principles for the educational work of the church. These fundamental principles were published in a study guide consisting of several parts, called *The Covenant Life Curriculum*.[3] As the title indicates, this curriculum has a broad perspective. It is focussed upon the all-embracing covenant life of the people of God in this world. With this new curriculum these churches have attemped to develop a program of study for both young and old which is truly relevant to the total life of the Christian community. In short, the broad aim of this curriculum holds a promise for the re-formation of all of life through the power of the Word of God.

The report, however, also gives rise to a number of fundamental questions. On the one hand the covenant life of God's people is described in the broadest possible terms, but on the other hand the covenant community is repeatedly identified with the organized church. But the institutional church as we know it today and as it

---

[2] For a survey of "religious" education in America see: M. J. Taylor, ed., *Religious Education: A Comprehensive Survey*, Nashville: Abingdon Press, 1960; P. H. Lotz, ed., *Orientation in Religious Education*, Nashville: Abingdon Press, 1950; J. M. Price, *et al.*, *A Survey of Religious Education*, New York: Ronald Press, 1959[2]. These works contain extensive bibliographies.

[3] *The Covenant Life Curriculum: Basic Paper; Foundation Papers; Curriculum Principles Papers*, Presbyterian Church in the U.S., Reformed Church in America, Moravian Church in America, 1960.

functions in our society clearly has a limited place and task. For next to the church we find the family, the school, the state, industrial organizations, and numerous other individual and communal relationships. *Obviously the church in its organizational structure cannot embrace the total life and witness of the church as the covenant community.* It is precisely at this point, the relation between the all-embracing covenant life of the people of God as it comes to expression in all areas of life *and* the organized church, that the *Covenant Life Curriculum* seems to suffer from a basic ambiguity.

The paper recognizes that the word "covenant" has reference to the new and life-giving *relationship* between God and his people. The covenant community, therefore, is the body of those whom God has graciously chosen to be his people. As God's people they are to live a life of service under the Lordship of Jesus Christ. The covenantal relationship must come to expression in every area of life and in every kind of activity, for the Christian faith makes a total claim upon man's life and does not allow any separation between the sacred and the secular. [4]

Nevertheless, the covenant community is repeatedly identified with the institutional church, with the result that the place and task of the church is grossly overestimated. Thus the authors look upon the Christian home as an integral part of the church, so that a significant aspect of its task must be accomplished in the home. The family is considered to be the most important educational agency of the church. [5] But why consider the family a part of the

---

[4] *The Covenant Curriculum: Basic Paper*, p. 14: "The principles grow out of the conviction that revelation occurs within a covenant relation; that is to say, God comes to man as to one with whom he wishes to enter into a relationship of mutual faithfulness." "He is concerned to enter into a profound and life-giving relationship with persons who will receive him as their God and receive life from his hands." *Foundation Paper*, II, p. 5: "The church is the body of those whom God has effectually called, or elected, or chosen to be his covenant people..." *Foundation Paper*, IV, p. 5f: "The gospel of the incarnation refuses a faith that separates the sacred from the secular, requiring instead the kind of response to God that claims the whole of life for him." "The Christian doctor must carry out his ministry of medicine under the Lordship of Christ, and the Christian laborer and storekeeper must minister to the world through laboring and trading in the name of Christ."

[5] *Ibid., Basic Paper*, p. 7: "An important part of the *church's* work of communicating the gospel will be accomplished in the home." "Under normal conditions the home is the most important educational institution of the *covenant community* for here a child assimilates the habits, values, attitudes, moral code, and religious sensitivity of his parents." (emphasis added) Cf. *Study Guide*, p. 6.

church, we are inclined to ask, and why only the family, why not other institutions as well? Are the school or other organizations less suitable to function as educational agencies of the church? A similar over-emphasis upon the organized church, becomes evident in the description of its task. The church, the report maintains, has been given power for the transformation of the world, which includes not only the lives of individuals but also the family, business, pleasure, politics, and every other area and situation in which men find themselves.[6] The church must address itself to the social, economic, political and moral issues of the day and through its educational program the people of God must be led to an understanding of the meaning of God's Word for the various areas of life. It is the task of the church as the covenant community to explore what it means to live under the Lordship of Christ.[7]

In keeping with this conception of the task of the church the curriculum places the major emphasis upon the education of adults, rather than the children or the young people. For it is the adults who are the church in the world and if they fail to live up to their calling there is no one else to represent the church.[8]

It is evident that the conception of the place and task of the church is determinative for the church's educational program. Thus it is hardly surprising to see that the ambiguity with regard to the church returns in the description of the curriculum. The adult

---

[6] *Ibid., Basic Paper*, p. 8: "The educational work of the church must be carried on courageously in the awareness that unique power for the transformation of the world has been given to the church. Gods works through his church to judge and transform the standards of human society." "The church must not fail to make provision for constant inquiry concerning the meaning of its faith for life in the family, in the world of business and pleasure and politics ..."

[7] *Ibid., Foundation Paper*, III, pp. 6 - 8. Cf. also IV, p. 6: "Thus the curriculum must through this third approach deal precisely with the call of Christ to serve the world wherever one is, and must provide resources for every individual to study the demands the gospel makes of him in the complex society of today." This third approach concerns "... the Christian Life, which is the response of the church, both corporately and individually, to the revelation of God in Jesus Christ as it lives its life under his Lordship and seeks to fulfill the mission entrusted to the church by Jesus Christ." See *Principles Paper*, III, p. 10: "The adult needs to explore what it will mean to *live* under the Lordship of Christ. This will include examining his various roles, such as husband, parent, or citizen, in the light of the gospel."

[8] *Ibid., Basic Paper*, p. 14: "The principles represent the conviction that a major emphasis should be placed on adults, for this emphasis, more than emphasis on any other single age group, will help the church develop the qualities of the covenant community in all areas of life." Cf. *Principles Paper*, III, p. 6.

program not only includes a systematic study of the Bible, of doctrine, and of church history, but also of the Christian life in all its aspects. But how, we wonder, can the broad aim of this curriculum ever be realized? Nearly every area of life and every profession is represented in an average congregation; how then shall the church in any relevant way establish the meaning of the Gospel for the covenant life in all its diversity? We must even consider the question whether the church is competent to do so. The paper recognizes that to accomplish this goal it will need to draw on the best insight of secular fields of knowledge. [9] Evidently the church has no particular competence or authority beyond the administration of the Word of God and the exposition of its confessions. For other information it is dependent on secular learning.

Taken seriously this broad aim of the adult educational program would lead to an "absolutizing" of the church in its organizational aspect. Moreover, it would make the "laity" permanently dependent upon the guidance of the church, and rob the people of God of the individual and corporate responsibility they have by virtue of the general office of believers. If *not* taken too seriously, this curriculum would once more be reduced to a study of the Bible, the church, and certain so-called moral problems, all narrowly conceived. But thus interpreted it could hardly be called the *covenant life* curriculum. [10] The fundamental ambiguity and the difficulties of this new curriculum forces us to reconsider the nature and function of the institutional church, especially in relation to the other areas of the Christian life.

Remarkably enough, the report pays very little attention to the *nature* of the church's instruction, a matter which is considered a major problem in the German literature on the subject. Christian education is defined as the *nurture* the church provides in the Christian faith. For that reason, the authors maintain, Christian education is quite unlike general education, since it has another, larger dimension and reflects the nature of the church of Jesus Christ. [11] The church as a whole can be thought of as the nurturing

---

9 *Ibid.*, Principles Paper, III, p. 10.

10 Gertrude Haan in her appreciative articles in the *Reformed Journal*, XIII, 4; 6 (May-June; July-August, 1963), entitled "New Frontiers in Religious Education" fails to consider the basic presuppositions and implications of this curriculum. We can readily agree that there is a place for adult education within the context of the organized church, but everything depends on how we conceive of the *place* and *aim* of such an educational program.

11 *The Covenant Life Curriculum: Foundation Paper*, V, p. 4: "Although

community of the faith. In all of its activities, its worship, its work, and its study, it seeks to nurture its members. A distinction must be made, therefore, between education in the broad sense of nurture and education in the specific sense of instruction. When it comes to the actual study of the content and meaning of the Christian faith, the church's education most closely parallels general education. [12] Regrettably nothing more is said about the nature or extent of the similarities between these two kinds of education, except that in the introduction the danger of secular views of man and society for Christian education is recognized. The church's teaching can be influenced by secular theories of education to such an extent that its message becomes distorted. That, however, was mainly in the past; with respect to the present the authors are confident that a Christian philosophy of education can be in harmony with the best scientific investigations on the nature of man and society. [13] Whatever the case, the methods of teaching used by the church must be in line with God's revelation. [14] In view of these few remarks a further elaboration of the nature of the church's teaching would certainly have been in place.

Finally we must take note of a feature characteristic of American "religious education" in general. Repeatedly basic biological, psychological, or general concepts are used in a "religious" sense without indication of their particular "religious" meaning. The *Covenant Life Curriculum* offers many striking examples of this tendency. Such concepts as "security", "growth", "experience", "need", "love", "acceptance", "nurture", "confidence", "maturity", etc., are used interchangeably in a psychic, social, and in a "religious" sense, so that often it is not clear what is meant. [15]

---

like other types of education in many respects, Christian education is unlike other types of education in that it is marked by a different and larger dimension and by the special interests that mark the church of Jesus Christ."

[12] *Ibid.*, VI, p. 6.

[13] *Ibid., Basic Paper*, p. 4.

[14] *Ibid.*, p. 11.

[15] *Ibid.*, p. 7: "The child in the family of faith will begin to know the meaning of love by experiencing the affection shown by his parents. From this creative and happy relationship he develops *a basic trust* in life *out of which faith in God naturally and readily develops*." Cf. p. 4: ". . . giving them a *foundation of security out of which grows freedom to respond in maturity to the will of God.*" See also *Foundation Paper*, V, p. 5: "God changes the *character* of man and brings him to *maturity*, ..." I, p. 9: "While the young child cannot express it, he can have very early in life the consciousness of being *accepted* as part of a community of life which centers in the church. This sense of *belonging* . . ." (emphasis added) Many other examples can be found throughout the report.

This unqualified use of analogical concepts to describe the faith-
life of man constantly threatens to reduce the unique character of
faith to organic, psychic, or social processes. Evidently the American school of religious psychology still has a widespread
influence. [16]

The studies prepared by the Lutheran Boards of Parish Education, [17] which we want to consider next, present even more striking
examples of this tendency to describe the faith-life of the believer
in terms of psychic and social categories. The authors of these
reports, however, give a rather detailed account of their understanding of the relation between a person's psycho-social experience
and the Word of God. For this reason their presentation merits
a further analysis.

In general it must be observed that this Lutheran long-range
program of parish education is an attempt to co-ordinate the
instruction of the various educational agencies of the church, such
as the Sunday school, family education, weekday education, and
vacation church school. All these agencies pursued different goals
and lacked an integrated curriculum. For a period of more than
ten years a great number of people — pastors, theologians, psychologists, educators, sociologists, and others — have co-operated to
come to a formulation of common objectives for the entire
educational program of the church. This endeavor involved four
stages: the development of fundamental objectives, the designing
of an all-inclusive curriculum, the production of new materials,
and the introduction of the entire program in the churches. The
tremendous amount of time, energy, and money devoted to this

---

[16] Cf. J. H. Ziegler, "Psychology of Religion and Religious Education", in
Religious Education, by M. J. Taylor, p. 34: "He [the psychologist] can speak
of the roots of faith attitudes in the developments of the child and the results
of faith in the personality structure." P. 35: "If we are to believe that religion
is an aspect of normal development, as we do believe, then we need to assume
that its form will be influenced by early experiences in the life of the child."
P. 42: "Further, additional understanding of the nature of the God-man
encounter is required to aid in the development of conditions which are
more favorable for the nurturing of religious experience." See also W. H.
Clark, *The Psychology of Religion*, New York: The Macmillan Company, 1958;
P. E. Johnson, *Psychology of Religion*, Nashville: Abingdon Press, 1959[2].
These volumes contain extensive bibliographies.

[17] *The Objectives of Christian Education; The Functional Objectives for
Christian Education*, The Boards of Parish Education of The American
Evangelical Lutheran Church, The Augustana Lutheran Church, The Suomi
Synod, The United Lutheran Church in America, 1957, 1959.

effort to come to a genuine and responsible renewal of the church's education certainly is noteworthy. Much can be learned in this respect from these reports.

The general aim of the entire educational endeavor of the church, according to the authors, is to *assist* the individual person in *his lifelong growth toward Christian maturity.*[18] As a person matures he gains a deeper understanding, develops more wholesome attitudes, and acquires more responsible patterns of action. Even though a person acts as a unity, yet, for educational purposes, it is helpful to distinguish the cognitive, affective, and executive aspects of his personality.[19] All three of these aspects of personality should be attended to during the process of education. This means that the learner's needs, interests, capacities, and level of maturation should all be taken into account.[20] The child or adult must be met at the level of his personal experience and circumstances. For no real learning, involving a change in personality, can take place unless the learner is actively engaged in the process of education.[21] In keeping with these educational principles the church must bring the Word of God in such a manner that it is meaningful to a person's particular situation.[22]

The proposed curriculum, therefore, gives a description of both the general experiences of people at different stages of their life *and,* corresponding with these common areas of life-involvement, opportunities for Christian learning.[23] In this way the curriculum can do justice both to the broad aim of the educational program, the life-long growth toward Christian maturity, *and* the nature of the learning-teaching act, involving the total personality. For example, when the fifteen-year-old is engaged in establishing friendships with age mates of both sexes (life-involvement), he must learn to find and make friends on the basis of Christian love and respect (Christian learning).[24] Or, to give another example, when the eight year old is involved in becoming independent while at the same time experiencing a need for guidance and approval, he must learn to understand that he is an independent person who can either rebel against or accept God's will and that he is secure

---

[18] *The Objectives,* p. 9.
[19] *Ibid,* p. 12.
[20] *The Functional Objectives,* p. 16.
[21] *Ibid.,* p. 15.
[22] *Ibid.,* pp. 20ff.
[23] *Ibid.,* pp. 26-43.
[24] *Ibid.,* p. 361.

in the forgiving love of God despite his self-assertion.[25] In this manner the most significant common experiences of each age-group of a personal, interpersonal, and impersonal nature are indicated and related to the church's teaching with regard to God, Bible, Church, fellow men, world, and self.[26] The things learned in this way at the various stages of life, the report maintains, should cause a person to grow toward Christian maturity, since they are intimately tied up with actual life involvements.[27]

This approach contains many valuable insights. It is incontestable, for example, that every form of education, including that of the church, must take account of the learner's circumstances and level of maturity. In the last chapter we shall have occasion to come back to this matter. For the moment, however, we must direct ourselves to a number of fundamental questions that arise with regard to the proposed objectives for the new curriculum; and with that we return to the last issue raised in connection with the *Covenant Life Curriculum*, namely, the relation between man's faith and his emotional life.

The educational principles presented in the volume on the functional objectives of the church's education are based upon a certain conception of the human personality. Personality, according to an earlier report, is the totality and the interrelation of an individual's "understandings", "attitudes", and "action patterns".[28] A change in one of these aspects will modify the whole personality. Such changes take place through a process of learning within the dynamic relationships in which a person finds himself. Thus the Christian may grow toward Christian maturity as he responds to God, the Bible, the church, his fellow men, the physical world, and himself. It is the task of the church to assist the individual in this response, so that he may come to a deeper understanding, develop more wholesome attitudes, and more responsible patterns of action.[29]

It is significant that the various reports make no reference to the believer's *faith*. The authors have limited themselves strictly to the use of such terms as "relationships", "response", "growth", and "Christian maturity". But, we are inclined to ask, is *"to believe"* not something more and other than to understand certain things

---

25 *Ibid.*, p. 294.
26 *Ibid.*, p. 22. Cf. the chart in *The Objectives*.
27 *Loc. cit.*
28 *The Objectives*, p. 12.
29 *Ibid.*, pp. 8, 12.

and to develop certain attitudes? No doubt the concrete act of believing has a physical, emotional, "mental", and social aspect — to mention only those aspects which the authors also distinguish [30] — but does this mean that faith can be reduced to these aspects, to knowledge, attitudes, or behavior? Is Christian maturity not something more and other than a particular configuration of an individual's personality? Is to "grow in grace" and to achieve "mature manhood", as Scripture uses these terms, not something more and other than the proper development and integration of the various aspects of personality? In other words, is not this the basic problem that these fundamental concepts are continually used in a psycho-social sense, or at best, in an indefinite and therefore ambigious sense?

The manner in which the authors of the different reports describe and employ these (psycho-social) categories points toward a specific conception of man. But since the various studies contain no explicit statements on anthropology, we shall not pursue this matter any further. It may be fruitful, however, to insert a general observation at this point concerning the widespread and commonly accepted way of thinking about man in America, a pattern which also dominates American psychology and education. In spite of many differences in approach and terminology and regardless of the great variety of personality-theories, there is nevertheless a basic unanimity with regard to the conception of man. In general this conception can be described as naturalistic and evolutionistic. [31] According to this view man is nothing more than a physical-chemical, bio-psychical organism that differs from the animal only in degree. Through the learning-process which takes place in the inter-action between the organism and his environment, the individual develops into a person or personality. Personality, therefore, is nothing more than the individual's total and integral response to his environment, or, the totality and particular con-figuration of his attitudes, thinking, and behavior. All the so-called higher aspects of man are acquired. They are the result of various (social) relationships. This deterministic and reductionistic way of thinking about man leaves no room for man as a religious being, created in the image of God, nor for faith as a unique and irre-ducible aspect of human life.

Nowhere do the authors of the Lutheran reports dissociate

---

30 *Ibid.*, p. 8.
31 Cf. A. Kuypers, *Een Paedagogische Beoordeling van het Amerikaanse*

themselves from this prevalent conception of man and the human
personality. On the contrary, they create the impression that they
have adapted this view of man to serve as the basis for a
"Christian" theory of education by simply adding another
dimension, namely the "vertical" relationship.[32] However this may
be, for our purposes it is sufficient to see that the ambiguity that
exists with regard to such basic categories as "individual", "relation",
"response", "growth" "personality", and "maturity" finds its
source in the influence of the commonly accepted way of thinking
about man. This observation holds true for other studies in religious
education as well.[33] Just as the German literature on the subject
cannot be understood apart from the influence of Karl Barth's
theology, so the peculiar nature of American religious education
cannot be understood without an awareness of this general tendency to describe man's faith in terms of organic, psychical, or
social processes.[34]

Persoonlijkheidsbegrip, Amsterdam: S. J. P. Bakker, 1951; C. Jaarsma, *Human
Development, Learning and Teaching*, Grand Rapids: Wm. B. Eerdmans
Publishing Company, 1961, p. 50: "These psychologists reason this way: We
begin with an organism in an environment. Events occur in the environment,
called stimuli; other events occur within the organism, called experience. The
events within and outside the organism form patterns of response and action
in the organism. The elements of these patterns we call personality traits, and
their aggregate we call personality. The essence of personality, then, is to
engage in *actions*." "It is held that as a biological organism man is in constant
tension with his environment. Events from within and events from without
must find equilibrium, balance to relieve the tension. In the interaction the
organism develops modes of adjustment in which conflicting events are brought
into balance. The various patterns of adjustment constitute the acquired traits
of behavior. It is the sum of these traits that constitute personality." "But this
is unacceptable from the Christian point of view. The person is not the
personality, and personality is not identical with actions." A similar analysis
was presented by Dr. R. J. Bijkerk in a paper read to the Calvin Seminary
Faculty and Student Body on March 4, 1960, entitled "Personality Dynamics".
Cf. also his *Psycho-Logica; Een Historisch Arrangement*, Amsterdam: Van
Soest, 1962, pp. 254ff., 310f., 373ff.

[32]   *The Objectives*, p. 5.

[33]   Cf. J. H. Ziegler, "Psychology of Religion and Religious Education", in
Religious Education, p. 39: "Is it not reasonable to assume that just as the
encounter between primitive drives of the id and objective reality results in
development of the ego, and as the encounter with the demands of culture
results in the development of the superego, so the encounter of the primitive
part of the personality with God results in the development of still another
part of personality? This might well be called the *spirit*."

[34]   Cf. A. E. Baily, "Philosophies of Education and Religious Education,"
in *Religious Education*, p. 33: "Can religious education handle the categories of
spirit without confounding them with either physical or mental processes?
It has not done so. Yet it may be that herein lies the key to many of the
paradoxes and problems that plague religious education." (emphasis added)

Before we conclude our discussion of the Lutheran reports we will briefly consider three other characteristic features of these studies. First it should be noted that, in keeping with the authors' conception of personality, education is concerned with the growth and development of Christian persons.[35] The church as an educating community must seek to bring about certain changes in the personality of the learner, and assist him in his growth toward Christian maturity.[36] Education, just as in the studies of the *Covenant Life Curriculum*, is used here in the broad sense of "nurture" and "forming". The authors do not deal separately with education in the specific sense of "instruction", something which could hardly be expected when the "learning-process" is primarily the link between the individual and his personality. One of the consequences of this approach is that the "subject matter" is pushed to the background and is first of all made to serve the development of the individual.[37] It is highly questionable whether the aim of education could ever be the development of personality, but since the nature and objectives of Christian education as set forth in these reports are directly related to the authors' conception of personality and its development, we shall postpone a further discussion of this matter to the chapter on education. For the moment we merely wish to draw attention to this characteristic feature of American religious education.

As in the *Covenant Life Curriculum*, and this is our second observation, so also in the Lutheran reports, the church, taken in its widest sense, as the fellowship of believers, is made to include the Christian home.[38] The proposed curriculum, therefore, gives directives for the different members of the family according to age-groups. It describes the opportunities for Christian learning within the family for the child's first years of life, as well as for old people.[39] The broad, undifferentiated concept of education enables the church to include the upbringing of the children in the home in its total educational program. This means that, even though the relative independence of the home is recognized,[40] the parents are nevertheless placed under the constant guidance and tutorship of the organized church. And once more we must ask whether the

---

[35] *The Objectives*, p. 3f.
[36] *Ibid.*, p. 5 Cf. also *The Functional Objectives*, p. 12.
[37] *The Functional Objectives*, pp. 13ff.
[38] *The Objectives*, p. 5.
[39] *The Functional Objectives*, pp. 221ff.
[40] *Ibid.*, pp. 80, 87.

church here is not overstepping its boundaries. For the suggested program does not merely provide for instruction in the fundamental Scriptural directives for family-life, but it provides detailed guidance for the upbringing of children as well. But with what right does the *organized church* (for after all, it is the organized church, the clergy, which provides the instruction and not the fellowship of believers in general) interfere with the authority and responsibility of the parents? Once more we are faced with the problem of the nature and place of the empirical church as the organized and institutionalized fellowship of believers.

The Christian community, the authors maintain, the church in its widest sense, includes the Christian family. For the family, although belonging to the secular realm as one of the "natural orders", can nevertheless become a redemptive community if its members are Christian. [41] But why only the family, we wonder, why cannot the school, for example, become such a Christian community, and why not other institutions and organizations as well? Is the structure of the family more suitable for becoming a Christian community than other institutions? Or, is the Word of God less relevant for the other "natural orders"? Evidently not, for the proposed curriculum not only suggests opportunities for Christian learning in connection with the personal and family-life, but also with respect to economic, political, and social structures. [42] But why should the Body of Christ, the Church in its widest sense, not "include" these structures as well? Does the reign of Christ not extend over all of creation? If this were acknowledged, then the question whether any empirical temporal institution could ever encompass the fullness of the Body of Christ would also have to be faced.

As it stands now the suggested objectives for Christian education can only lead to the absolutizing of the church in its organizational aspect. This means that all of life is permanently subject to the supervision and leading of the empirical church, and that the "laity" is dependent upon the constant guidance of the clergy. But is the organized church competent to give guidance with respect to problems of economic justice and the structure of the economic system? [43] Can it teach us how to interpret the political structure and how to accept the political responsibilities of Christian citizenship? [44] Is it able to show us how to make use of the cultural

---

[41] *Ibid.*, pp. 87, 91, 93.
[42] *Ibid.*, p. 38f.
[43] *Ibid.*, p. 39.
[44] *Ibid.*, p. 43.

heritage in a Christian manner and how to exert influence on the cultural developments?[45] Is it qualified to tell us how to develop Christian discrimination and judgement with regard to social mores and values?[46] It would seem that all of these tasks are the direct responsibility of the fellowship of believers in general, the church in its widest sense, which can never be incorporated by the empirical church or any other Christian institution. This does not mean that the organized church has no educational responsibilities with regard to the family, and the economic, political, and social structures, but that is a different question. In the second chapter we shall return to this question, for without a clear understanding of the place and task of the church in general, it is impossible to determine the extent and limit of its educational responsibilities.

Finally it must be observed that this long-range program of the Lutheran churches is an attempt to reform and co-ordinate the instruction of the various educational agencies of the church. To accomplish this purpose the authors have made a sociological study of the potentialities and limitations of the existing agencies.[47] To come to some useful division of labor and to avoid duplication of efforts, the agencies are assigned distinct tasks. In general the Sunday schools are to concentrate on the areas of emotion and action patterns, while the weekday schools are to focus their attention upon intellectual growth. The distinction between the different agencies was bound to be rather vague and arbitrary, since the existing situation was largely taken for granted.[48] However, it would seem that a genuine renewal and integration of the educational program would require more than a (sociological) appraisal of the possibilities and limitations of the existing institutions. For such a renewal the agencies themselves should be subjected to a critical analysis. Then it would become apparent whether the training in the family, the Sunday school, the weekday school, catechetical instruction, and the vacation church school are simply historically grown institutions and complementary forms of instruction which often overlap, or whether there is a distinctive place and task for each of these agencies. The criteria for such an analysis could only be found in the general nature and aim of the church's education. This brings us back to our original questions, namely: "what is the place and nature of religious education?"

---

[45] *Loc. cit.*
[46] *Loc. cit.*
[47] *Ibid.*, pp. 10, 77ff., 125ff., 145ff.
[48] *Ibid.*, pp. 249, 267, 288, 305, 322, 351.

Summarizing our findings thus far, we can say that in order to determine the place and nature of "religious" education as carried on by the church we must first of all have a clear conception of the place and task of the church in general. Only then shall we be able to determine the scope and aim of the educational program of the church. Secondly, it has become apparent that we must have a basic understanding of the general nature of education before we can say something about the unique character of the church's instruction in the faith.

B. THE GERMAN DILEMMA

In many ways the German discussions about the church's instruction in the faith are the counterpart of the debates on "religious" education in America. If the American literature manifests an overemphasis upon the educational aspect, the German publications exhibit a preoccupation with the "faith"-aspect of the church's education. For the discussions of the last thirty years in Germany have been strongly influenced by Karl Barth's conception of "proclamation".[49] Contrary to Barth's own intention,[50] the uncritical use of this theological concept in catechetics, gave rise to the thesis that "the church's instruction must be proclamation". But with this emphasis upon "proclamation" it became rather difficult to account for the educational aspect of the church's instruction. For if the Word of God is not at man's disposal but depends upon God's initiative for its occurrence among man, how can the Gospel really be *taught,* many argued, since teaching always involves human planning, educational objectives, and the mastery of subject matter? As a result of this change in emphasis the place of "religious" education in the school was also subjected to a critical

---

[49] K. Barth, *Die Kirchliche Dogmatik*, I-1, Zollikon: Evangelischer Verslag, 1932, pp. 50ff.

[50] Cf. K. Barth, *Church Dogmatics*, Vol. I-1, Edinburgh: T. & T. Clark, 1960, p. 55: "... Church *instruction of youth* cannot as such pretend to be proclamation." The church has no mandate to proclaim through instruction. In this respect preaching is different from all the other ministries of the church. "As such, instruction of youth has to teach, not to convert, not 'to bring to a decision'; and to that extent not to proclaim." This does not mean that from time to time instruction cannot change into proclamation and must not "... pass over at a definite place, though one not easy to define outwardly, into *worship by youth,*" See also p. 90. For a summary and discussion of Barth's conception see R. Dross, *Religionsunterricht und Verkündiging*, Hamburg: Furche-Verslag, 1964, pp. 94-97.

analysis, since many children and young people in Germany receive their "religious" training in the public school. As long as "religious" education was conceived of as moral instruction, or as a general introduction to Christianity, this subject presented no problems. But as soon as "Religionsunterricht" was changed to "kirchliche" or "evangelische Unterweisung", the place and function of this "subject" became rather doubtful. For if the church is responsible for the "instruction" in the Christian faith, and if this "instruction" is to be thought of as a form of "proclamation", how can such "instruction" ever be realized within the school situation, or, as some have asked of late, with what right does the church enter the public school at all? Seemingly it was not possible to do justice *both* to the church's instruction as a form of "proclamation" *and* the structure of the school with its educational objectives. Education and "proclamation", the school and the church, seemed to be mutually exclusive categories. This constitutes the German dilemma. [51]

The various attempts of the past thirty years to solve this dilemma make a fascinating study. [52] By way of illustration we shall examine a few of the proposed solutions, keeping in mind our questions concerning the nature and place of the church's educational program. The first illustration is from a group of authors, who, in one way or another, [53] have continued to adhere to the thesis

---

[51] R. Dross, *Religionsunterricht und Verkündiging*, p. 14, formulates the dilemma as follows: "Lassen sich Evangelium und Unterricht überhaupt miteinander vereinigen? Muss hier nicht notwendig entweder die Lehr- und damit Schulsituation oder die Evangeliumsgemäszheit verfehlt werden? Besteht noch ein Recht, sich in Raume der Schule aufzuhalten, wenn nicht eine Unterrichtsstunde, sondern ein Gottesdienst vonstatten geht? Oder bleibt von dem Evangelium noch etwas übrig, wenn die 'Verkündigung des Wortes Gottes' so tiefgreifed verwandelt wird: im Vorgang in eine Lehre, im 'Stoff' in ein Bildungsgut?" And on p. 15: "Eine eindeutige Lösung dieser Fragen wäre offenbar nur dann möglich, wenn eines von beiden aufgegeben würde, der Erziehunsanspruch, damit die Unterrichtssituation und der schulische Rahmen, oder die Evangeliumsgemäszheit und damit der Verkündigingsmodus. Im ersten Falle wäre es nur konsequent, ein solches Unternehmen gansz aus der Schule auszugliedern und in angemessenen kirchlichen Räumen den hierfür besonders ausgebildeten und dazu berufenen Kräften anzuvertrauen. Im zweiten Falle aber müszte das 'Evangelium' als Gegenstand oder Lehrstoff fallen und an seine Stelle etwa die Bibel als literarisches Dokument oder das unsere gegenwärtige Kultur prägende 'christliche Gedankengut' treten."

[52] For a survey see: H. Kittel, *Vom Religionsunterricht zur Evangelischen Unterweisung*, Hannover: Schroedel, 1957[3]; F. Grässmann, *Religionsunterricht zwischen Kirche und Schule*, München: Chr. Kaiser Verlag, 1961: R. Dross, *Religionsunterricht und Verkündiging*, Hamburg: Furche-Verlag, 1964. These works contain extensive bibliographies.

[53] A. Burkert, E. Müller, H. Diem, K. Frör, H. Angermeyer, *et al.* Cf. bibliography for the publications of these authors.

that the church's instruction is essentially "proclamation". One of
these authors, H. Angermeyer, has attempted to escape the dilemma
by making instruction a form of "proclamation". The Word of
God, according to Angermeyer, can be administered in many ways,
as is evident from the New Testament.[54] Teaching is one of these
ways and therefore on a *par* with preaching and pastoral care. All
three are to be considered forms of proclamation.[55] He dissociates
himself from the view that the church's education can only be
preparatory to the real proclamation that takes place in preaching.
Since teaching is simply another way of communicating the Gospel,
it remains proclamation. The educational aspect of the church's
teaching may not be contrasted to the aspect of proclamation. To
teach, unfold, or explain are acceptable and even mandatory ways
of proclaiming the Word of God.[56]

From this it would seem that Angermeyer has overcome the
dilemma between education and proclamation. Actually, however,
the problem remains, for proclamation, according to the author, as
the highest category, refers to the *meaning* of the teaching process,
which must be distinguished from the educational *structure* of the
activity. One cannot derive specific educational principles from the
thesis that instruction in the faith is proclamation.[57] But in that
case it becomes all the more urgent to indicate *in what sense* this
instruction can be considered proclamation and *how this claim can
be realized in the actual classroom situation*. This the author fails
to do. He does point to the relationship between baptism and instruction, and the fact that the children are members of the congregation,[58] and he does stress the importance of the teacher and
the intention with which he approaches Scripture,[59] but he does
not clearly indicate how these various considerations must function
in the teaching-process. Thus he still faces the problem of the
identity, *or* the difference, between the *teaching* of the church and
the *teaching* that takes place in the school.

---

[54] H. Angermeyer, *Die evangelische Unterweisung an höheren Schulen*,
München: Chr. Kaiser Verlag, 1957, pp. 16ff.

[55] *Ibid.*, p. 24.

[56] *Ibid., p. 19:* "Die Form des Erzählens, Entfaltens, Erklärens, Sichausein-
andersetzens steht *selbständig* neben der anderen Form des Anredens, Einladens,
Anrufens..." (emphasis added)

[57] *Ibid.*, p. 24: "Man musz die Ebene der Sinngebung und die Ebene der
pädagogischen 'Struktur' unterscheiden,..." "Es ist ein Irrtum, wenn aus dem
Begriff der Verkündigung methodische Grundsätze entwickelt werden."

[58] *Ibid.*, pp. 25ff.

[59] *Ibid.*, pp. 37ff.

With the aid of the Lutheran notion of the two-fold reign of God he constructs a radical division between general education and the church. General education can never lead to redemption and only the church can instruct in the Christian faith. [60] Public education is an expression of God's care for this fallen world. It can be an aid in becoming genuinely human and as such it is to be evaluated positively by the Christian, even though it is not governed by the Gospel but by Law. The school must teach the children to develop and to care for God's creation and to respect and help one another as fellow human beings. This calling pertains to all men, so that education can never be specifically Christian. [61] This does not mean that the Christian does not have a task with regard to public education. First of all he must oppose idealism as well as every attempt to absolutize creation. Secondly, the minister who teaches "Bible" must stimulate the dialogue between the school and the church, between the aims of the different subjects that are taught and the Gospel's. [62] This does not imply that "religious" education could ever become an integral part of the school; on the contrary, the radical difference between the church and the public school always remains. [63]

But if on the one hand there is a fundamental distinction between the aim of the school and the church, and if on the other hand "religious" education and public education are both forms of instruction and to that extent exactly alike, how must we conceive of this teaching-process they are said to have in common? At times the author seems to consider the teaching-process a *formal* aspect of the church's instruction, [64] while in other instances he maintains

---

[60] *Ibid.*, p. 46: "Die Erziehung ist keine 'magische Kraft', sie führt niemals zur Erlösung." And p. 69: "Der evangelische Lehrer hat bei seinen Unterricht in keinesfalls die biblische Botschaft auszurichten. Seiner Aufgabe ist streng sachbestimmt. In einem Unterricht geht es um die Welt." "Das Evangelium bringt die Gabe der Vergebung der Sünden, die Wiedergeburt und die endliche Erlösung; die Erziehung bringt die Bildung zum Zweck der Erhaltung des natürlichen Menschen."

[61] *Ibid.*, p. 45: "Erziehung ist vom Evangelium her positiv zu bewerten. Sie steht im Dienste der göttlichen Hilfe an dieser gefallenen und dem Ende zueilenden, aber von Gott gehaltenen und geliebten Menschheit und musz an jedem Menschen geübt werden." See also p. 46f.

[62] *Ibid.*, pp. 50ff., 60ff.

[63] *Ibid.*, p. 69: "Vor allem durch das strenge Festhalten an der theologischen Einsicht, dasz zwischen Erziehung und Verkündigung ein unüberbrückbarer Gegensatz besteht."

[64] *Ibid.*, p. 58: "Die kirchliche Unterweisung kann ihren von Gott gegebenen Auftrag nur durch Teilnahme an der Erziehung und Bildung erfüllen. Das gilt einmal *formal* hinsichtlich der *Art* und *Weise,* in der das Evangelium gelehrt wird." (emphasis added)

that every educational method has its own philosophical presuppositions. [65] He urges the pastor to examine the various theories to see whether or not they can be used for "religious education". But he does not tell us which methods have an unfavorable effect upon the church's teaching, nor does he tell us what criteria must be applied to select the most suitable procedures. At this decisive point the author leaves us in the dark. [66] We can only conclude that Angermeyer has failed to demonstrate how the initial thesis, that the church's teaching is a form of proclamation, can be realized in practice. Furthermore he has failed to answer the question with what right the church enters the public school at all. The two-realm theory, which allows only one kind of "religious" education, namely that given by the church, [67] aggravates the problem even more. If "religious" instruction always remains a *Fremdkörper* within the school, [68] it is difficult to see how the church can vindicate its right to teach the Gospel in the public school. If the church is allowed to enter the school at all, this "right" must of necessity be subject to the permission of the government and the approval of the parents. [69]

Next to Angermeyer several others have attempted to integrate proclamation and instruction. But all of these attempts have failed, [70] and we could add, *had* to fail. Given these descriptions of instruction and proclamation *the dilemma is indeed inescapable.* So long as the teaching-process is thought of as a formal, neutral activity, or as belonging to the secular realm, it is impossible to integrate proclamation — however defined — with instruction. Or, conversely, so long as proclamation is considered to belong to the

---

[65] *Ibid.*, p. 113: "Das heiszt allerdings nicht, dasz die Methode völlig neutral sei. Vielmehr ist jede Methode Ausflusz einer bestimmten philoophischen Grundhaltung." "Der Religionslehrer ist dann genötigt, die weltlichen Methoden von seinem Auftrag her eigenständig zu entwickeln."

[66] Cf. F. Grässmann, *Religionsunterricht*, p. 29.

[67] Angermeyer, *op. cit.*, p. 216: "Die erste Folgerung musz lauten: Dem schulischen Religionsunterricht kommt kein anderer Character zu als dem kirchlichen." "Darum ist es völlig gleichgültig, ob sie durch den Pfarrer in kircheneigenen Räumen oder durch den Religionsphilologen im Schulzimmer gegeben wird."

[68] *Ibid.*, p. 59: "Der religionsunterricht darf nicht aus vollem Herzen teilhaben am Bildungsvorgang der Schule. Er vergiszt sonst, dasz er nicht wezensmäszig in der Schule angesiedelt ist. Er hat seine Heimat nicht in der Schule, sondern in der Kirche."

[69] *Ibid.*, p. 217. Cf. G. Hummel, *Religionsunterricht und Schule*, München: Chr. Kaiser Verlag, 1964, p. 8.

[70] For an analysis of other attempts (by Burkert, Frör, Diem) to solve the dilemma, see R. Dross, *Religionsunterricht*, pp. 131-138.

spiritual realm, or to be of another order than education and other human activities, there can never be anything more than an uneasy tension between proclamation and instruction.

Nevertheless, whenever "religious" education is thought of as a form of teaching, the educational aspect of this instruction must be accounted for and *such* methods will have to be found as are in keeping with the nature of the Gospel. In a study dealing with educational methods used in "religious" education F. Grässmann has demonstrated how little has been accomplished in this respect. [71] This should hardly surprise us, since, as we saw in Angermeyer, the educational aspect of the church's teaching immediately confronts us with the relation between proclamation and education in general, or, even more broadly, between the so-called secular realm and the spiritual, or between the church and the world, between grace and nature, between theology and the other sciences. And so long as proclamation and education are thought of as belonging to different realms, or as being of a different order, the dilemma remains insoluble.

During the last decade, however, a number of writers have come to the fore who believe they can do justice to both the school situation and the nature of the Gospel. [72] Their writings can be seen as a reaction to the preoccupation with proclamation and to the role of the church in "religious" education. [73] In his study *Religionsunterricht und Verkündigung*, R. Dross has given us a survey of this development by analyzing the various ways in which the term "proclamation" has been used. Contrary to previous writers, the authors belonging to this last group are no longer concerned about the general thesis that "religious" instruction must be proclamation. Their only concern is that the actual text of Scripture is faithfully and accurately explained and interpreted. Anything more or other may not be required of the teacher. The general (theological) question of proclamation is thereby reduced to a question about what happens when Scripture is actually interpreted. Dross, *et al.*, believe that this new approach offers a genuine

---

[71] F. Grässmann, *Religionsunterricht*, pp. 96-110 (summary).

[72] H. Stock, *Studien zur Auslegung der synoptischen Evangelien im Unterricht*, Güterloh: C. Bertelsmann Verlag, 1963³; G. Otto, *Schule, Religionsunterricht, Kirche*, Göttingen: Vandenhoeck & Ruprecht, 1961; —————, *Handbuch des Religionsunterrichts*, Hamburg: Furche-Verlag, 1964; I. Baldermann, *Biblische Didaktik*, Hamburg: Furche-Verlag, 1964²; R. Dross, *Religionsunterricht*.

[73] Cf. G. Hummel, *Religionsunterricht*, p. 8f.

solution to the dilemma between proclamation and education. [74]
But whether this is so remains to be seen.

To interpret Scripture these authors make use of the hermeneutical principles developed by R. Bultmann, E. Fuchs, and G. Ebeling.
It would take us too far afield to give an account of the different
ways in which these principles are worked out; for this we must
refer to their own publications. [75] One thing is clear; all these
authors accept the historical-critical method of interpretation. The
text of Scripture is subjected to the same historical-grammatical
analysis as any other document. In this respect "religious" education
does not differ from general education and must indeed be considered an integral part of the school. But besides a historical-
grammatical analysis the teacher must engage in an "existentiale"
interpretation, which is first of all an exposition of human
existence. [76] These two methods, which are said to be in complete
harmony with each other, [77] actually exclude and presuppose one
another, because they stand in a dialectic relation to each other. [78]
This means that the dilemma is now inherent in the method of interpretation. For this group of authors „religious" instruction has
become primarily a hermeneutical problem. Of the various solutions
this last one is most deceptive, for, pretending to do both, it does
neither justice to the school (since the exposition does not limit
itself to a historical-critical analysis as is done in other subjects)
nor does it do justice to the Gospel (since Scripture is made
subservient to the "existentiale" interpretation). [79]

Summarizing this brief survey of the German situation we can only
conclude that the dilemma between proclamation and education, the
church and the school, remains unsolved. Every solution that has
been proposed so far leads to insoluble problems, if not antinomies.

---

[74]   R. Dross, *Religionsunterricht*, pp. 17, 126ff., 157ff.

[75]   See note 72. Especially the fascinating study of I. Baldermann must be
mentioned here. Doing justice to these publications would require a separate
study.

[76]   Cf. R. Dross, *Religionsunterricht*, p. 128; and S. U. Zuidema, *Van Bultmann naar Fuchs*, Franeker: T. Wever, n.d., p. 51.

[77]   Cf. Zuidema, *op. cit.* pp. 9, 13, 33, 73ff.

[78]   *Ibid.*, p. 77: "De verhouding tussen existentiale en historisch-kritische
interpretatie is derhalve een dialektische, waarbij het laatste en eerste woord
aan de existentiale interpretatie is, en deze existentiale interpretatie aan de
historisch-kritische methode een *vrijbrief* en een *opdracht* geeft..." See also pp.
30ff., 53ff. Cf. by the same author "Openbaringsinhoud en existentie in de
theologische hermeneutiek van R. Bultmann," *Mededelingen van de Vereniging
voor Calvinistische Wijsbegeerte*, (December, 1964), 2-7.

[79]   Cf. Zuidema, *Van Bultmann naar Fuchs.* p. 51.

The emphasis upon the Word of God, the *kerygma*, and the insistence upon the *Christian* character of "religious" instruction in the public school, certainly must be evaluated positively, especially when seen in contrast to the American situation. Nevertheless, both the dilemma and the suggested solutions are unacceptable. "Religious" education which wants to be genuinely *Christian* will always be out of place in, if not at odds with, the public school. For public education simply cannot be neutral with regard to the Gospel. The driving force behind public education, which is often overlooked or underestimated,[80] is undeniably of a religious character. This is not to say that "religious" education which seeks to do justice to the Word of God, is not allowed at the public school,[81] nor that at certain places or at times such instruction cannot be effective. But it does mean that "religious" education within the public school will always be a hybrid situation and that it can never be more than an emergency measure. In this respect we agree with Grässmann that *today's* "religious" instruction in the public schools must be looked upon as an "evangelism" project.[82]

Only to the extent to which a school offers genuine *Christian* education can the instruction in the Christian faith become an integral part of the total curriculum. The prevailing dualism between proclamation and education, however, precludes the very possibility of developing an educational system which is motivated and directed by the Christian faith instead of by some other religious conviction like the neutrality postulate. Consequently "religious" instruction can never be integrated with the aim of the school and the objectives of the other subjects. The most that could be achieved would be the type of "dialogue" described by Angermeyer,[83] (for any other solution as worked out by Stock, Otto, Baldermann, *et al.*, involves a reduction and compromise of the Gospel). But a critical analysis along the lines of K. Schaller[84] would soon bring to light the utter incompatibility of public edu-

---

[80] Cf. K. Schaller, *Die Krise der humanistischen Pädagogik und der kirchliche Unterricht*, Heidelber: Quelle & Meyer, 1961.

[81] To evaluate the German situation correctly one must take into account the (still) prevalent idea of the *corpus christianum*. Cf. S. C. W. Duvenage, *Kerk, Volk en Jeugd*, Vol. I, *De Verhouding van Kerk tot Volk*, Zaandijk: J. Heijnis Tsz., 1962, p. 103f. The American situation, in contrast, reflects a completely different way of thinking about the relation between the church and the school.

[82] F. Grässmann, *Religionsunterricht*, pp. 147-171, 184.

[83] H. Angermeyer, *Die evangelische Unterweisung*, pp. 60-65.

[84] K. Schaller, *Die Krise der humanistischen Pädagogik*.

cation and instruction in the Christian faith, which in turn would have to lead to Grässmann's conclusions ('evangelism'), or to abandoning the school. But both the solution of Grässmann and restricting "religious" education to catechetical instruction leaves unanswered the question how to give form to a view of instruction that is in keeping with the nature of the Word of God.[85] Unless the dualism between proclamation and education is completely abandoned, there is little hope that this perplexing problem can be solved. A brief analysis of some of the Dutch publications will confirm this thesis.

C. DEVELOPMENTS IN THE NETHERLANDS

By far the most significant study in catechetics that has appeared in the Netherlands is the dissertation of P. ten Have. His inquiry confronts us once more, although in a slightly different context, with the German dilemma, but at the same time his thinking reflects the developments in the Netherlands. Dr. ten Have's study, therefore, serves both as an epilogue and as an introduction. Keeping in mind our two questions concerning the nature and place of the church's instruction, we shall briefly examine the central thesis of his dissertation.

From the outset Dr. ten Have maintains that catechetical instruction belongs to two areas, namely that of the church and education.[87] This assertion immediately brings us to the heart of the matter. For if it is true that catechism belongs both to the church and education, we may legitimately inquire about the nature of these two spheres and their relationship. It is precisely these two questions that Dr. ten Have sets out to answer, particularly in his second chapter.

As an aspect of the total ministry of the church, catechism must be seen primarily as a form of *proclamation*, according to the author.[88] In all its activities, and not in the last place in its teaching,

---

[85] Cf. F. Grässmann, *Religionsunterricht*, p. 191.

[86] P. ten Have, *Een Methode van Bijbelse Catechese.*

[87] *Ibid.*, p. 15: "De catechese, als kerkelijk onderwijs, behoort tot twee terreinen: tot het terrein der kerk, en tot dat der opvoeding."

[88] *Ibid.*, p. 9: "Nu is de kerk er terwille van de prediking, de *verkondiging* van Jezus Christus." "In al haar levensuitingen, in woord en daad, is ze als het goed is, een getuige van Gods barmhartigheid in Jezus Christus. Dat geldt zeker het kerkelijk onderwijs, . . ." "Wij aarzelen zelfs niet dit het centrale gezichtspunt der catechese te noemen, omdat het hierin toch wezenlijk en uiteindelijk om het doel der verkondiging gaat."

the church must testify to the grace of God in Jesus Christ. This is the first and most important thing that can be said about the church's education. But catechism can also be looked at from another point of view, namely that of education, and then it must be considered a form of *instruction,* even though it be the official instruction of the church in the Christian faith.[89] Catechetical instruction, therefore, is as it were school and church in one, *formally* it belongs to the school, but as far as *content* goes it belongs to the church. It is a mixed marriage, in which proclamation and education are only outwardly united, since a real integration between two totally different categories is impossible. There is always an inner tension between these aspects of catechetical instruction.

The form-content scheme, which ten Have employs, seems to offer a genuine explanation of the relation between proclamation and education within catechism. The church determines the content of what is to be taught and the school provides a suitable method. However, far from solving anything, this form-content scheme leads to insoluble contradictions.

Dr. ten Have takes note of the fact that the words for "preaching" and "teaching" in Scripture are closely related, often appearing in the same context, and that in "teaching", the whole man is addressed and not just the intellect.[91] Yet he assumes a hierarchical order between general education, "religious" education in the school, catechism, and preaching. The first category, general education, is the most formal and peripheral one, and the last division, preaching, the highest and most central, while the two middle ones have some of each category. Such a division between the higher and the lower, the central and the peripheral, proclamation and education is hardly consistent, since "pure" proclamation and "pure" education do not exist.

"To proclaim" and "to preach" are *human* activities, which involve the total person, his faith as well as any other aspect, and as such they can be called forms of public address. On ten Have's basis one would have to conclude that there is an inner tension within

[89] *Ibid.,* p. 15: "De catechese is de school der kerk..." "...open en eerlijk geldt het dit feit te erkennen, dat de catechese *onderwijs* is, onderwijs der kerk, en ook op het woord *onderwijs* moet de nadruk gelegd, school!" Cf. p. 151.

[90] *Ibid.,* p. 26: "Daarom bevat dit woord, dit begrip, deze zaak ["religious" education], een grote, innerlijke spanning. Het is als het ware kerk en school in énen, materieel kerk, formeel school, een gemengd huwelijk, dat daarom nog geen ongelukkig of zelfs maar onvruchtbaar huwelijk behoeft te zijn. Al is het wel nodig zich voortdurend van de spanning bewust te blijven." Cf. p. 216.

[91] *Ibid.,* pp. 6, 10.

preaching between form and content, and that preaching is a mixed
marriage between the rostrum and the pulpit. On the other hand
ten Have has to admit that education cannot be completely separated from proclamation.[92] Apparently there is a similar tension
within education. Furthermore, "religious" education in (high)-
school is given such a central position that the result could only be
Christian education.[93] These inconsistencies completely destroy any
hierarchical order and any principle differences between preaching
and teaching. For both are *religious* activities, governed by the
Word of God.[94] Prof. Dooyeweerd's remarks with respect to Brunner's view of church-law can also be applied to Dr. ten Have's
construction. "The famous form-matter scheme, in its neo-Kantian
sense, is thus called in here to elucidate the problem concerning the
essential character of Church-law (and we might add: catechetical
instruction). This scheme however, is anything but appropriate. It
owes its origin to a misconception and disruption of the divine
world-order, and must always end in an internally contradictory
dualism."[95] The source of this division between form and content
is to be found in the nature-grace dualism and as long as "... this
dualism keeps ruling thought, it is impossible to gain an insight
into the individuality-structure of the temporal Church-institute,"[96]
or, for that matter, into the structure of the church's education. The
obvious distinctions between different human activities cannot be
explained by the form-content scheme, which is based upon the
nature-grace dualism, but must be accounted for quite differently.
A genuine insight into the peculiar nature of preaching, catechizing,
and teaching, to mention only these three (for the same holds true
for any other activity), presupposes an analysis of the structure of
reality and an understanding of the interrelationship and inter-
dependence of its various aspects.

---

[92] *Ibid.*, pp. 20-22.
[93] *Ibid.*, p. 28f: "Dit schoolse onderwijs heeft een ander doel, nl. het
fundament te vormen van het overige onderwijs, te doen verstaan, waarvan
dit mag uitgaan, de geestelijke band te vormen, die de onderscheiden leervakken
samenbindt."
[94] *Ibid.*, p. 20f: "Het lijkt ons ook een te theoretische scheiding, die men
in de praktijk niet kan volhouden, enerzijds te willen verkondigen en anderzijds
te willen opvoeden, beide vanuit hetzelfde Evangelie." "Evenzeer als de verkondiging ingrijpt in de opvoeding, grijpt deze in de verkondiging in, ..."
[95] H. Dooyeweerd, *A New Critique of Theoretical Thought*, Vol. III, Am-
sterdam/Philadelphia: H. J. Paris, The Presbyterian and Reformed Publishing
Company, 1957, p. 553.
[96] *Loc. cit.*

Since the form-content scheme does not clarify the essential nature of catechetical instruction, it is not surprising to see that at decisive points ten Have seeks to overcome the inner tension and dualism of this scheme. Thus methodology is not quite as formal a matter as one might expect, in fact, principle and method are really quite closely related, even so much so that the unique character of the church's education demands a genuine *catechetical method*. [97] The content which the church wants to convey apparently has certain implications for the manner in which it is done; or, approached from the opposite end, the method that is employed apparently does something to the content of what is being taught. The usefulness, therefore, of certain educational principles and methods must be examined in the light of the nature of catechetical instruction. [98] If pursued to the end this would mean a fruitful procedure for developing a catechetical method. For not only does it force one to reflect upon the unique nature of the church's education, but it also demands an analysis of the presuppositions and implications of educational theories and practices. Regrettably ten Have discontinued his theoretical analysis at a point where it became most fruitful and promising and settled prematurely for the methodology developed by prof. Ph. Kohnstamm and his followers.

Although hampered by a misleading conception of the relation between proclamation and education, Dr. ten Have sought to do full justice to the *distinctive nature* of catechism as a *form of education*, taking both aspects seriously. In spite of many differences he considered both the school and catechism to be forms of education and therefore basically alike. [99] In keeping with this he paid a great deal of attention to the educational aspect of cate-

---

[97] Ten Have, *op. cit.* p. 48f: "Daarom moet bij de methode nooit vergeten worden, dat het methode is van de *catechese*, dat is *gods*dienstonderwijs. Het eigen karakter der catechese binnen het kader van het onderwijs zal voortdurend een waarschuwingssignaal moeten zijn om het eigen karakter der catechetische methode te bewaren. Ook om die reden is nauwgezette studie der catechetische didactiek geboden."

[98] *Ibid.*, p. 131: "Wie het bijbels-reformatorisch karakter der kerk, en daarmee der catechese als verkondiging, hiervoor centraal houden ..., hebben zich serieus af te vragen, of de catechese waarlijk meer gediend is van een didactiek, steunend op de denkpsychologie, boven een die voortkomt uit associatie-psychologische opvattingen. Met andere woorden: past de theologische instelling, die we in het eerste deel in het bijzonder in het eerste hoofdstuk gaven, bij de paedagogisch-didactische, in het tweede hoofdstuk gegeven, ...?"

[99] *Ibid.*, p. 129: "Immers, hoe groot de verschillen ook mogen wezen, de overeenkomst blijft bestaan, nl. dat zowel school als catechese vormen van onderwijs zijn, dat in beide wezenlijk dezelfde functie wordt uitgeoefend, ..."

chism, but he did not reflect sufficiently on the peculiar nature of this education. The religious ground-motive which dominated ten Have's thinking prevented him from gaining a clear insight into the structure of the church's education.

Long before Dr. ten Have wrote his dissertation quite another conception had been developed by Dr. Abraham Kuyper. In principle Dr. Kuyper had broken with the scholastic nature-grace dualism and returned to Calvin's biblical view of the radical nature of sin and grace. [100] We shall briefly consider Kuyper's contribution to catechetics and trace the developments that took place during the next fifty years. Already in 1894 Dr. Kuyper presented a programmatic outline of what the church's education ought to be like. [101] His views demonstrate a remarkable insight into the significance and meaning of catechetical instruction. Regrettably his basic conceptions were never worked out systematically or applied consistently.

First of all Kuyper called attention to the larger context of this particular ministry of the church. According to the author, the life and practices of the church in general have a forming influence upon its young members, and this subtle and unintentional training constitutes the immediate background for the actual instruction in the Christian faith. In this connection it should be noted that Kuyper would have preferred discussing the general (ecclesiastical) office of believer before dealing with the special offices, had that been feasible in his day. [102] Applied to catechism this would have meant that the forming influence of being a part of the fellowship of believers, witnessing and sharing in its activities, should be constantly kept in mind. In keeping with this Kuyper saw a close relation between Catechetics and Homiletics, since catechism must also introduce the young people to the church's preaching. [103] The consequences of this viewpoint would be that, in order to be fruitful, catechism must take into account the child's experiences in the church, his familiarity (or lack of it) with its services, and his understanding of the role of the minister and the other office-bearers. Next to the general influence of the church's activities, Dr. Kuyper maintained, there are other specific educational enterprises which should be considered. The Sunday school, young people's societies,

---

100   Cf. Dooyeweerd, *A New Critique,* I, pp. 516, 523f.
101   A. Kuyper, *Encyclopaedie der Heilige Godgeleerdheid,* Vol. III, Kampen: J. H. Kok, 1909², pp. 503-510.
102   *Ibid.,* pp. 481-483.
103   *Ibid.,* p. 486.

or young adult study groups, may precede, accompany, or follow catechism. Finally, basic to all the efforts of the church to guide and instruct its youth is the Christian upbringing in the home. Kuyper did not deal systematically with this larger context of catechetical instruction, but these few remarks are worth noting. Without the support of the home and the general educational influence of the church's services catechism would be doomed to failure and to remain a sterile, isolated, and ineffective under-taking.

Catechism then, according to Kuyper, is the official introduction and initiation of the young members in the confessions and life of the church, and is completed when the catechumens gather with the congregation around the communion table. The communal and individual aspect are inseparably united in this description, since the young people must be considered as *members* of the *fellowship* of believers. They must be taught in such a manner that they are prepared to take up their responsibilities as mature members in the midst of the congregation.

As the church's ministry to her youth, catechism is a unique kind of instruction. It is unique not because it can be called Christian education, but because it intends to introduce and initiate into the life of the *church*. This emphasis upon the distinctive character of catechism does not mean that thereby it stops being genuine in-struction; on the contrary, as a form of instruction it is just as much subject to the general rules of education as any other kind of instruction. The church's teaching cannot be separated from human life in general. But (and here Kuyper touches on a fundamental issue), the general educational principles must be transformed and adapted in such a way that full justice can be done to the special nature of the church's instruction.

Basically catechism, according to Kuyper, should be the same for everybody, yet the instruction should be geared to any social dif-ferences that may exist between groups of catechumens. Likewise the individual differences between persons should be taken into account.

With regard to the curriculum Kuyper considered the intro-duction to the Scriptures to be of primary importance. In passing he took note of the fact that teaching "Bible" requires a method that is in keeping with the nature of the Word of God. Further-more, the young people should be made familar with the tradition, history, liturgy and confession of their church. Each of these sub-jects requires a different method of instruction. Finally, a pastoral attitude should characterize all teaching and find overt expression in song and prayer.

A review of the existing catechism booklets used in the Reformed churches makes it abundantly clear that Kuyper's insights are still highly relevant today. Above all he has provided us with a criterion to distinguish meaningfully between catechism and other forms of instruction in the faith. This should prove to be of great value, for it is one thing to claim a distinctive place for this ministry of the church, but it is quite another thing to realize this thesis in practice.

A number of years later prof. P. Biesterveld gave a further exposition of the peculiar character of catechetical instruction.[104] He maintained that there are similarities between general Christian education and catechism. From the relation between nature and grace in general one could expect as much.[105] Educating children for a life of service is a religious activity and can only be done in the light of the Word of God. The subject matter and method of general education must likewise be governed by the principle of redemption.[106] Not only the church engages in *religious* education, but also the school, for in both instances the education is subject to the Word of God. In this respect there is no difference between the church and the school. Neither does the difference necessarily lie in the subject matter, for the Christian school may also have a course in "Bible". Both, the school and the church, can give instruction in the Christian faith. But in the first instance this instruction is entirely qualified by the nature and task of the school and in the second instance by that of the church.[107]

---

[104] P. Biesterveld, *Het Karakter der Catechese*, Kampen: J. H. Kok, 1900.

[105] *Ibid.*, p. 58: "Dit vloeit vanzelf voort uit de verhouding van natuur en genade in het algemeen. God heeft ook wetten gegeven voor de onderwijzing der kinderen; wetten, wier kennis onvolledig en verdorven is door de zonde, maar die bij het licht der Godsopenbaring weer moeten opgespoord." Cf. also his *Het Object der Ambtelijke Vakken*, Wageningen: N.V. Drukkerij "Vada", 1902, p. 38f.

[106] *Ibid.*, *Het Karakter der Catechese*, p. 60: Het is geen geringe arbeid de kinderen zo te onderwijzen en te vormen, dat zij als mensen Gods tot alle goed werk toegerust Hem dienen in het natuurlijke leven." "En dat zelfs kan ook alleen gedaan in het licht van Gods Woord. Stof en methode, ook van het gewone onderwijs moet beheerst door het beginsel der verlossing, die in Christus Jezus is."

[107] *Ibid.*, p. 63: "Het stempel wordt op de catechese gedrukt door de aard der kerk zelve." Cf. also p. 62: "Zij heeft bepaaldelijk tot doel in te leiden in de denk- en levens-sfeer van de kerk zelve." "Zij moet ... zelf haar kinderen inleiden in haar eigen denken, in de wijze van haar bestaan; zelf hen vormen voor het belijdend leven in het midden der kerk." "Van uit dat oogpunt bezien, zal ... ook hare methode van onderwijzen eene eigene zijn."

Thus catechism is a unique kind of instruction, which has its own aim and method, but at the same time it is related to general education. Biesterveld did not want to subordinate catechetical instruction to education, neither did he simply want to borrow from the school whatever seemed suitable. Rather he insisted that the principles and methods of general education should be reworked and thoroughly integrated with the nature and aim of catechism. Only after the educational principles have been transformed can they be applied to the church's teaching.[108] His conception of the relation between "nature" and "grace" in general is indeed decisive for his approach to the education of the church.

At this point it is important to note that the terms "nature" and "grace" as used by most of the authors of that time,[109] can easily lead to confusion. W. Heyns, for example, speaks of a special "realm of grace", to which the church and its ministries belong, and an "area of common grace", in which he places the school. As a result he calls catechism, in contrast to general education, a form of *religious* instruction.[110] One might conclude from this that the school is a non-religious institution and solely orientated to this temporal life. Nothing could be further from the truth, however, for the child should be reared and educated by the light of the Word of God and prepared for a life of service.[111] The terminology plainly confuses the issues.

A similar obscurity can be found in Hoekstra's presentation of the matter. Psychology and education belong to the "realm" of

---

[108] *Ibid.*, p. 93: "Bij de methode komt van zelf het meest uit, het verband tussen Catechese en de algemene Paedagogiek of Didactiek. Het is onderricht en daarom ook gebonden aan de eisen van het algemeen onderwijs, maar dan, niet slechts door het bijzonder karakter van de Catechese genuanceerd, *doch bepaald door dat karakter zo beheerst, dat zij alleen in een bepaalde vorm op dit terrein gelden kunnen.*" (emphasis added)

[109] Cf. P. A. E. Sillevis Smitt, *De Betekenis van het Gereformeerde Beginsel voor de Ambtelijke Vakken*, Amsterdam: H. A. van Bottenburg, 1912, p. 27; T. Hoekstra, *De Psychologie der Religie en de Ambtelijke Vakken*, Kampen: J. H. Kok, 1913, p. 30; W. Heyns, *Handboek voor de Catechetiek*, Grand Rapids: Eerdmans-Sevensma, n.d. (1916?), p. 106.

[110] Heyns, *Handboek*, p. 105: "Vooreerst is het eis van het Genade-Verbond, dat haar onderwijs uitsluitend *religieus* onderwijs zal zijn."

[111] *Ibid.*, p. 105f: "Dragen de Pedagogie en de school een Christelijk karakter, zodat zij zich door Gods Woord laten voorlichten, dan zullen zij zulk een opvoeding van het kind bedoelen, dat het ook zijn natuurlijk leven naar de eis Gods zal inrichten, en ook op dat terrein God als Koning zal huldigen en Hem zal dienen." Cf. also p. 180: "*De rechte Waardering van het Natuurlijke Leven.* De Schrift leert ons, dat wij geheel ons leven tot godsdienst hebben te maken, door in geheel ons leven de Souvereiniteit Gods te erkennen, en geheel ons leven te brengen onder zijn heerschappij."

"nature" and deal with "temporal life", while catechism only pertains to the *religious* life of the child. [112] Nevertheless there is a relation between catechetics and education, just as there is a relation between "nature" and "grace". At another place, however, Hoekstra asserts that education is always of a *religious* nature and that a Christian must train his children to serve God in all things. [113] According to this description Christian education clearly belongs to the "sphere of grace". [114] If both education and catechism belong to the "sphere of grace", that is, if both activities are of a religious nature, subject to the Word of God, how then are they related and how then can the church make use of the insights gained in the school? These questions remain unanswered. The use of the terms "nature" and "grace" in this context only serves to obscure the basic problem.

"Nature" and "grace" are two entirely different categories. "Grace" has reference to God's favorable attitude toward sinners. As the opposite of "grace" one might have expected "wrath", but not "nature". "God's attitude" and "nature" can hardly serve as criteria for dividing life into two realms, and when so used this terminology can only lead to confusion. [115]

In view of this development it is not surprising to see that the main contributions of Kuyper and Biesterveld were soon lost out of sight and were never worked out systematically.

Following in the footsteps of Dr. T. Hoekstra in this respect, Prof. J. Waterink became preoccupied with the "psychology and sociology of religion" as *integral aspects* of the disciplines dealing with the church's ministry. This great interest in the "psychology

---

[112] T. Hoekstra, *Psychologie en Catechese*, Nijverdal: E. J. Bosch Jbzn, 1916, p. 21: "Paedagogiek en catechetiek werken alzo in de weg van onderwijs ieder aan op een eigen doel, gene op een doel in het natuurlijke, deze op een doel in het religieuze leven . . ." Cf. also p. 22f.

[113] *Ibid.*, p. 16: "Welke taak de mens in deze wereld heeft te vervullen, welke de bestemming is van de mens op aarde, wat dus het doel is van de opvoeding, wordt beheerst door onze religieuze overtuiging. Dienovereenkomstig stelt de Christelijke paedagogiek vast, dat het de roeping is van de volwassen mens God te dienen met alle gaven en krachten, dat de opvoeding tot doel heeft de jeugdige mens op te leiden tot een mens Gods tot alle goed werk volmaaktelijk toegerust."

[114] *Ibid.*, p. 17: "De Christelijke paedagogiek gaat voorts uit van de heerlijke belijdenis, ons in het stuk van het genadeverbond gegeven, dat de Here de God is van Zijn Volk en van hun zaad. De verbondsgedachte moet in alle Christelijke paedagogie voelbaar zijn."

[115] Cf. D. H. Th. Vollenhoven, *Het Calvinisme en de Reformatie van de Wijsbegeerte*, Amsterdam: H. J. Paris, 1933, p. 45f. See also his *Isagogè Philosophiae*, College-dictaat, Amsterdam: Uitg. Theja, n.d., p. 74.

of religion" and a "psychological method" for "practical theology" found its source in his conception of the "soul", and directly related to this, of "psychology" *(zielkunde)*. [116] In order to find a *theoretical basis* for his "psychological method" Dr. Waterink extended Kuyper's principle of God's *organic* activity, and applied it to the ministry of the church. God works *organically* in saving man, which indicates that He uses means to accomplish His purposes, in this instance, the special ecclesiastical offices. Furthermore, man responds *organically* to God's Word, which suggests that man is totally involved in his religion. The word "organic" draws attention to a very important state of affairs, but at the same time it is also a very deceptive term. For this "principle" of God's organic activity and man's organic reaction does not explain anything; on the contrary, it tends to hide the real problem, namely *how* man is totally involved and *how* the office-bearers can use a "comprehensive" approach that does justice to the distinctiveness of their ministry. The term "organic" calls attention to the unity of man and his total involvement, but is does not *explain how*, within this unity, man's psychic and faith life, for example, are interrelated, much less does it *theoretically establish* the need for a "psychological method" in "practical" theology.

This latter point tends to be overlooked, as M. Hugen's unwarranted conclusions illustrate: "God's organic activity in saving man,

---

[116] J. Waterink, *Plaats en Methode van de Ambtelijke Vakken*, Zutphen: Drukkerij Nauta & Co., 1923, p. 149f: „De betekenis van de ziel, haar waardij en haar wezen, kunnen voor de Gereformeerde theologie alleen uit de Schrift worden gekend. Van dichotomistisch standpunt en naar de uitspraken der Openbaring Gods, zijn ook de vermogens der ziel te bepalen. Ook de religieuze psychologie heeft haar kenbron ten materiële en ten formele allereerst in de H. Schrift." Cf. also p. 178: "De theologie geeft dan ook, ... in het principiële deel de lijnen aan, lange welke de psychologie van de religie zich moet bewegen." For his view of psychology in general see his *Ons Zieleleven*, Wageningen: N.V. Gebr. Zomer & Keuning's Uitg., n.d.[6] (1946[5]), p. 10f: "De zielkunde ... is de wetenschap, die het wezen der ziel en de organisatie van het zieleleven bestudeert." "Dat de ziel des mensen een eigen substantie heeft en geformeerd is voor de eeuwigheid, leert de Schrift ons duidelijk." For an extensive discussion and critique of this (scholastic) view of the soul and psychology, see: Vollenhoven, *De Eerste Vragen der Psychologie*, Loosduinen: Drukkerij Kleywegt, 1930; by the same author: *Inleiding tot de Wijsgerige Anthropologie*, College-dictaat, Amsterdam: Uitg. Theja, 1958; Dooyeweerd, "Kuyper's Wetenschapsleer," *Phil. Ref.*, IV, 3 (1939), 129-150; by the same author: *A New Critique*, II, p. 111f; cf. also A. Dirkzwager, "Wereldbeschouwing, Theorievorming, Psychologie," *Phil. Ref.*, XXVII, 3, 4 (1962), 97-105. Regrettably Dr. Waterink has never seen the need to respond to this fundamental criticism or to defend his viewpoint. For a further discussion of Dr. Waterink's conception, see Chapter III, pp. 94ff.

man's organic reaction ... *require* that poimenics ... include sociological and psychological studies as *constituent* elements. Without
these it is an incomplete science. The scope of the church's ministry
to the individual is much more extensive than only that of the
direct ministry of proclamation." "The church feels no inconsistency in attempting to remedy injustice, in promoting psychic and
physical health, and in giving guidance to men with personal
problems."[117] The very thing that needs explaining, the relation
between the social and psychic aspect of man *and* his faith, and the
relation between the different sciences *and* theology, is presupposed
and not subjected to a further analysis. It can readily be admitted
that there is such a relationship, but it is questionable whether
psychology or sociology are *constituent* elements of poimenics.

Dr. Hugen rightly appealed to Waterink for his conception of
poimenics, since Waterink did consider "psychology and sociology
of religion" to be necessary areas of study for the theologian.[118]
Dr. Waterink's conception, however, was based not so much on the
principle of God's organic activity as on the inseparable connection
between the subject matter of the "psychology of religion" and
"practical theology". Scripture itself, Waterink maintained, provides the basic material and the main principles for a study of the
"soul" and "religion", and since Scripture is the *principium* of
theology, the disciplines dealing with these subjects must be
regarded as legitimate sub-divisions of theology, even though they
can also be granted a certain independence.[119] Hugen, on the other
hand, based his view primarily on the notion of "organic" in order
to make room, *within theology*, not for the "psychology of religion",
but for (positivistic and pragmatic?) psychology and sociology in
general.

This preoccupation with psychology and sociology has caused
the central issues of "practical theology" to remain in the background. Prof. Waterink did acknowledge that the results of the
"psychology of religion" should be applied in keeping with the
nature of liturgics or catechetics, and so forth, but he did not
subject the *nature* of worship and catechism *itself* to a further
inquiry.[128] A similar tendency can be found in Dr. Hugen's approach to poimenics. The proclamation of the Word of God

---

[117] M. D. Hugen, *The Church's Ministry to the Older Unmarried*, Grand
Rapids: Wm. B. Eerdmans Publ. Co., 1959[2], pp. 14, 15f. (emphasis added)
[118] Waterink, *Plaats en Methode*, p. 192.
[119] *Ibid.*, pp. 178, 184, 186.
[120] *Ibid.*, p. 185. Cf. also pp. 195ff.

"... may indeed be the kernel of the church's ministry to the individual, but its area is much more extensive. The investigation of the social and psychic aspects of man and his problems is a legitimate and even essential part of the theological science of poimenics." [121]

The increasing use of the nature-grace scheme and the subtle shift in emphasis meant a regression with respect to Kuyper's and Biesterveld's approach to "practical" theology. Conceivably a very different development would have been possible if their conceptions had been worked out. Then there could have been a growing awareness of the distinctive nature of the church's ministry as compared to somewhat similar activities in other areas of life, and as a result a more genuine integration and transformation of the findings of the other disciplines. Such a development, however, could not have taken place without a deeper understanding of the relation between "nature" and "grace" in general, or rather, between Scriptural revelation and creational revelation.

It must be acknowledged that all the publications we have encountered thus far manifest a great concern for the welfare of the church and its youth. The primary aim of every author has been to reform the church's education and to achieve a genuine renewal. This concern for the spiritual growth of the young members of the church must be fully appreciated and can only be shared. In this light our orientation and critical analysis must be understood. It has been motivated by the question why different attempts at reformation have not been successful and why the various solutions and perspectives do not satisfy. We have asked ourselves where they fall short and in what sense they fail; how we can gain a true insight into the nature and place of the church's education; how we can instruct the church's youth in such a manner that they are truly built up in the faith.

Confronted by these questions we can only conclude that as long as a dualistic scheme dominates thought, it is impossible to achieve a genuine reformation. Any attempt to come to a renewal of "religious" (!) education that is motivated and directed by a dialectic religious ground-motive is bound to fail. The inner tensions and contradictions these dialectic ground-motives give rise to cannot be solved unless there is a return to a Scriptural understanding of creation, sin, and redemption. The religious choice we make at this fundamental level has far-reaching consequences and

---

[121] Hugen, *The Church's Ministry*, p. 15.

manifests itself everywhere. Of course, like ten Have and Angermeyer and many others, one can choose for a dualistic conception,
but then let it be acknowledged that such a conception involves a
religious choice, and, as prof. Dooyeweerd has remarked once, let
it be shown then that such a viewpoint is founded on the Word of
God. [122]

At the same time that Dr. Waterink began to work out his basic
conception of psychology and education, prof. H. Dooyeweerd and
prof. D. H. Th. Vollenhoven began to reflect upon the relation
between "nature" and "grace". Under the inspiration of Dr. Abraham Kuyper's writings and through Calvin they were gripped by
the Scriptural ground-motive: the integral and radical meaning of
creation, the fall into sin, and the restoration in Jesus Christ. [123]
Motivated and directed by this religious understanding they began
a systematic study of the dynamic structure of reality, its unity and
diversity, and the interrelationship between its various aspects.
With the aid of these insights, developed in numerous writings, we
would in turn seek to gain a deeper understanding of the structure
and scope of the church's instruction in the faith.

To accomplish this purpose, as became apparent from our
orientation, we must first of all explore the place and task of the
church in general. Without such a structural analysis of the church
it is impossible to find an inner criterion to distinguish meaningfully between the instruction in the faith of different institutions
and organizations (home, school, church, youth organizations). To
avoid duplication and overlapping and to come to a delineation of
the typical aim of the church's educational program, it is imperative
that a norm be found that will enable us to differentiate between
the various types of faith-instruction. Certainly the church does not
have the prerogative in this respect, nor is the church (normally)
the first to instruct the child in the faith; therefore it is important
that we find the boundaries and scope of its task.

To gain an insight into the unique character of faith-instruction,
the necessity of which the American and German studies illustrate,

---

[122] Dooyeweerd, "De Wijsbegeerte der Wetsidee en de 'Barthianen'," *Phil.
Ref.,* XVI, 4 (1951), 161: "De barthianen zullen hunnerzijds bereid moeten zijn
hun dialectisch grondmotief inderdaad aan de critische vuurproef van Gods
Woord te onderwerpen en dus moeten aantonen, dat de radicale en integrale
opvatting van schepping, zondeval en verlossing on-bijbels is en dat in dit
centrale motief *naar de H. Schrift zelve* een verborgen tweespalt aan het licht
treedt, die de dialectische opvatting rechtvaardigt."
[123] Cf. Dooyeweerd, *A New Critique,* I, pp. 52-68, 170-188, 508-526; Vollenhoven, *Het Calvinisme,* pp. 13-67.

we must, in the second place, devote some time to the structure of education in general. Without such an analysis of education the peculiar nature of catechetical instruction will remain in the dark. This provides us in principle with an outline for the following chapters: The Church and its Ministry (Ch. II), The Nature of Education (Ch. III), The Church's Instruction in the Faith (Ch. IV). However, before we can pursue this course of study, there is another question that demands our attention.

D. A PRELIMINARY QUESTION

The preliminary question that must be answered before we can undertake a systematic analysis of the church's educational ministry concerns the nature of "Catechetics" as a theological discipline. From the very beginning the New Testament church has been engaged in teaching the first principles of the Christian faith. With this educational ministry the church shared in the task that had been given to the people of God from of old.[124] Throughout the ages servants of God have responded, more or less faithfully, to the divine charge to expound the good news of the Kingdom of Heaven. In all its weakness this ministry contains the mystery of the continuation of Christ's church from generation to generation. For it is the Lord himself who preserves and upholds his Body and who adds to its members those who are being saved. In view of this mystery we must ask ourselves whether a systematic study of this teaching-ministry is even possible. Shall not the very secret of the church's education escape us when we attempt to analyse it theoretically? And, if possible at all, what can we expect from such a systematic discipline? Is not the actual practice of the church something more than any theoretical analysis of this activity?[125] Certainly life consists of more than theoretical abstractions, and

---

[124] Cf. such passages as Deut. 4:9f; 6:7, 20ff; 11:19; 31:12; Ex. 10:2; 12:26ff; 13:8, 14ff; Josh. 4:6ff, 21ff; Ps. 78; and Lev. 10:11; Deut. 17:11; 24:8; 23:10; II Chr. 15:3; 17:7ff; 35:3; Ezra 7:10, 25; Neh. 8:2 8f., 28. See W. Jentsch, *Urchristliches Erziehungsdenken,* Gütersloh: C. Bertelsmann, 1951.

[125] Ten Have, *Een Methode,* p. 9: "Overtuigd van de waarde van het woord, doet dit ons enerzijds beseffen de noodzaak ons hiervan te bedienen om de zaak te omschrijven, maar anderzijds niet minder de moeilijkheid het wezenlijke in woorden weer te geven, hierin als het ware op te vangen. Omdat de volheid van het leven nooit in woorden adaequaat is weer te geven, kunnen we kleur en fleur, leven en bloei, nuance en toon van de catechese ook niet in een definitie verdisконteren, en moet elke begrips-bepaling daarom ook cum grano salis worden gelezen, willen we het eigenlijke niet missen."

no one could ever grasp, rule over, or control reality with his
scientific analysis. Such is perhaps the history of Western civilization, but it cannot be our approach. Our knowledge is limited
and represents but an aspect of reality, but of course that is no
reason to discredit theory in general. Theory and practice need
not be opposed to one another. Systematic reflection upon this
ministry of the church can lead to genuine knowledge and deepen
our understanding of the church's practice. To discredit all theory
with regard to catechetical instruction would be very impractical,
as the history of this teaching-ministry amply illustrates. Everything depends on how we conceive of Catechetics and what we
expect from this discipline. In this section, therefore, we want to
give a *brief account* of our conception of Catechetics as a theological discipline.

Anyone who begins a study of "practical" theology immediately
faces a baffling number of problems. The name itself, "practical"
theology, already leaves one guessing what to expect, and considering the history of the term one may well object to its use.[126]
The disagreements and confusion in this area are rather discon-
certing, especially when one takes into account national and
denominational differences. More than sixty years ago, prof.
P. Biesterveld already complained that there were hardly two
authors to be found that agree with one another.[127] This is true
of the past and it is true even today. Since the publication of
Dr. J. Waterink's dissertation in 1923,[128] which dealt with the
place and method of "practical" theology, no major study has
appeared on this subject within the Reformed community in the
Netherlands. Most of the writings after that,[129] treating one of
the "diaconological" subjects, have taken prof. Waterink's exposition, which in turn was largely based on Dr. Abraham Kuyper's
conception of theology and encyclopedic system,[130] for granted.

In 1939, however, prof. H. Doyeweerd presented a critical

---

[126] Cf. Waterink, *Plaats en Methode*, pp. 89-105.
[127] Biesterveld, *Het Object der Ambtelijke Vakken*, p. 9: "Maar er zijn er
geen twee te noemen, die, wat uitgangspunt en methode betreft, met elkander
overeenstemmen. Ook zij niet, die anders op het terrein der beginselen samen-
gaan. Er heerscht hier eene schier hopeloze verwarring".
[128] Waterink, *Plaats en Methode van de Ambtelijke Vakken.*
[129] Cf. J. G. Fernhout, *Psychotherapeutische Zielszorg*, Baarn: Bosch &
Keuning N.V., n.l., pp. 11, 12, 77; C. Gilhuis, *Pastorale Zorg aan Bejaarden*,
Kampen: J. H. Kok N.V., 1956, pp. 5, 7; M. D. Hugen, *The Church's Ministry
to the Older Unmarried*, pp. 1, 2; C. G. Kromminga, *The Communication of the
Gospel through Neighbouring*, Franeker: T. Wever, 1964, pp. 108-119.
[130] A. Kuyper, *Encyclopaedie der Heilige Godgeleerdheid.*

analysis of Dr. Kuyper's conception of theology and of science in general, drawing attention *both* to scholastic influences *and* to genuinely Scriptural and reformational insights. [181] But until now his critique and positive contributions have not yet been assimilated or worked out, nor have other conceptions of ("practical") theology been set forth, with the result that a serious lag exists in the area of *prolegomena*. [182] This vacuum and lack of clarity with regard to the very basis of ("practical") theology manifests itself everywhere and presents a major obstacle to any detailed study of a particular theological problem.

In the meantime other significant studies have appeared by such differently orientated authors as S. Hiltner, H. Diem, and A. D. Müller, to mention only these three. [183] The works of the first two authors may well serve as an example of the developments within "practical" theology, since they present alternative viewpoints. Dr. Hiltner's book entitled *Preface to Pastoral Theology* may be seen as typical of a functional approach to "practical"

---

[181] Dooyeweerd, *Phil. Ref.*, IV, 4, 193-232. See also Vollenhoven, "De souvereiniteit in eigen kring bij Kuyper en ons," *Mededelingen van de Vereniging voor Calvinistische Wijsbegeerte,* (December, 1950), 4-7; ————, "Norm en Natuurwet," *Mededelingen,* (Juli, 1951), 3-6; ————, "De visie op de Middelaar bij Kuyper en ons," *Mededelingen,* (September, 1952), 3-9, (December, 1952), 3-4; K. Schilder, D. H. Th. Vollenhoven, *Van "Oorzaken en Redenen":* Minderheidsnota inzake Algemene Genade, Genadeverbond, De onsterfelijkheid der ziel, Pluriformiteit der kerk. Vereniging der twee naturen van Christus, en Zelfonderzoek, Kampen/Amsterdam: (stencil), 1939; J. Stellingwerff, "Kritiek op K. Schilder als Filosoferend Dogmaticus," *Phil. Ref.*, XXVII, 3, 4 (1962), 124, note 6. Within Reformed theology Dooyeweerd's and Vollenhoven's analysis of Kuyper's conception has not yet received the attention it deserves. The passing references to Dooyeweerd's critique made by Dr. W. H. Velema in his *De Leer van de Heilige Geest bij Abraham Kuyper*, 's-Gravenhage: Van Keulen N.V., 1957, p. 81, note 80, can hardly be considered adequate. As F. H. von Meyenfeldt has remarked: "Als Dr. Velema Dooyeweerd had willen bestrijden op dit punt, had hij moeten aantonen dat deze eenheidsconceptie niet gevonden wordt bij Kuyper, maar dat daarentegen de genoemde scholastieke dichotomie voor Kuyper het een en het al is." "Zo is de problematiek van de Kuyperinterpretatie door dit proefschrift m.i. nog niet opgeheven." *Phil. Ref.*, XXIII, 4 (1958), 183, 184.

[182] The remark the Rev. E. G. van Teylingen makes with regard to Dr. Berkouwer's *Dogmatische Studiën* can be applied to Reformed theology in general: "Daarom doen zijn boeken over de eschata des te dringender de behoefte blijken aan de behandeling van de prolegomena der dogmatiek." *Gereformeerd Theologisch Tijdschrift*, "Futurum en Futurisme," LXIV, 2 (Mei, 1964), 107.

[183] S. Hiltner, *Preface to Pastoral Theology*, New York/Nashville: Abingdon Press, 1958; H. Diem, *Theologie als kirchliche Wissenschaft*, Vols. I-III, München: Chr. Kaiser Verlag, 1951-1963; A. D. Müller, *Grundriss der Praktischen Theologie*, Gütersloh: C. Bertelsman Verlag, 1950.

theology, while prof. Diem's three-volume work *Theologie als kirchliche Wissenschaft* reflects, in the main, Karl Barth's conception of theology. These two publications manifest a contrast similar to that which we encountered between the American and German studies on "religious" education. Neither conception, in our estimation, can give an adequate account of the nature of the church's practice. Dr. Hiltner's approach fails to do justice to the normative aspect of the church's ministry and is constantly in danger of reducing the Christian faith to psycho-social processes.[134] Dr. Diem's conceptions on the other hand, cannot do justice to the structural aspect of the church's ministry.[135] Both theories, however, deserve separate treatment, and are too important to deal with in passing. For now we merely want to call attention to these alternative approaches to ("practical") theology.

Against this background and keeping in mind the aim of this study, we want to give a *brief account* of our starting-point and an indication of our conception of Catechetics as a theological science. In several books and many articles prof. Dooyeweerd has presented a genuinely Scriptural foundation for theology.[136] His challenging

---

[134] In this work Dr. Hiltner deals with an important state of affairs, which, when recognized and assimilated, has far-reaching consequences for our understanding of "practical" theology. In many ways our present study is an attempt in the area of catechetical instruction (but the same holds true for other areas of the church's ministry as well) to integrate and account for the "structural" aspects Dr. Hiltner has brought to the fore. For a short summary and critique of Dr. Hiltner's main thesis, see C. G. Kromminga's introduction to *The Pastoral Genius of Preaching*, by S. Volbeda, Grand Rapids: Zondervan Publ. House, 1960. Although we cannot agree with Dr. Kromminga's own solution, he has rightly drawn attention to the basic problem of the functional or the "operation-centered" perspective of Dr. Hiltner.

[135] In as much as H. Diem's conception and presuppositions reflect K. Barth's view of theology, his theory is subject to the same objections Dooyeweerd has made with regard to Barth. Cf. Dooyeweerd, *Phil. Ref.*, XVI, 4 (1951), 145-162; ——————, *Phil. Ref.*, XXIII, 1, 2 (1958), 1-21, 50-84; ——————, *In the Twilight of Western Thought*, Philadelphia: The Presbyterian and Reformed Publishing Company, 1960, pp. 113-172. Cf. also S. U. Zuidema, "Theologie en wijsbegeerte in de 'Kirchliche Dogmatik' van Karl Barth," *Phil. Ref.*, XVIII, 2, 3 (1953), 77-138.

[136] Dooyeweerd, "Kuyper's Wetenschapsleer," *Phil. Ref.*, IV, 4 (1939), 193-232; ——————, "De vier religieuze grondthema's in den ontwikkelingsgang van het wijsgerig denken van het Avondland," *Phil. Ref.*, VI, 4 (1941), 161-179; ——————, "De leer der analogie in de Thomistische wijsbegeerte en in de Wijsbegeerte der Westidee," *Phil. Ref.*, VII, 1, 2 (1942), 45-47; ——————, "De idee der individualiteitsstructuur en het Thomistisch substantie-begrip," *Phil. Ref.*, VIII, 3, 4 (1943), 65-99; IX, 1, 2 (1944), 1-41; X, 4 (1945), 25-48; XI, 1 (1946), 22-52; ——————, "Het wijsgerig tweegesprek tussen de Thomistische philosophie en de Wijsbegeerte der Wetsidee," *Phil. Ref.*, XIII, 1, 2, 3 (1948), 26-31, 49-58; ——————, "De Wijsbegeerte der

and positive contributions regarding the religious and philosophical presuppositions of theology provide us with a valuable perspective for our theologizing. For the dilemma is not whether or not theology must take its starting-point in certain philosophical presuppositions, but whether or not these philosophical presuppositions are Scripturally founded and orientated. As a science theology cannot do without religious and philosophical presuppositions. [187]

A truly Scriptural theology, according to prof. Dooyeweerd, [188] must be founded in a true knowledge of God and ourselves. This knowledge can only be worked by the Holy Spirit through the operation of the Word of God in our hearts, as the religious root and center of our existence. True self-knowledge, which is dependent upon our knowledge of God as Calvin already maintained in the first part of his *Institutes,* is the key to all other knowledge both practical and theoretical. This central principle of knowledge is not of a theological nature and cannot be made into a theological problem, since it is the very presupposition of all Scriptural theologizing. The theologian can only acknowledge his starting-point

---

Wetsidee en de 'Barthianen'," XVI, 4 *(1951),* 145-162; ——————, "De trancendentale critiek van het theoretisch denken en de theologia naturalis," *Phil. Ref.,* XVII, 4*(1952),* 151-184; ——————, "De verhouding tussen wijsbegeerte en theologie en de strijd der faculteiten," *Phil. Ref.,* XXIII, 1, 2 *(1958),* 1-21, 50-84; ——————, *A New Critique,* Vols. I-III, *1953-1957, passim;* ——————, *Vernieuwing en Bezinning,* Zutphen: J. B. van den Brink & Co., 1959, *pass.;* ——————, *In the Twilight, 1960,* pp. 113-172.

See also Vollenhoven, *Het Calvinisme;* J. P. A. Mekkes, *Scheppingsopenbaring en Wijsbegeerte,* Kampen: J. H. Kok N.V., 1961; F. H. von Meyenfeldt, "Enige algemene beschouwingen gegrond op de betekenis van het hart in het Oude Testament," in *Wetenschappelijke Bijdragen door leerlingen van Dr. D. H. Th. Vollenhoven,* Franeker: T. Wever, 1951, pp. 52-67; J. M. Spier, "De norm voor ons geloven," in *Wetenschappelijke Bijdragen,* pp. 72-89; ——————, "Het veld van onderzoek voor de theologie," *Phil. Ref.,* XV, 4 (1950), 169-178, XVI, 1, 2 (1951), 1-15; E. G. van Teylingen, "Over terminologie in de theologie," *Ger. Theol. Tijdschrift,* LXI, 4, 5 (1961), 117-130; J. Stellingwerff, "Kritiek op K. Schilder als filosoferend dogmaticus," *Phil. Ref.,* XXI, 1, 2 (1956), 1-44; *et. al.;* many other articles can be found in *Mededelingen en Correspondentiebladen.*

[187] Dooyeweerd, *Phil. Ref.,* XXIII, 2, 69: "Het dilemma voor de theologie is niet: of ze al of niet wijsgerig gefundeerd moet zijn, maar of ze haar wijsgerige grondslagen in een schriftuurlijke, dan wel in een onschriftuurlijke philosophie zal zoeken. Want zij *kan* als wetenschap niet zonder wijsgerige grondslagen bestaan."

[188] For a more detailed description we must refer to prof. Dooyeweerd's own writings. See note 136.

and bear witness to its radical meaning, since it involves a religious choice. [139]

It is the Holy Spirit through the power of the Word of God who opens our eyes to the claim God has upon us as creatures made in His image, who leads us to acknowledge our radical corruption and spiritual death as fallen man, and it is He who leads us to surrender our lives to God's service, following in the footsteps of our Master. The Word of God revealed in the Scriptures is a divine spiritual Power, regenerating our hearts and renewing our lives. Thus God's Word is the central principle of knowledge and the foundation of the Christian life, both in its practical and scientific activity. In communion with his fellow-believers, each Christian has the calling to hear, interpret and apply the Word of God, for it is by this Word that he shall live.

The central theme of the Scriptures in their integral unity can be formulated in what Dooyeweerd has called the Scriptural

---

[139] Dooyeweerd, *In the Twilight*, pp. 120ff; —————, *Phil, Ref.*, XVIII, 1, 3ff. His remarks in *Verkenningen in de Wijsbegeerte, de Sociologie en de Rechtsgeschiedenis*, Amsterdam: Buijten & Schipperheijn, 1962, pp. 12, 14, may well serve as a summary of his entire (religious) perspective. There he writes: "Wat bedoelde immers Kuyper toen hij het reformatorisch beginsel, dat Calvijn dreef, weer als een heel het leven omvattend principe in het licht stelde en tegenover iedere dualistische scheiding van een 'Christelijke' en een 'wereld-se' sfeer, weer erkenning eiste van het universele koningschap van Christus over alle terreinen van het leven? Het ging hem in diepste zin om een leven en denken vanuit die centrale eenheid der Heilige Schrift, die zich boven de divergentie der menselijke opvattingen en interpretaties verheft, omdat zij niet uit de mens voortkomt, maar, als de geestelijke *dunamis* van het goddelijk Woord, *bezit* neemt van de mens en onvoorwaardelijke zelf-overgave eist. Van die geestelijke dunamis gaat de centrale werking uit op het menselijk hart, 't zij in aantrekkende, 't zij in afstotende zin, maar nog vóór alle theoretische overlegging van het menselijk denken." "Het gaat hier echter niet slechts om de individuele mens, maar om de gemeenschap van de in Christus gewortelde nieuwe mensheid, om het koninkrijk Gods, dat in de van God afgevallen wereld een rusteloze strijd heeft te voeren tegen het rijk der duisternis. De gehele wereld in al haar verschillende levensgebieden is het terrein van deze strijd, die vanuit de religieuze wortel zich in het tijdelijke leven voortplant." "Daarom raakt de centrale greep van het Woord Gods ... alle menselijke samenlevings-verhoudingen, de staatkunde, de cultuur, de wetenschap, de wijsbegeerte. De erkenning van deze radicale en integrale betekenis van de Christelijke religie mag niet als een specifiek Calvinistisch standpunt worden voorgesteld. Zij dringt zich vanuit het centrale grondmotief der Heilige Schrift, ... onweer-staanbaar op en het is alleen te wijten aan de inwerking van on-bijbelse mo-tieven, wanneer die erkenning plaats maakt voor de aanvaarding van een 'eigenmachtigheid' of 'autonomie' van het 'natuurlijk' of 'wereldlijk' leven. Kuyper drong achter de theologische en wijsgerige strijdvragen door tot de diepste en volstrekt centrale geestelijke drijfkrachten, die het menselijk leven en denken bewegen en die als zodanig niet in het vlak der theoretische of weten-

ground-motive. The Word of God is the revelation of *an integral creation, the radical fall, and the equally radical restoration in Jesus Christ.* This Scriptural ground-motive is not to be interpreted as a static, formal summary of the teachings of Scripture, but as a *religious ground-motive,* that is, as an indication of the driving and directing force of our life, as that which motivates us and holds us in its grip. It is nothing less than a reference to the Power of the Word of God operating in our hearts through the Holy Spirit. [140]

As the central principle of knowledge the Word of God is directed to the heart of man as the religious concentration-point of his entire existence. Always and everywhere man stands before the face of the Lord, addressed by His Word. It is impossible to consider him apart from this relationship to God, for he is a religious being created in the image of God. "Right at the beginning God bound man to himself both in the structure of his being and in his

---

schappelijke problematiek kunnen worden gebracht, omdat elke theortische bezinning zich reeds bij voorbaat in hun greep bevindt." "Hier, in de volstrekt centrale sfeer der religie wordt de uiteindelijke antithese openbaar, die van daaruit ook in de gehele levens- en denkhouding van de mens een onontwijkbare positiekeuze eist.

De Wijsbegeerte der Wetsidee gaat, wanneer zij deze zuiver bijbelse gedachte van Kuyper volgt, er van uit dat het centrale, radicale en integrale motief van de Heilige Schrift, dat van schepping, zondeval en verlossing door Jezus Christus als het vlees-geworden Woord, als de sleutel der kennis, niet afhankelijk is van menselijke theologische interpretatie. Het staat niet ter beschikking van de mens, maar het beschikt over de mens." Any critique of prof. Dooyeweerd's conception of theology, it would seem, must begin at this fundamental level.

140 Dooyeweerd, *A New Critique,* I, pp. 173-188. See also Berkouwer, *Phil. Ref.,* XXI, 86ff; H. E. Runner, "The Relation of the Bible to Learning," in *Christian Perspectives,* Pella: Pella Publishing, Inc., 1960, p. 112f.; K. J. Popma, "Het systematisch karakter van de theologische dogmatiek," *Phil. Ref.,* XXV, 1, 2 (1960), 30ff. Both Dr. Runner and prof. Popma have responded to Dr. C. A. van Peursen's obvious misunderstanding of Dooyeweerd's formulation of the Scriptural ground-motive in his *Filosofische Oriëntatie,* Kampen: J. H. Kok N.V., 1964[2]. In spite of a further exposition by Dooyeweerd, Dr. van Peursen has seen no need to change his presentation of Dooyeweerd's intention in the second edition of his book! Cf. C. A. van Peursen, "Vragen bij 'A New Critique of Theoretical Thought'," *Phil. Ref.,* XXIV, 3, 4 (1959), 167; Dooyeweerd, "Van Peursen's critische vragen bij 'A New Critique of Theoretical Thought'," *Phil. Ref.,* XXV, 3, 4 (1960), 99-105; Van Peursen, "Antwoord aan Dooyeweerd," *Phil. Ref.,* XXVI, 4 (1961), 198-200; Mekkes "Wet en subject in de wijsbegeerte der wetsidee," *Phil. Ref.,* XXVII, 3, 4 (1962), 152ff., 179ff.

With Berkouwer we can only conclude ". . . dat het Dooyeweerd niet te doen is om een *quantitatieve* abstractie van een bepaalde waarheid (of van waarheden) uit de openbaring Gods om dan vanuit deze waarheid zijn systeem op te bouwen, maar om een 'existentiële' betrokkenheid van de ganse mens op de

assigned task." "Essential therefore to religion is the idea of office
which means that man is everywhere and always the servant of the
Lord, called to obedience and placed in a position of responsibility
and trust."[141] Centered in the heart of man, religion concerns
man's entire being and not merely one of his aspects. The direction
of his heart expresses itself in *all* his functions and is decisive
for all his activities, including his theologizing.[142]

Man's religion, therefore, must be distinguished from his belief.
"As the absolutely central sphere of human existence, religion
transcends all modal aspects of temporal reality, *the aspect of faith
included*. It is not at all a temporal phenomenon which manifests
itself within the temporal structure of human act-life." "Therefore
with respect to its inner essence, religion can never be described
'phenomenologically'." "It is the *ex-sistent* condition in which the
ego is bound to its true or pretended firm ground. Hence, the mode
of being of the ego itself is of a religious character and it is nothing

---

openbaring Gods in de kracht des Geestes," "Van enige 'self-sufficiency' van
de mens in het grondmotief is in het geheel geen sprake, omdat juist hier —
in het hart — alles op het spel komt te staan." "Het religieus a priori is niet een
vervanging van de onderworpenheid aan het Woord Gods, maar de *om-
schrijving* van die onderworpenheid. Liever nog: die onderworpenheid zelf."
Phil. Ref., XXI, 1, 2, 36f. See also note 139.

[141] P. G. Schrotenboer, *The Nature of Religion*, Hamilton: The Association
for Reformed Scientific Studies, 1964, p. 13.

[142] Cf. Von Meyenfeldt, *Wetenschappelijke bijdragen*, p. 59: "De religie
van de mens is niet een zaak van een zijner vermogens of functies of belevenis-
sen of wat ge wilt; maar de religie is zaak van de authentieke, de onvervalste
mens; m.a.w. de religie is zaak des harten." See also G. C. Berkouwer, *De Mens
het Beeld Gods*, Kampen: J. H. Kok N.V., 1957, p. 220: "... *in* het hart gaat
het om de ganse mens, die juist daarom niet aangesproken wordt als een los
agglomeraat van functies, maar in zijn geconcentreerde eenheid. Het is dan
ook de mens zelf, die leeft en werkt in al z'n functies." And p. 221: "In het
hart gaat het om de *totale* oriëntering, gerichtheid, concentratie van de mens
in en vanuit zijn hart, om de diepte-dimensie, waardoor 's mensen volle bestaan wordt geleid en gestempeld. En wie zijn *hart* aan de Heer geeft, geeft zijn
ganse leven." See further H. N. Ridderbos, *Paulus: Ontwerp van zijn Theologie*,
Kampen: J. H. Kok N.V., 1966, p. 127: "En gelijk God Zich door zijn openbaring aan des mensen hart betuigt, als het eigenlijke centrum van zijn wezen,
zo is ook dit hart het subject van het antwoord, dat de mens op deze openbaring geeft, hetzij positief, hetzij negatief; dat door God daarop ook wordt
doorzocht, beproefd, openbaar gemaakt, ..." "Maar in al dit veelvuldig gebruik van het woord hart, in de meest beslissende uitspraken, die aangaande
de mens gedaan kunnen worden, wordt tot uitdrukking gebracht, dat de mens
ten diepste vanuit een punt geleid en bestuurd wordt, daarin het eigenlijke
mens-zijn vertoont, zowel in zijn vatbaarheid voor de openbaring van God als
in zijn verantwoordelijkheid voor zijn denken, willen en handelen."

in itself. Veritable religion is absolute *self-surrender.*"[143] This conception of religion does not reduce man's nature to a relationship, but, in keeping with the Scriptural witness, it implies that we cannot talk about man's nature apart from his relationship to God, and the religious direction of his heart.[144] Religion therefore should not be taken in the sense of a separate area of human life, nor should the concentration-point of our existence, the heart, be thought of as a "religious center" with a "separate function". All dualism, speculation, or mysticism with regard to religion and our selfhood must be radically rejected.[145]

Our relationship to God, concentrated in our hearts, can only come to expression *in* our temporal functions, *within* the act-structure of our human bodies.[146] It is only through *faith* therefore that the heart directs itself to the Lord and that we have knowledge of our relation to Him. It is through *faith* that divine Revelation enters our temporal horizon. Within the act-structure it is our faith, as the leading function, that governs and directs all of our activities, however they are qualified.[147] Faith, in this context, has reference to what Dooyeweerd has called the "pistical" function of man and as a *function* it can never be *identified* with religion, which refers to the direction of man's functions and not to the structure or the functions *as such*.

---

[143] Dooyeweerd, *A New Critique*, I, p. 57f. Cf. Von Meyenfeldt, *Kerkelijk Vooruitzicht*, Wageningen: N.V. Gebr. Zomer & Keunings, n.d., p. 126: "Religie is dus niet een van de vele bestaanswijzen van de mens, zoals het kerkelijk leven er een is. Voor de Schrift is immers de situatie van de mens zo, dat God in Christus contact met hem opneemt in wat het meest wezenlijk is voor de mens, de diepste verborgenheid van zijn bestaan. We bevinden ons hier op een ander niveau dan bij het kerkelijk belijden. Want als zodanig is de religieuze relatie en wat wij daarin meemaken onuitsprekelijk. Alle formulering zal tekort schieten wanneer het er om gaat onder woorden te brengen wie God voor mij is in Christus Jezus."

[144] Cf. Berkouwer, *Phil. Ref.* XXI, 30ff; ————, *De Mens*, pp. 32, 287ff; ————, *Conflict met Rome*, Kampen: J. H. Kok N.V., 1953³, pp. 137ff. This touches upon a central issue of Christian philosophy. Cf. H. van Riessen, "Betekenis van de wetsidee in de wijsbegeerte," *Phil. Ref.*, XXX, 3, 4 (1965), 161ff; Mekkes, *Phil. Ref.*, XXVII, 3, 4, 126-190.

[145] Dooyeweerd, *A New Critique*, II, p. 303. Cf. also Mekkes, *Phil. Ref.*, XXIV, 3, 4 (1959), 186.

[146] Dooyeweerd, *A New Critique*, III, 87-89.

[147] Cf. A. Troost, *Casuïstiek en Situatie-ethiek*, Utrecht: Drukkerij Libertas N.V., 1958, p. 126: "Door de geloofs-functie, die als modaal levensaspect in directe zin is toegeordend aan het Woord Gods als de 'wet' voor het geloof, vindt de religieus bepaalde volle levenswerkelijkheid haar bewuste betrekking op God en Zijn openbaring in Christus Jezus, alsmede op zijn koninkrijk"

The modal faith-aspect should be distinguished from the concrete act of believing. The "pistical" function pertains to a fundamental *manner* of experiencing, distinct from all other modes
of experience, and belongs to the order of creation.[148] As a modal
aspect the "pistical" function can only be *theoretically abstracted*
from the full and integral act of believing. The concrete act, on the
other hand, functions in all the modalities and is only qualified
by the faith-aspect, giving it a typical character. Although belonging to the order of creation the faith-aspect occupies an
exceptional position as the limiting aspect of this order, and "refers
beyond the temporal order to the religious center of our existence
and to the divine Origin of all that has been created."[149] For this
reason Dooyeweerd describes the modal kernel of the faith-aspect
as *"that ultimate mode of certitude within the temporal order of
experience which refers to an indubitable revelation of God
touching us in the religious center of our existence."*[150] Thus there
is an inseparable relation between faith and Revelation.[151]

The emphasis upon the leading role of faith, which is sometimes
overlooked, the distinction between the "pistical" function and the
concrete act of believing, and the exceptional place of the

Mekkes, *Phil. Ref.*, XXIII, 4 (1958), 188: "Het is in het geloof dat de mens
de actualisering van zijn tijdelijk leven aanvangt, hetzij persisterend in de afval
dan wel telkens zich bekerend tot God. De Heilige Geest spreekt hem door de
Woordopenbaring aan in zijn geloof en via dat geloof voor *heel* zijn bestaan.
Door het geloof worden al zijn akten en handelingen, modaal ethisch dan wel
anders gekwalificeerd, ontsloten en toegesloten. De strijd der antithese in het
hart treedt in de geloofsstrijd naar buiten. In zijn op God gericht geloof ver-
wacht het herboren hart bij uitsluiting alles van Hem Die dit geloof in ons
plant en Die het voleindt." Compare also his remarks in *Phil. Ref.*, XXIV,
3, 4 1959), 186: "Het geloof niet als een *geïsoleerde* functie — wie het zo zou
zien, heeft het aan eigen analytisme te danken als hij met het geloof geen weg
meer weet — doch als dat wat geheel het bestaan beheerst en de richting van
elke akt en handeling bepaalt. Van onze radicale verhouding tot de Schepper,
waardoor wij als mens zijn gekwalificeerd, weten wij eveneens slechts door het
geloof. Niet slechts elke speculatie maar ook elke mystiek inzake de wortel
van ons bestaan wordt door de Woordopenbaring afgewezen. Wie de weg naar
God zoekt, zal uitsluitend door het geloof leven."

[148] Dooyeweerd, *In the Twilight*, p. 137; —————, *A New Critique*,
II, p. 289; —————, *Phil. Ref.*, XXIII, 1, 14.

[149] Dooyeweerd, *In the Twilight*, p. 138.

[150] *Loc. cit.* See also *A New Critique*, II, p. 304, and *Phil. Ref.*, XXIII,
2, 50.

[151] Dooyeweerd, *Phil. Ref.*, XXIII, 2, 49: "Het geloofsaspect echter anti-
cipeert in zijn *modale kern* onmiddellijk op de absolute Oorsprong aller dingen,
die de tijd *te boven gaat*, en die zich slechts door *zelf-openbaring* aan de mens
kenbaar maakt." "Het geloof is dus steeds op Godsopenbaring betrokken. Die
betrokkenheid behoort tot zijn *wezen*, tot zijn *onuitwisbaar karakter*"

"pistical" modality, as the limiting aspect referring beyond the temporal order both to God's revelation and to the religious center of our existence, should dispel the reluctance of some to recognize a faith-aspect in distinction from religion as the concentration-point of all aspects. The failure to recognize this distinction between religion and the concrete human act of believing qualified by the faith-aspect is not without consequences. *Invariably it leaves room for a more or less docetic or spiritualistic conception of faith, and, consequently, a dualism between faith (religion) and creation.*[152] The primary question, therefore, with respect to Dooyeweerd's arguments for distinguishing religion from the human act of believing, qualified by the faith-aspect, is "... whether Christian belief can function outside of the temporal order of creation in which the modal aspect of faith has an essential and undeniable terminal position."[153]

The only legitimate basis for Christian theology is the *a priori*, pre-theoretical, religious basic motive of Scripture: creation, fall, and redemption in Jesus Christ in communion with the Holy Spirit. The theologian must be in the grip of this driving force of God's Word before he can truth-fully reflect upon the teachings of Scripture in relation to the confessions of the church. In other words, for a genuine Biblical theology it is necessary that the theologian

---

[152] Cf. Von Meyenfeldt, *Wetenschappelijke Bijdragen*, p. 62; Van Teylingen, *G.T.T.*, *LXI*, 4, 5, 126: "Nu is het waar dat het spreken van geloof-als-functie *kan* getuigen van een tergende oppervlakkigheid, alsof niet juist in de *activiteit* van het geloof zich het geheim van de ontmoeting tussen God en de mens, het geheim der religie, verbergt." "Het is wel zo dat de mens in zijn prae-functionele religie des harten boven de tijd uitgrijpt, maar hij ontsnapt nimmer aan de tijd: daarom betekent geloven ook *menselijk functioneren*. Anders moet men terugvallen in een *dualisme* tussen de *functionerende mens* en zijn *religie* of ook tussen *schepping* en *verbond*." (emphasis added) We fear, therefore, that the . distinction prof. Popma makes between religion and our creatureliness will lead us back — unintentionally — to some kind of dualism. Cf. K. J. Popma, *Inleiding in de Wijsbegeerte*, Kampen: J. H. Kok N.V., 1956, p. 91: "Religie en geschapenheid zijn beide relaties (betrekkingen) tot God. Tegen deze gemeenschappelijke achtergrond onderscheiden we religie en geschapenheid als de relatie tot *God de Here* en de relatie tot *God de Schepper*." (emphasis added) And by the same author *Correspondentiebladen*, XVI (Mei, 1952), 8. With respect to this tendency prof. Mekkes remarked: "Men wil gaarne in dit tijdelijk bestaan nog een aparte (sit venia verbo) 'functie' aan een 'religieus' centrum toekennen". *Phil. Ref.*, XXIV, 3, 4, 186. With Dooyeweerd we can only conclude that: "Compared with all these misunderstandings Kuyper's really Biblical conception of faith as a temporal function must be considered as breaking new ground." *A New Critique*, II, p. 303.

[153] Dooyeweerd, *A New Critique*, II, p. 302.

be *constantly guided by* his *actual believing* in subjection to the
norms for his faith laid down in the Word of God.

These presuppositions of a truly Scriptural theology cannot be
made into a theological problem, for they are always presupposed
and escape all theological concepts. Our actual belief through
which we know with *ultimate certainty,* is not subject to theoretical
reflection. Neither can the Word of God as the central principle
of knowledge become the object of *theoretical* thought. Our acceptance or rejection of God's powerful Word is a matter of life or
death, and not a question of theological research. God's revelation
of Himself is always existential, touching the center of our
existence. [154] Here we are beyond the scientific problems of theology, or, for that matter, of any science. [155]

All that has been said up till now about the pre-theoretical
religious basis of theology has far-reaching implications. First of
all, it means that we must carefully distinguish between the Word
of God as the central principle of knowledge *and* the scientific
object of theological exegesis. [156] Scripture in its central religious
sense directs itself to the heart of man and cannot become the
theoretical object of theological interpretation. When God addresses us, we cannot dissociate ourselves, not even for a moment, from
God's Word to determine its meaning. He demands a wholehearted response. A Scripturally directed *scientific* interpretation of
the Bible already presupposes that we are in the grip of the active
and renewing Word of God. Only the Holy Spirit operating
through this powerful Word can open our hearts and enlighten our
minds to the true meaning of Scripture, and not the exegete. In
his *theoretical* interpretation the exegete himself is constantly
directed and guided by his religious commitment and actual
belief. [157]

---

154   Dooyeweerd, *In the Twilight*, p. 125. Compare note 139.

155   Cf. Van Teylingen, *G.T.T.*, LXI, 4, 5, 122: "Onze diepste kennis van de
mens en zijn geheim, van de ware mens, is religieuze kennis; zij berust op openbaring en hangt met onze kennis van God volstrekt samen. Ze is voorwaarde
voor alle wetenschappelijke kenniswerving, maar kan er nooit inhoud van zijn."
See also Mekkes, "Boekbespreking: Dr. H. Berkhof, God voorwerp van wetenschap?" *Phil. Ref.*, XXVI, 4 (1961), 219-223; and his *Scheppingsopenbaring,*
pp. 50-60; Dooyeweerd, *Phil. Ref.*, XXV, 3, 4, 100ff.

156   Dooyeweerd, *In the Twilight*, p. 136, likewise in *Phil. Ref.*, XXIII,
13, 53.

157   Cf. Von Meyenfeldt, *Wetenschappelijke Bijdragen*, p. 56: "Een mens
komt met zijn ideeën en begrippen tot het woord van de tekst en zijn verstaan
van dat woord geschiedt mede vanuit zijn ideologie, zouden wij kunnen zeggen." "De exegeet zij er van overtuigd, dat hij bepakt en gezakt zijn veld van
onderzoek betreedt." Cf. also S. U. Zuidema, "Openbaringsinhoud en existentie

The basic theme of Scripture as the key to knowledge is always presupposed in Christian thought and cannot be subjected to *theoretical* analysis. The failure to recognize or account for this fact can only lead us astray. Therefore we cannot accept Dr. R. Schipper's description of the so-called "hermeneutic circle".[158] Once we are in the grip of God's Word, our daily use of Scripture can indeed deepen our understanding of the integral unity and meaning of Scripture, and, *vice versa*, our knowledge of the central meaning of Scripture can indeed aid us in interpreting its various parts. However, this is not a theoretical question, but a matter of faithful listening to God's Word, an activity which takes place on the level of faith. No *theoretical* analysis, however enlightening or Christian, can help us to get into this "hermeneutic circle" correctly. A correct understanding of the Word of God is the sole result of the operation of the Holy Spirit in our hearts.

To talk of a "hermeneutic circle" on the theoretical level is, to say the least, misleading. For all *scientific* exegesis is directed by religious and philosophical presuppositions, and not by a *theoretical* conception of the total meaning of Scripture. Neither can the basic theme of Scripture be established by a *theoretical* study of its various parts, since these scientific studies *themselves* are founded in a *religious choice* with regard to the central meaning of the Word of God. This does *not* mean that exegetical studies are of little significance for the believer. On the contrary, these studies can greatly enhance and deepen his knowledge of Scripture. There

---

in de theologische hermeneutiek van R. Bultmann," *Mededelingen*, (Dec., 1964), 2-7, who concludes his article with the following statement: "... dat Bultmanns theologische hermeneutiek er een zoveelste bewijs van is, dat theologie, in elk geval zoals zij in onze Westerse kultuurwereld reilt en zeilt, steeds weer aan filosofische presupposita gebonden blijkt te zijn, en dat niemand een theologische visie en werkwijze, zoals die van Bultmann, in haar wortel kan peilen, als men deze wijsgerige presuppositie niet onderkent en deze presupposita op eigen, d.i. op *wijsgerig* terrein, in diskussie stelt." See below pp. 65, 66.

158 R. Schippers, *De geschiedenis van Jezus en de apocalyptiek*, Kampen: J. H. Kok N.V., 1964. In this address Dr. Schippers deals with the relation between *Christian faith* and *scientific exegetical knowledge* (p. 3). To interpret Scripture, prof. Schippers maintains, one is in need of a hermeneutic principle. 'Dat laatste moet dan wél aan de te onderzoeken en onderzochten teksten worden ontleend en door hen worden gerechtvaardigd." (p. 7) For this reason Dr. Schippers wants to see if the (theoretical?!) conception of E. Käsemann "... kan helpen op de goede wijze binnen de hermeneutische cirkel te komen'." (p. 8) To a great extent prof. Schippers can go along with Käsemann's analysis. At the end, however, he dissociates himself from Käsemann's view by making a religious choice. (p. 22, 24)

What makes this appeal to faith necessary, we wonder, is it because the diffe-

is *no opposition* between the believer's integral understanding of the Word of God and the theoretical expositions of the theologian. These two different kinds of knowledge may not be played off against one another. They are simply of a different order. A detailed exegetical study is of no use to the believer unless it is transposed and re-integrated with his full and integral understanding of the Word of God. In this way theoretical exegetical studies can indeed be of great value to the believer and deepen and broaden his "practical" (integral and total) knowledge of Scripture. This conception implies that the theological interpretation of Scripture can never be the final authority for the believer, since *theology itself is directed by a pre-scientific understanding of Scripture. Purely* exegetical arguments, therefore, do not exist, because they are always based upon and guided by a religious conviction with regard to the central meaning of the Word of God. Theology has scientific (no more and no less) and not religious authority, so that, in the end, the community of believers can always appeal to their religious understanding of the Scriptures. And it is for this reason that we cannot really talk about a hermeneutic *circle,* even though it remains true that one part of Scripture may help us to explain another part and vice versa.

Secondly, the recognition of the *a priori* religious basis of theology means we must distinguish between the *knowledge of faith and the theoretical knowledge* resulting from the systematic reflection of the theologian. The failure to observe the distinctive nature of these two kinds of knowledge can only result in

---

rence of opinion with Käsemann cannot be cleared up "... bij de stand van het heden voorhanden instrumentarium der onderzoekmethoden..." (p. 22)? If so, there is some hope that Dr. Schippers and Käsemann will come to a certain agreement in the future. Or is the method of interpretation itself, the "form-geschichtliche methode" and its presuppositions, rather questionable? (p. 20) In that case we can only expect a further clarification from a critical analysis of the method itself.

In the meantime we cannot suppress the thought that the relation between faith and the scientific analysis of the text of Scripture is left in the dark. The question remains, how do we get into the "hermeneutic circle" in the right way? Is it by faith, or is it ultimately, even though the hermeneutic principle is derived from Scripture itself, by means of a *theoretical analysis* of the texts of Scripture? But if the hermeneutic principle can be derived from Scripture through *systematic exegetical study* ("de te onderzoeken en onderzochte teksten" p. 7!), what then is the nature of this theoretical activity and what are its presuppositions? Is this activity not directed by our faith and the religious direction of our heart?

confusion.[159] Recently this has become evident in the writings of
Dr. H. M. Kuitert.[160] Dr. Kuitert fully recognizes the peculiar
character of our knowledge of God, but he leaves us in the dark
when it comes to the nature of *theological thought*. To know God,
according to Kuitert, is to have fellowship with Him, which is
virtually equal to loving, obeying, and serving Him, for God
reveals Himself as a *covenant-God*.[161] Scripture contains no
theoretical information and no general statements about God, man,
or the world.[162] Our knowledge of God and of ourselves is
characterized by the intercourse between God and man, and is of
a practical nature. In other words, it is knowledge gained through
actual believing, through our fellowship with God; it is faith-
knowledge.

After having observed this peculiar nature of faith, Dr. Kuitert
goes on to describe the place and task of "theology".[163] Since God
demonstrated Himself as a covenant-God first of all to the
people of Israel, His deeds and words are recorded in their
language. In view of the special character of the Hebrew language
— the language of men who lived in actual fellowship with the
covenant God — *our* language must be "trans-formed" before we
can understand God's revelation. At this point Dr. Kuitert sees a
task for theology. In as much as theology seeks to understand the
particular nature of the language of Scripture, it can be of service
as "translator". In fact, this service to the church is its only
vindication.

This description, however, of the task and place of "theology"
gives rise to many questions. For how are we to conceive of such
a "theology"? Is it a *systematic* discipline and of a *scientific*
nature? Does it share the *theoretical* attitude of thought of all
scientific endeavor and does it claim a place for itself among the

---

159 Van Teylingen, *G.T.T.*, LXI, 4, 5, 121f: "Hoe groot is de verwarring die
aangericht wordt door een critickloos door elkaar halen van geloofskennis, belijdenis, wijsbegeerte en theologie!" "Wetenschap is actie en resultaat van de
'beschouwelijke' theoretische kennisverwerving en begripsvorming. Als zodanig
kan wetenschap als wetenschap van mensen nimmer de mensen-maat te buiten,
laat staan te goven gaan." „*Daarom is wetenschappelijke kennis van God een
onmogelijkheid.*" "Dat wil natuurlijk niet zeggen, . . . dat kennis van God onmogelijk is. Hier treedt altijd weer verwarring op, omdat men niet in de aard
van onze kennis onderscheidt. Wij mogen God kennen in zijn Zelfopenbaring
door het geloof . . ."
160 H. M. Kuitert, *De Mensvormigheid Gods*, Kampen: J. H. Kok N.V., 1962.
161 *Ibid.*, pp. 285ff.
162 *Ibid.*, pp. 291ff.
163 *Ibid.*, pp. 294-302.

other sciences at the university? If so, what are its presuppositions
and how can such a theology, with its theoretical concepts, deal
with the full reality of God's speaking to man? Or, to take the
alternative, must we conceive of this "theology" as a more or less
practical activity, closely related to preaching and catechizing? If
so, can it still have a legitimate place at the university?

Dr. Kuitert is well aware of these questions, but for the time
being he has *chosen* not to answer them.[164] But is it not high time
that these fundamental problems which concern the very basis and
nature of theology receive serious attention, including Dooyeweerd's rather extensive (comparatively speaking!) contributions?
The alternatives are few, and each *choice* has far-reaching
consequenses.

Prof. Dooyeweerd's conception of theology has been presented
and elaborated on more than one occasion both by himself and
others.[165] His main contention is that theology is a special science
with a limited field of inquiry. Theological thought, like all other
scientific analysis, must move within the boundaries of the temporal order of our experience. The different fundamental ways in
which we experience reality can be investigated by the special
sciences. For theology this is the "pistical" modality. The arguments
for distinguishing such a fundamental mode of experiencing

---

[164] *Ibid.*, p. 302, where he distances himself from Dooyeweerd's conception
of theology. One cannot, however, dissociate himself from Dooyeweerd's
arguments so easily and without seriously considering the alternatives. See
also his remarks in "Kroniek," *G.T.T.*, LXIV, 4 (1964), 240-252. There he
obeserves: "Want het gaat in de vraag naar de theologische methode eigenlijk
om de wetenschappelijkheid van de theologie, en daarmee om haar rechtmatige
plaats aan de universiteit." (244) In view of this how shall we interpret his
remark: "Ik vraag mij alleen nog af hoe lang wij m.n. in West-Europa de
theologische faculteit — deze onmiskenbare vracht van het *corpus christianum* —
nog kunnen bewaren?" (248) Finally Dr. Kuitert asks: "Is er in de theologie een
hygiënische objectiviteit, in de zin van onbevooroordeeldheid mogelijk, . . . ?
Voor mijn besef staan we hier wel eens al te gauw klaar met het antwoord dat
objectiviteit niet bestaat; dat vooroordelen op veronderstellingen berusten;
en dat onbevooroordeeldheid dus een fictie is. Voordat ik mij met zo'n antwoord eens verklaar, wil ik er eerst een poosje tegen zijn." (249) "Theologie
heeft m.i. iets wetenschappelijks (laten we verder voorlopig maar niet gaan)
voorzover ze niet in handen van deze beiden extremen [wij-hebben-nu-eenmaal-
een-standpunt *en* de illusie van de onbevooroordeeldheid] valt." (250)

As a reaction to a certain kind of theologizing we can understand, and to a
certain extent, appreciate this attitude, but as soon as we take the scholarly
studies of prof. Dooyeweerd with respect to the presuppositions and nature of
theology (1939-1960!) into account such a response seems hardly adequate.

[165] See note 136.

pertaining to the act of believing have already been referred to in the previous pages. [166]

As a systematic discipline theology is bound to the *theoretical* attitude of thought. This implies that the theoretical object of theological analysis is limited to the "pistical" aspect of such concrete phenomena as the Scriptures, the act of believing, or the organized institutional church. Theological abstraction is based upon the *pre-theoretical* experience and knowledge of faith. Full reality as it is given in our experience and as we have immediate knowledge of it in its integral character and totality, escapes scientific analysis. The object of theoretical thought is the result of *theoretical abstraction.* Only *analytically* can we dissociate the various aspects of our integral experience of reality. [167] Thus the Word of God can only become the object of theological research as it manifests itself within the faith-aspect of our experience, and not in the full reality wherein it presents itself to us.

The inquiry into the *structure* of the "pistical" modality is of a philosophical nature. Theology itself, as a special science with a limited point of view, cannot establish the place and boundaries of its own field of investigation and the inner coherence of the faith-aspect with the other modalities. Theology, therefore, is not only religiously directed, but also philosophically founded. The insights gained into the structure of the "pistical" aspect serve as the philosophical pre-suppositions of theology.

In keeping with its nature as a special science, theology cannot be satisfied with a mere modal analysis of belief, but must direct all its attention to the source, norm and content of the Christian faith. Because of the exceptional place the faith-aspect occupies in the temporal order of our experience, theology is indeed a unique discipline. However, precisely because theology deals with the limiting aspect of the *temporal order of our experience,* it is implicitly bound to the modal structure of creation. This comes

---

[166] See above p. 45f.

[167] It should be noted that basic to prof. Dooyeweerd's conception of theology is not only his distinction between religion and the faith-aspect, but also his theory of the nature and (limited) place of theoretical thought, or, better, that his view of religion is also determinative for his epistemology. It is far beyond the scope of this study, however, to present even a summary account of prof. Dooyeweerd's theory of knowledge and the discussion it has evoked (Stoker). Cf. *A. New Critique,* II, pp. 430-598. This does not mean that the epistemological problem is unimportant for theology; the contrary is true.

to expression particularly in the basic concepts of which it avails itself. Without an analysis of the modal structure of the faith-aspect, theology cannot give an adequate account of its analogical concepts. As a starting-point, the philosophical presuppostions play a decisive role in theological investigations.

In keeping with this brief account of the nature and place of theology we can describe catechetics (as a part of theology), as a systematic discipline which focusses all its attention upon the *church's instruction in the faith as a "pistically" qualified activity.* [168] Catechetics, therefore, presupposes the actual catecheti-cal instruction of the church. From this full and integral activity it can theoretically abstract the faith-aspect by which this ministry of the church is qualified and seek to give a systematic account of the norms and content of catechetical instruction and the typical nature of the church's teaching.

Catechetical theory presupposes the church's practice and can in no way replace actual instruction. For centuries the church has taught the Way without any kind of systematic knowledge of this activity, and even today, if forced by circumstances, the church could do without a theoretical analysis of its educational practice. Catechetical theory has a subordinate and limited place. In view of the history of Western thought it is good and probably even necessary to keep reminding ourselves of this state of affairs. But once we are thoroughly aware of this situation we may also call attention to the great value of theoretical knowledge. A Scrip-turally founded and guided catechetical theory can indeed deepen our understanding and greatly enhance our knowledge of catechet-ical instruction. The full, integral, on-going activity will always (in spite of the claims of positivism and phenomenology) escape our theoretical analysis and description, but a study of its various aspects can indeed be very fruitful. The assertion that in Catechet-ics the church's educational ministry is viewed from a specific ("pistical") point of view certainly needs further elaboration. Such an exposition, however, will be more meaningful after we have presented our analysis of the educational structure of the church's teaching-ministry.

In view of the limited place and function of catechetical theory, we can legitimately focus all our attention in this study upon the place and typical structure of the church's education without for

---

168 Cf. Dooyeweerd, *In the Twilight,* pp. 128 f., 137ff; and J. M. Spier, *Phil. Ref.,* XVI, 1, 2, 4ff.

the moment considering the other fundamental aspects of this ministry. We need not, as we may be inclined to think at first include an investigation of the *norms* for the church's teaching and the *content* of its instruction. For this we may simply refer to those parts of the confessions and the church order in which the divine charge to proclaim and to teach the Gospel have been formulated and positivized. The church's ministry is in no way dependent on a theoretical verification of its mandate or on the theological exegesis of relevant passages of Scripture. The norms for the church's instruction are founded in God's revelation and demand first of all faithful obedience and continual reformation of the church's practice. This does not mean that theological reflection upon the church's understanding of its mandate is impossible or unfruitful. On the contrary, when we consider the uncertainty and confusion with regard to infant baptism, the "covenant", the requirement of making profession of faith before partaking of the Lord's supper, the relation between teaching and preaching, etc., a study of the norms for the church's instruction could indeed be very helpful. Our point is that we may legitimately exclude this aspect from our investigation at this time, since the educational ministry does not depend on a demonstration of the validity of its mandate.

Since the determination of the function and the *typical structure of the church's education* appears to present a major obstacle and has as yet received little attention, we have singled out this particular aspect for further investigation. Moreover, we are convinced that an analysis of the structural aspect of the church's education can clarify similar problems in pastoral care, homiletics, and evangelism. In our estimation only a structural analysis can give us an insight into the typical nature of these activities and avoid *both* a "docetic" or "spiritualistic" conception *and* a purely psychological or sociological interpretation.

CHAPTER II

THE CHURCH AND ITS MINISTRY

In order to determine the nature and place of the church's educational ministry, we must first of all seek to gain an understanding of the structure and the functions of the church in general. Without a fundamental insight into the unique character of the church it is impossible to determine the nature and the scope of its educational program. [1] It is evident that this state of affairs is usually recognized, since many publications dealing with the church's education contain a section, or at least some introductory remarks, about the church in general. Dr. R. Bijlsma, for example, begins his *Kleine Catechetiek* with a short description of the church and its ministry. [2] His conception of the church as "apostolicity", of which he does not give an account, serves as a basis for his analysis of catechetical instruction. But since there are many differences of opinion with regard to the basic structure of the church, something more and other than a summary statement of one's conception of the church is needed.

---

[1] Cf. K. Dijk, *De Dienst der Kerk*, Kampen: J. H. Kok N.V., 1952, p. 17: "Waar het op aankomt is bij het object der diaconia recht te verstaan wat we als kerk te zien hebben, hoe we die kerk moeten beschouwen en wat ze voor ons is naar het Woord Gods; tasten we ten opzichte van dit primaire in het duister, dan beweegt zich heel de ambtelijke dienst in de nevelen, en geraakt de kerk haar blijvende betekenis voor het mensenleven *en* voor het koninkrijk Gods kwijt." See also p. 119: "Wie over het doel der catechese, d.i. over het doel van het kerkelijk jeugdwerk spreekt, heeft onmiddellijk te doen met het *wezen* der kerk zelve;..." Similarly, D. van der Plas, "De Belijdeniscatechisatie II," *Mededelingen van het Studiesecretariaat van de Raad voor de Catechese der Ned. Herv. Kerk*, 21/22, Den Haag: Boekencentrum N.V., 1963, p. 5: "Het doel van de catechese blijkt sterk samen te hangen met het kerkbegrip, en uit deze samenhang komen belangrijke vragen voort."

[2] R. Bijlsma, *Kleine Catechetiek*, Nijkerk: G. J. Callenbach N.V., 1962, p. 14: "Het apostolaat behoort tot het allesomvattende wezen van de kerk en kan niet als één van haar facetten worden aangemerkt." "Het getuigenis ten overstaan van de wereld is immers niet een bepaalde zijde van het leven der kerk, maar omvat haar ganse bestaan en al haar arbeid."

This presents us with the difficulty of procedure. Certainly it cannot be our intention to engage in an exegetical study of the word *ecclesia* and its synonyms, or in a systematic analysis of various ecclesiologies. Even though we want to take the results of such inquiries into account, in themselves they cannot provide us with a basis for an examination of the structure and the function of the church's education. For these theological studies also have a foundation, as we have contended in the last section of the previous chapter. All theological reflection is motivated and driven by certain (differing) religious presuppositions, which also manifest themselves in the exegetical and systematic studies dealing with the church. In view of this fact, "Catechetics" cannot take its starting-point in ecclesiology. The differences of opinion with regard to the structure and the functions of the church direct us to a more fundamental level, namely that of the pre-theoretical religious commitments. But since we have already given a brief account of our religious starting-point in the last chapter, we can limit ourselves in this chapter to a consideration of the implications of our main perspective for our conception of the church.

A. THE CENTRAL ISSUE

"The essential nature of the Church eludes precise definition," Dr. L. B. Smedes once wrote.[3] This, of course, applies to any definition, since a description can never encompass the fulness of concrete reality, whether this be a thing, an event, or a communal relationship. Apparently Dr. Smedes had something else in mind when he wrote these words. By referring to the "mysterious inner life" of the church he meant to point to the "real identity, the inner selfhood, the essence of the church", to "its living relationship to its living Lord."[4] Or as the Rev. S. G. de Graaf once wrote: "In the church we meet the work of the Lord, with the miracle of His grace in the re-creation of mankind in Jesus Christ. This miracle can be known only by faith."[5] Indeed this is a great mystery, for

---

[3] L. B. Smedes, *The Nature of the Church and Some Problems in Evangelism*, Grand Rapids: Christian Reformed Publishing House, 1958, p. 7.

[4] *Ibid.*, pp. 10, 7.

[5] S. G. de Graaf, *Het Woord Gods en de Kerk*, Zutphen: J. B. van den Brink, 1935, p. 37: "We hebben in de Kerk met het werk Gods te doen, met het wonder Zijner genade in de herschepping der mensheid in Christus. Dit wonder is alleen door het geloof te verstaan."

the Church is the very body of Christ. She has her origin in Him and even today exists by the power of His Spirit. His people share in His anointing and they are endowed with the gifts of His Spirit.[6]

This mystery, the continuation of the Church throughout the ages and the living relationship of the body with her living Lord, can be seen and experienced only by faith. Without faith we see nothing but her "transitory, historical, and often tattered forms" (Smedes[7]) and "the doings of sinful human beings" (de Graaf[8]). But the Church is much more than that which meets the eye, more than what can be observed and described. Through faith we understand "that the Son of God, out of the whole human race, from the beginning to the end of the world, gathers, defends, and preserves for Himself, by His Spirit and Word, in the unity of the true faith, a Church chosen to everlasting life."[9] The Church is the work of God, therefore we *believe* "one holy, catholic, and apostolic Church, the communion of saints."[10] In all our thinking about the Church this *confession* must remain our starting-point.

The Church then is first of all to be conceived of as the new humanity, the people of God, or the body of Christ. "Jesus, as the Messiah, as the Son of Man and the Servant of the Lord, is the great Representative of the people of God. What he creates is not a new religion or a new morality, but a new people of God, a New Covenant, the *ecclesia* of the Messiah." "Christ is the second Adam; the church is the new mankind and is as such the body of which Christ is the Head. Belonging to Christ means belonging to His body."[11] The Church is not a new creation, but the re-constitution of mankind in Jesus Christ.[12] The believers, united in Christ, constitute the new humanity; they are the citizens of the Kingdom of God, the very body of Christ, in one word, the Church.[13]

In several of his publications Dr. H. N. Ridderbos has demonstrated that the word *ecclesia* in the New Testament is used in at

---

6   *Ibid.*, p. 8.
7   Smedes, *The Nature of the Church*, p. 10.
8   De Graaf, *Het Woord Gods en de Kerk*, p. 47.
9   *Heidelberg Catechism*, L.D. XXI.
10   *Apostles' Creed*, IX.
11   H. N. Ridderbos, "The unity of the Church," *International Reformed Bulletin*, VIII, 20, 21, 22 (Jan., Apr., July, 1965), 24. Cf. also his *De Komst van het Koninkrijk*, Kampen: J. H. Kok N.V., 1950, pp. 304ff.
12   Cf. A. Kuyper, *Encyclopaedie der Heilige Godgeleerdheid*, III, pp. 205, 218.
13   Cf. H. N. Ridderbos, *Paulus*, pp. 364ff., 415, 439.

least two different senses. Usually *ecclesia* refers to the local congregation or to the congregation gathered together for worship. In other instances, however, the word has a much broader meaning, as in Matt. 16 : 18 for example, where Jesus talks about the Church in the *ideal* sense of the word, the so-called *invisible* church.[14] In the same way the apostle Paul refers to the Church in her *totality*, to the *universal Church*, which is not to be understood as the confederation or union of individual congregations.[15] The universal Church as the people of God or the body of Christ realizes itself in the life and worship of the local congregations and for that reason the word *ecclesia* can be used both for the people of God in general and for the Christian community at a certain place. The Church, therefore, refers first of all to the people of God or the body of Christ in its totality.[16] In the second place the word *ecclesia* can be applied to the local congregation (gathered together for worship), since each congregation is a manifestion and representation of the body of Christ.

At this point, however, we encounter a peculiar difficulty in the exegetical, Biblical theological, and dogmatic reflections upon the Scriptural Revelation concerning the Church. Usually it is assumed that whatever Scripture reveals about the Church applies exclusively to *the church as we know it today, as a distinct communal relationship with a limited place and function.* The validity of this assumption is hardly ever questioned. Nevertheless, this question constitutes the major problem of ecclesiology, since it is directly related to the central meaning of the Word of God. It seems quite obvious that the church in its organizational structure as it exists today next to the family, the school, the state, industrial organizations, and numerous other societal relationships cannot possibly

---

[14] Ridderbos, *De Komst van het Koninkrijk*, p. 309: "Jezus spreekt hier dus van zijn gemeente, *zijn* volk, zonder daarmee nog een bepaalde of ook zelfs algemene organisatie aan te duiden. Het gaat hier over de ekklesia in de ideële zin van het woord." Cf. also pp. 313, 318, 175.

[15] Ridderbos, *Paulus*, p. 367: "... onweersprekelijk is o.i., dat Paulus van meet af in zijn brieven meer dan één betekenis aan de titel *ecclesia* toekent: naast die van plaatselijke (huis-)gemeente en godsdienstige vergadering óók die van gemeente in het algemeen, kerk als totaliteit." "... de meermalen voorgestane opvatting, als zou de samenvoeging of confederatie der afzonderlijke gemeenten bedoeld zijn, ... is te verwerpen."

[16] *Ibid.*, p. 368: "... dan is duidelijk, dat voor Paulus ... in héél zijn prediking de gedachte van de universele kerk primair is en dat de plaatselijke gemeente, de huisgemeente en de godsdienstige samenkomst dáárom als *ecclesia* kunnen worden aangeduid, omdat daarin de algemene *ecclesia* zich openbaart en zich representeert."

embrace *the total life and witness* of the covenant community. But doesn't Christ make a total claim upon the lives of His people? Doesn't He regenerate the hearts of the members of His body through His Spirit, so that their entire existence is re-directed? Didn't He come to proclaim the good news of the Kingdom of Heaven, and doesn't this Kingdom embrace all of creation? To whom then is the Gospel addressed? To the church, certainly; but to the church as we know it today with its limited place and function?

The answer we give to this question, implicitly or explicitly, is determinative for our understanding of the Word of God in general, and, consequently, for our view of the place of faith and religion in life. To our knowledge Dr. F. H. von Meyenfeldt is the only author who has dealt with this question and considered the meaning of the word *ecclesia* as used in the New Testament *in relation to* today's place and function of the church. "Is the Word of God addressed to the church?" Dr. von Meyenfeldt asks in his more or less popular book on the church.[17] This is a difficult question, says the author, since the empirical church we are acquainted with differs radically from the New Testament church. During the centuries great changes have taken place in the cultural life of mankind. As the result of a process of cultural differentiation many tasks that were originally performed by the family, the tribe, the state, or the church have now been taken over by relatively independent institutions and organizations.[18] All through Scripture the traces of this process of cultural unfolding can be found.[19] Thus the New Testament was written at a time

---

17   F. H. von Meyenfeldt, *Kerkelijk Vooruitzicht,* pp. 59-69.

18   *Ibid.,* p. 60: "Deze vraag is niet zo eenvoudig te beantwoorden, omdat — als we het zo eens mogen uitdrukken — het een vraag is van het jaar 1959 aan het jaar 0. Wij leven immers in een cultuurperiode waarin de samenleving zich heeft gespreid in een grote hoeveelheid van betrekkelijk zelfstandige verbanden. En met name de samenleving der christenen heeft vele vormen gevonden om er zich in uit te drukken. De wetenschap, het onderwijs, handel en bedrijf, de kunst en het ontspanningsleven, allerlei verenigingen en organisaties kwamen tot ontplooiïng buiten de overkoepeling door het kerkelijk instituut."

19   *Ibid.,* p. 64: "Er groeit reeds een begin van arbeidsverdeling in het volk Israël. Het zou interessant wezen de geschiedenis van Israël eens te bezien vanuit dit gezichtspunt: overal zouden we dan de symptomen van dit proces kunnen aanwijzen. Alleen: het is en blijft onder Israël een *begin.*" Likewise p. 68: "De grote arbeidsverdeling is immers begonnen sinds Pinksteren. Dat is dus al een heel belangrijke zaak die het evangelie ons leert: het mensenwerk in de kerk heeft slechts een beperkte plaats in het leven. En deze beperking is niet betreurenswaardig, maar hartverheffend en vrucht van de Pinkstergeest."

when the communal life of the Christians was largely centered around the worship services and the mutual love and care for one another. [20] But since that time much has changed; the Christian community has found many ways to give expression to its corporate responsibility and witness. It is in the light of this development that the Word of God and the Scriptural references to the church must be read and understood. One cannot legitimately say, therefore, that the Scriptures are addressed to the church, *if* one means by this the organized church of today, nor can one maintain that the Scriptures only refer to the empirical church with which we are acquainted. [21]

By calling attention to this important state of affairs, Dr. von Meyenfeldt has made a valuable contribution to our understanding of the church. Without some such perspective as he has presented, we cannot do justice to the New Testament. For if we interpret the word *ecclesia* and its synonyms as referring exclusively to the (organized) church (of today), we are bound to misinterpret the Word of God in many other respects too. Then the Bible becomes a "pulpit-Bible" or a "church-book", which is limited in its meaning and relevance to man's faith or to the "spiritual" realm.

If in our theological reflection upon Scripture and its teaching concerning the *ecclesia* we are not to be led astray, we cannot do without some worked-out conception of the process of cultural differentiation, which during the centuries has resulted in the free development of various societal structures. The exegete's conception of the (interrelation between) different organizations and institutions, or, more vaguely, his general view of society, is bound to enter in when he seeks to determine the meaning of the New

---

[20] *Ibid.*, p. 60: "De bijbel is geschreven in een tijd waarin de christenheid pas aan het begin stond van zijn historische ontplooiing." "De nieuwe gemeenschap drukte zich slechts uit in wat ten nauwste samenhing met de eredienst en de onderlinge liefde." And p. 61: "Wel laat de bijbel duidelijk merken, dat het genoemde differentiatie-proces reeds aan de gang was."

[21] *Ibid.*, p. 61f: "Het zal echter nu al duidelijk wezen, dat het niet juist zou zijn, wanneer men uit het eenvoudige spreken van de Schrift de conclusie trok, dat de bijbel zich slechts richt tot de kerk." "Wie deze gedachte koestert, vergeet, dat wat wij nu kerk noemen wel heel sterk verschilt van de kerk die in de bijbel is verondersteld. De toenmalige kerk verkeerde in het oer-stadium, waarin de latere verscheidenheid van het christelijk leven nog niet tot de volle ontplooiing gekomen was." "Het komt er dus op aan voor de kerk van deze tijd om de bijbel zorgvuldig te lezen, wanneer zij tot een verantwoorde opvatting van haar taak wil komen." Indeed, and it would be a great service to the church and the Christian community in general if this state of affairs were consciously taken into account in exegetical studies and commentaries. Cf. also S. G. de Graaf, *Het Woord Gods en de Kerk*, p. 9.

Testament references to the church, or for that matter, to marriage and the family, or to the state. The theologian simply cannot speak meaningfully about the nature and the function of today's church without a basic understanding of the development of Western society. The theologian, therefore, should not be chided for making use of a certain (philosophical) conception of the development of Western civilization, for he cannot do without such a theory, whether he knows it or not.[22] What we should be concerned about is whether the religious starting-point, upon which these presuppositions concerning human society are based, is in keeping with the central meaning of the Word of God. A view of reality, including the (normative) process of cultural development, which is not directed by the Scriptural ground-motive will distort one's interpretation of Scripture and particularly the Scriptural references to the *ecclesia*.[23]

The empirical church, according to prof. Dooyeweerd, can never be identified with the fulness of the body of Christ, the Church in its central religious sense, for our relationship to Christ transcends all communal relationships. Nor can the church as we know it today and as it functions in our differentiated society encompass the total life and witness of the covenant community. The present-day church has a unique but clearly limited place and task. "It is beyond doubt that the latter, in its inner nature, is not to be viewed apart from the *corpus Christi* in its transcendental religious sense as the radical communion of reborn mankind in Jesus Christ. Nevertheless, it may be identified neither with the religious fulness of the body of Christ, nor with the temporal expression of the latter in those societal relationships which as such have a radically different type from that of the organized Church-institution."[24]

These two trends, which time and again have obscured a Scriptural understanding of the church, still constitute the major

---

[22] This also means that theology must renounce any claims to an independent, autonomous place among the other disciplines at the (Christian) university and acknowledge the inter-dependence of all the (special) sciences. Cf. Troost, *Casuïstiek*, pp. 356, 363.

[23] Troost, *Casuïstiek*, p. 356: "Wij zouden dat gaarne extra willen onderstrepen en het ook met deze woorden willen herhalen, dat niet slechts de algemene openbaring tegenover de bizondere openbaring verzelfstandigd mag worden als een aparte kennisbron, maar dat ook omgekeerd de Heilige Schrift niet verstaan kan worden, zonder te letten op Gods zelfopenbaring en op zijn wilsopenbaring in 'natuur en geschiedenis'." See also the discussion below, p. 84f. and note 80; and p. 118-123, and notes 58-65 of chapter III.

[24] Dooyeweerd, *A New Critique*, III, p. 215.

problem of ecclesiology today. On the one hand there is a tendency to contrast the Church in its central religious sense to the institutional church in such a way that the latter is completely relativized, or considered to be of only secondary importance.[25] Especially in this connection there has been a general reaction to the term "invisible", since it can easily be interpreted in the sense of "a spiritual, inner essence" over against "the merely outward, natural, earthly forms."[26] Over against this trend to minimize the significance and the unique function of the institutional church there has been a renewed emphasis in our day upon the inseparable unity between the inner nature and the organizational structure of the church. *In* the "visible" manifestations, *in* the organization of the offices and services it must become apparent that the church is a community of faith. In the very life, *in* the activities and *in* the mutual relationships of the church-members it must become evident that they constitute a fellowship of *believers*. In the light of the history of the church this is a wholesome corrective, which has led to a new appreciation and deeper understanding of the institutional church and its inner nature.

The reappraisal of the empirical church through a rediscovery of its inner nature has not warded off the other trend, however, of absolutizing the institutional church by *identifying* it with the fulness of the body of Christ.[27] This equally disastrous tendency has traditionally manifested itself in the church's attempt to dominate and rule over all of life (the *corpus christianum*). But

---

[25] Cf. S. C. W. Duvenage, *Kerk, Volk en Jeug*, Deel I, *Die Verhouding van kerk tot Volk*, Zaandijk: Drukkerij J. Heijnis Tzn., 1962, pp. 54, 100-105; Dooyeweerd, *A New Critique*, III, pp. 509, 512-515.

[26] Ridderbos, *Int. Ref. Bulletin*, VIII, 20, 21, 22, 24: "As long as the essence of the church is sought in its invisibility and as long as the body of Christ in interpreted merely as a mystical unity it is no surprise that, both in the pietistic and the liberalistic concept of the church, the so-called 'external church' has become a matter of secondary import, and has indeed been left to arbitrary human discretion. The Scriptures, however, do not contain such a dichotomy. The body of Christ is really a *body*, that is, a visible manner of existence."

[27] Dr. Smedes, for example, although recognizing one evil ("making the organism an unseen ghost detached from the earthly body of the church") has failed to see the real issue in the tendency he is opposing. As a result he tends to go in the opposite direction of identifying the fulness of the body of Christ ("the organism" in Dr. Smedes' terms) with the institutional church. "Paul gives us no reason to suppose that he is speaking of an organism in distinction from the institution. He refers to one entity: the organism in its living fellowship. He knows only the Church." *The Nature of the Church*, p. 10. Prof. Ridderbos, however, also with reference to Paul, comes to quite different conclusions. See above p. 59f., and notes 14, 15, 16 of this chapter.

since the inner nature of the church as a community of faith called
to proclaim the Gospel does not allow of such an expansion of
its territory and jurisdiction, its guardianship could and can never
be more than an external supervision based upon an outward bond
with the other areas of life. The free development of political life,
art, science, trade, social and family life simply could not and
cannot tolerate the church's tutorship and interference, since the
church lacks competence in these areas. [28] Regrettably this tendency,
although different than during the Middle Ages, still manifests
itself today in the practices and pronouncements of many churches,
both in the Roman Catholic Church and in the Protestant
Churches. [29] The result is that many of the statements made by
councils, assemblies, and synods, are often quite irrelevant, since
they are neither competent political, social, or economic pronouncements nor genuine testimonies of faith. [30] Such declarations are
rightly ignored by both Christians and non-Christians.

Today, largely in reaction to the idea of the *corpus christianum*
and under the influence of modern secularism, this tendency of
identifying the church with the fulness of the body of Christ
demonstrates itself also in the seemingly opposite trend of limiting
the Christian life to the area of the church or to the spiritual realm.
Usually this un-Scriptural division of life into a secular and a
spiritual sphere is justified with the aid of some form of the
(Lutheran) two-realm theory. Even though the church, according
to this conception, has a limited place and function, at least in
theory (in practice there is often a tendency to extend its authority

---

[28] Cf. Von Meyenfeldt, *Kerkelijk Vooruitzicht*, p. 22: "En nadat de kerk
eeuwenlang de positie van voogd over de gehele samenleving heeft ingenomen,
maakt het leven zich nu los uit die voogdij en komt het tot een alzijdige ontplooiing. En de christen die aan de kerk die hegemonie over het hele leven
wenst terug te geven, is in feite reactionair en houdt de voortgang van Christus'
werk tegen. De kerk wordt dan inderdaad tot een pure lastpost in de samenleving. Ze compromiteert Christus omdat ze in Zijn naam het leven knecht."

[29] Cf. Duvenage, *Kerk, Volk en Jeug*, p. 285; writing about the Reformed
Church in the Netherlands he concludes: "Hulle sal óf met Rome die Christelike
karakter van die nie-institutêre kerklike lewe moet soek in 'n uitwendige binding
aan die kerklike instituut, óf die mening toegedaan raak dat *natuur* en *genade*
'n teëstelling vorm, en dan kom tot die verwêreldliking van die hele lewe buite
die kerklike instituut en tot die beperking van die koningkap van Christus enkel
tot die instituut." "Die terrein buite die kerk word dan dikwels verklaar tot
neutrale of saaklike gebied waar geloofsbeslissinge, lewens- en wêreldbes-
skouing geen rol speel nie."

[30] Cf. Troost, *Vermogensaanwasdeling en Sociale Ethiek*, Kampen: J. H.
Kok N.V., 1964, p. 10: "Men zoekt hier een weg *tussen* kerkelijk spreken met
gezag en vrijblijvend meepraten, een weg *tussen* kerkelijk spreken met en kerkelijk spreken zonder ambtelijk gezag."

over other areas of life), the empirical (and local?) church is still identified with the Church in its central religious sense, the Church in its "totality".

However divergent these various trends may seem, in reality they have a common basis, since they originate from the dualistic separation between "grace" and "nature", the "spiritual realm" and the "secular realm", between theology and the other sciences. [31] And as long as the real source of these tendencies to minimize or to deify the institutional church is not recognized, the one trend is bound to be succeeded by the opposite tendency. The religious ground-motive of nature and grace itself, with its inner tension, gives rise to this pendulum movement from one pole to the other, repeating itself in endless variation. Unless this dualism is completely abandoned, there is little hope of escaping the existing dilemmas forced upon us by the inner dialectic of this religious ground-motive. Nevertheless, the choice is not between invisible or visible, between the inner essence of the church or its institutional form, between a spiritualistic (individualistic) view or a universalistic conception, nor between the *corpus christianum* or some form of secularism. Only a radical rejection of every expression of the nature-grace dualism can deliver us from the force of these dilemmas.

Prof. Dooyeweerd's distinction between the Church in its central religious sense as the new humanity in Jesus Christ and the

---

[31] Writing about the tendency to identify the fulness of the body of Christ with the institutional church, Dr. Troost concludes: "De gevolgen daarvan zien we niet slechts in de rooms-katholieke ontwikkeling van kerkleer en praktijk, maar in onze naaste omgeving, nl. bij de doorsnee opvattingen van vrijge-maakten en hervormden. Daar wreekt zich, op verschillende wijze, een visie op de kerk en op de samenleving, alsmede op de plaats van de kerk in de samen-leving, die zich innerlijk niet radicaal heeft kunnen losmaken van de traditio-nele twee-sporige denkwijze: een christen leeft in twee werelden, twee rijken, op twee terreinen, één daarvan is het koninkrijk Gods, de ander is het rijk van 'déze wereld'. Als christen belijden we dan uiteraard dat er maar één Heer over beide rijken Koning is, maar daarmee hebben we dan ook temeer ons het uitzicht belemmerd op de grote geestelijke antithese in de éne religieuze diepte-dimensie van het leven." *Sermo*, X, 9 (Juni, Juli, 1963), 13. Cf. also his *Casuïstiek*, pp. 364, 366. See further Van Riessen, "De Christen en deze We-reld," *Mededelingen*, (Juni, 1965), 1-4; Dooyeweerd, *Vernieuwing en Bezinning*, pp. 9-13, 111-142; and his *A New Critique*, I, pp. 65, 180ff., 508-527; III, pp. 510-512. For a further analysis of these tendencies, especially with reference to Barth's, Brunner's. Tillich's, Van Buren's, and Cox's conception of the church, see the article by J. H. Olthuis, entitled "Must the Church become secular?" to be published in the next issue of the *International Reformed Bulletin*, X, 28 (January, 1967).

empirical church as the veritable expression of the body of Christ
with a unique but limited place and function (which can only be
understood in the light of the cultural process of integration, differentiation, and individualization) is the theoretical development
of a fundamental insight of Dr. A. Kuyper. Before we present prof.
Dooyeweerd's conception in somewhat greater detail, therefore, it
may be helpful to include a brief description of Dr. Kuyper's understanding of the church.

The Church, according to Dr. Kuyper, is not a new creation,
but the re-constitution of mankind in Jesus Christ. And as such,
as the new humanity, the Church comes to expression everywhere.
The believers, united in their common faith, constitute a people,
a community. They do not only function as such within and as
members of the institutional church, but they *are* the people of
God and the body of Christ, which must necessarily come to
expression in all the activities of the community of believers and
not only in their church-life. Wherever there are people of God,
there the Church is to be found. Dr. Kuyper was constantly aware
of the danger and the far-reaching consequences of limiting the
ecclesia to the institutional church.[32] Over against this tendency
he posed the radical unity of life and the absolute kingship of
Jesus Christ over all of creation. Christ's rule in the hearts of His
people must come to expression in all that they do in every area
of life.

With this view of the Church as the new humanity in Christ
Jesus, Dr. Kuyper had basically overcome the dualistic separation
between (a sphere of) nature and (a sphere of) grace. To clarify
his viewpoint, however, he took recourse, ". . . in a really confusing
terminological way . . .," to the terms "church as organism" and
"church as institute".[33] Many, quite rightly, have criticized and
rejected this terminology, since it has given rise to a great deal
of misunderstanding and confusion.[34] At times Kuyper placed the

---

[32] Kuyper, *Encyclopaedie*, III, p. 204: "Alle denkbeeld, alsof de Ecclesia
alleen in het instituut visibilis zou zijn, moet derhalve met wortel en tak uit-
geroeid, en duidelijk behoort te worden ingezien, dat de Ecclesia *visibilis* is
op tweeërlei wijze: én als organisme én als instituut; als organisme door hetgeen
uitkomt in de Christelijke metamorphose van het persoonlijk, huiselijk, zedelijk
en maatschappelijk leven; en als instituut door de formatie van een corporatie
ad hoc." Cf. also p. 307: "Het is toch een grove dwaling te menen, dat de Kerk
alleen in haar institutairen vorm visibilis zou zijn."

[33] Dooyeweerd, *A New Critique, III*, p. 524.

[34] Cf. Vollenhoven, *Isagogè Philosophiae*, p. 79: "Deze wijze van onder

two ("organism and "institute") next to each other, leaving room for the idea of two more or less separate churches one of which could then be considered of greater importance than the other. But a careful reading makes it abundantly clear that no separation between "organism" and "institute" is intended, nor a devaluation of the "institute"; rather the opposite is true.

With regard to the relation between the "organism" and the "institute" Kuyper maintained that the variety of ways in which the *ecclesia* expresses itself may be distinguished but never separated. It would therefore be quite wrong to place the "institute" over against or next to the church as "organism". The *one* body of Christ, the *"Organism"*, expresses itself both in the "institute" and in the church as "organism", that is, in all the other spheres of human life. [35] The "invisible" Church as the reborn humanity or the body of Christ is one and reveals itself in the entire "visible" church, in the total life and witness of the people of God, including their worship and the organization of the ecclesiastical offices and services. The emphasis upon the "invisible" Church, the "Organism", or the body of Christ did not lead to a depreciation of the "visible" church (which includes the "institute"). It is precisely the "institute" that has a unique and central place in the lives of the people of God. [36] Through the administration of the

---

scheiding is niet bijzonder gelukkig: 'organisme' ligt voor het plantenleven, 'instituut' voor resultaat van juridische actie vast. Daarom spreke men liever van Kerk en kerk, of — wat wellicht nog duidelijker is — van Christenheid en kerk. Intussen vergete men niet, dat de critiek op minder heldere termen het verschil, dat ze beogen te formuleren allerminst opheft. Dat is vooral in dit verband van belang, daar anders het gevaar dreigt dat men alle christelijke actie zou willen verkerkelijken." See also Duvenage, *Kerk, Volk en Jeug*, p. 62, note 117.

[35] At one place Kuyper even corrects his own formulation and writes: "...of, om nauwkeuriger te spreken, ... de tweeërlei openbaring van het organisme der Kerk, de ene organisch en de ander institutair." The one body of Christ realizes itself in many ways, not only in the church but also "... op allerlei wijze in de verschillende energieën van het menselijk leven." It would be quite wrong, therefore, "... de Kerk als instituut naast de Kerk als organisme te plaatsen. De Kerk is één, en krachtens haar wijzen, waarop deze Kerk zich openbaart, hoort ook de openbaring in institutaire gestalte." *Encyclopaedie*, III, pp. 218, 192, 195, 306.

[36] Kuyper, *Encyclopaedie*, III, p. 215: "Het instituut dient het organisme, en is in zoverre slechts instrumenteel..." but *as such* it is of central importance. For whenever the people of God manifest themselves as such in the various areas of life, this always happens "... onder centrale beheersing van de ge-institueerde Kerk..." (p. 192) "Die organisatie toch is er geheel op ingericht, om *centraal* het bewustzijn der gelovigen te bewerken, opdat *hun stand voor God* aan het Woord conform zij." (p. 196)

Word of God and the sacraments Christ Himself would gather
His people, transform their lives, and commit them once again
to wholehearted service of God. But since this re-formation of all
of life can only come about through the power of the Word of God,
the "institute" can be "nothing more" than an instrument in the
service of the "organism". The "institute" can only *administer* the
Word of God and the sacraments, but from this *administration*
one may expect great things!

From the preceding references[37] it is evident that Kuyper used
the word "organism" in two different senses: as a synonym for the
"invisible" Church or the body of Christ in *all* its "visible"
manifestations, *and* as an indication of the activities of the community of believers *outside* of the sphere of the institutional church
with its ecclesiastical offices. Because of this double meaning of the
word "organism" Kuyper's terminology, even apart from the terms
themselves, is indeed confusing and could better be avoided. Yet
his *main* intention is plain enough and can still have our full
approval, because the relationship of the believers to Christ
transcends all communal relationships and because the church as
we know it today cannot possibly embrace the total life and
witness of the covenant community. As prof. H. N. Ridderbos
remarked recently: "It is my conviction that this distinction gives
expression to an important truth". ". . . because in this manner the
maturity *(Mündigkeit)* of the church-members can clearly come to
light in order to reveal that this, too, *without the direct accom-
paniment of the ecclesiastical offices,* is an expression of the body
of Christ." "There would be, in my view, less confusion on this issue
if it were seen that this office of all believers is not confined within
the limits of the institutional church but that it penetrates every
area of life. And there would be less need to speak about **the**
problem of the laity if the communal activity of the believers in
the world were also viewed as an expression, *Gestaltung,* of the
church."[38]

Kuyper's distinction, however badly formulated, is indicative of
a genuine insight into the universal significance of Christ's
redemptive work. The kingship of Christ requires the re-formation
of all life, and it is the cosmic dimension of His work, its
universal blessing demonstrating itself primarily in the preservation

---

[37] See also note 35.
[38] Ridderbos, *Int. Ref. Bulletin*, VIII, 20, 21, 22, 27. Cf. also his article in
Anti-Revolutionanre Staatkunde, XXV, 11, 332.

of creation and its law-order ("common grace"), which makes such a reformation possible. With his distinction between the new humanity and the institutional church and his refusal to identify the two, and with his conviction that the body of Christ must also come to expression outside the sphere of the institutional church, Kuyper had in principle overcome the dualism between nature and grace, the church and the world, theology and the other sciences; this in spite of the fact that he did not consistently work out his main insight and, as a result, continued to use rather confusing and misleading terminology.

But apparently not all can agree with these conclusions. Dr. R. Schippers, in a *Wending* article,[39] has not only criticized Kuyper's terminology but also taken issue with the entire structure of his ecclesiology. The main difficulty centers around the word "organism". Dr. Schippers does not seem to be aware of the fact, or at least he does not mention, that Kuyper used this term in a double sense. Yet the *ambiguous* use of this term touches upon the heart of the matter. For thereby Kuyper left room for a very narrow interpretation of the church as "organism", namely, as only another way of looking at the institutional church rather than the broad perspective of the new humanity in Christ. But even though Kuyper was not consistent in developing his central viewpoint and to that extent was still influenced by a scholastic division of life, it is evident that the Church in its central religious meaning as the new humanity or the body of Christ, the Church as "Organism", is the basis of his ecclesiology.

Dr. Schippers, on the other hand, in rejecting the term "institute",[40] creates the impression that in *his* thinking about the "organism" he takes his starting-point in the *institutional church*

---

[39] R. Schippers, "De weg van de christelijke organisaties," *Wending*, XVI, 10 (December, 1961), 583-594.

[40] *Ibid.*, *Wending*, XVI, 10, 587: "De Schrift spreekt, zo zou men kunnen zeggen, reeds dan zo mystiek en eschatologisch over de kerk, dat de wat kerkrechterlijk aandoende aanduiding der kerk als instituut het heilsgeheim van de kerk teveel verschraalt, in elk geval *het te zeer binnen de tijd haalt, binnen menselijke organisatiepatronen en samenlevingsverbanden.*" (emphasis added) With the criticism of the term "institute" we can readily agree, as we have already indicated, but the last part of this remark raises some serious questions. If we formulate the problem this way, are we then not in danger of again lifting the temporal Christian community of faith out of the temporal world-order and hypostatizing it to the "supra-natural", which then has no *internal* connection with the "natural" order? (Dooyeweerd) How shall we account for these temporal aspects which the church undeniably has, as merely formal and external aspects? Cf. Dooyeweerd, *A New Critique*, III, p. 513.

(as we know it today with a limited place and function), rather than in the all-inclusive relationship of the people of God to Christ which must come to expression in all their activities and relationships. How else must we understand his remark about the Christian politician, for example, who supposedly would not like to have his work considered as being done within the confines of the church, *even though this be the church as "organism"?*[41] Looked at from the perspective of the institutional church such a statement would indeed be objectionable. But Kuyper, when talking about the church as „organism", had first of all reference to the new humanity as it manifests itself in the different spheres of life. A Christian always lives and works as a member of the body of Christ. To say, therefore, that a Christian politician does his work within the confines of the church (as "organism") would be the same as saying that he does his work as a member of the body of Christ and therefore in a Christian manner and in co-operation with the community of believers. And if the words "Christian politician" are to have any meaning at all, there could hardly be any objection to such a statement.

Thus conceived it is true, of course, that the church as "organism" in the broad sense of the body of Christ in *all* its manifestions, and the "organic" subjects dealing with these different activities of the people of God and the re-direction of every aspect of life, do not belong under "ecclesiology" as a theological discipline.[42] This confusion is the direct result of Kuyper's failure to distinguish properly between theology and philosophy in his *Encyclopaedie.*[43]

Considering the activities of the "laity" under ecclesiology indeed poses an insoluble problem, *if* this ecclesiology is conceived of as dealing only with the institutional church, or, at the most, with the members of the instituted church in their mutual relationships. Such an ecclesiology cannot possibly do justice to the "world" or "cosmology".[44] But Kuyper, although mistakenly dealing with these matters under "ecclesiology" (broadly conceived!), did not approach the place and task of the Christian in the world from

---

[41] Schippers, *Wending*, XVI, 10, 588.
[42] Kuyper, *Encyclopaedie*, III, p. 312. Cf. J. M. Spier, *Phil. Ref.*, XVI, 1, 2, 7: "Het is echter beslist onjuist, wanneer Kuyper het veld van onderzoek voor de ecclesiologie uitbreidt tot ver buiten de grenzen van de geinstitueerde kerk."
[43] Cf. Dooyeweerd, *Phil. Ref.*, IV, 4, 225ff; and *Phil. Ref.*, XXIII, 1, 11-15; see also his *In the Twilight, p. 131.*
[44] Schippers, *Wending*, XVI, 10, 590.

the point of view of the "institute", but rather from the perspective of the new humanity in Christ Jesus and His kingship over all of creation. Without considering this broad perspective and the central issue that is at stake here one cannot possibly do justice to Kuyper's "ecclesiology". Regrettably, Dr. Schippers has not explicitly dealt with Kuyper's view of the body of Christ as the re-constitution of mankind in Jesus Christ, the second Adam. *Regrettably*, for we could all have profited from a thorough discussion of Kuyper's starting-point, especially against the background of the New Testament references to the last Adam, the body of Christ, and the all-embracing character of Christ's redemptive work. [45]

This fundamental insight into the Church in its central religious sense as the new humanity in Christ which Dr. Kuyper took as his starting-point lies also at the foundation of prof. Dooyeweerd's conception of society. Mankind, according to Dr. Dooyeweerd, is a religious unity, ". . . all humanity is spiritually included in Adam. In him the whole human race has fallen, and in mankind also the entire temporal cosmos, which was concentrated in it. In Jesus Christ, the entire *new* humanity is one in root, as the members of one body." [46] No communal relationship can embrace or give expression to this *religious* unity and solidarity of mankind. The true and full community is only revealed in Jesus Christ. "By laying bare the religious root of mankind in creation, fall and redemption, it has revealed the meaning-fulness of the idea of community, in opposition to all narrow-minded nationalism and

---

[45] Cf. Ridderbos, *Paulus*, pp. 33f., 56-63, 96-104, etc.

[46] Dooyeweerd, *A New Critique*, I, p. 60. Cf. Von Meyenfeldt, *Kerkelijk Vooruitzicht*, p. 126f: "Wij beleven in de religie dan ook niet slechts een particulier intieme verhouding tot God. Maar in Christus zijn we zo ook verbonden met onze medemensen in de diepste zin van het woord. Het is de oergemeenschap krachtens welke we delen in Adams val en krachtens het herstel van die religieuze gemeenschap delen we ook in Christus' verzoenend werk. Zo gewaagt de bijbel van het verbond als een gemeenschap die de wisseling der generaties overkoepelt en de eeuwen te boven gaat, naar het bekende woord aan Abraham (Gen. 17:7): 'Ik zal Mijn verbond oprichten tussen Mij en u en uw nageslacht, tot een eeuwig verbond om u en uw nageslacht tot een God te zijn.' Het is duidelijk, dat we deze oergemeenschap moeten onderscheiden van de belijdenis-gemeenschap in het kerkelijk leven. De religie is de essentie van de mens; dat is van het kerkelijk leven niet te zeggen." This conception also throws new light upon the doctrine of original sin. Cf. Troost, *Altijd Bereid tot Verant-woording; Kort Commentaar op de Nederlandse Geloofsbelijdenis*, Aalten: N.V. Uitg. De Graafschap, 1961, p. 86f, and therefore we cannot accept the alternatives posed by Dr. Kuitert in the same publication, pp. 91-98.

to all kinds of deification of particular temporal societal relation-ships."[47] Neither the family, the church, the state, the labor union, nor any other organization can demand absolute loyalty. Instead, each institution and organization is under divine charge to give expression — each in its own unique way — to the radical religious unity and communion that exists in Jesus Christ.

Neither the universalistic nor the individualistic conceptions of human society can do justice to this state of affairs. The dilemma posed by these conflicting theories can only be solved from a Scriptural point of view, in which all societal relationships are ultimately related to the radical spiritual solidarity of mankind and the new humanity in Jesus Christ. Man is neither to be conceived of as a self-sufficient individual nor as an organic member of some absolutized societal whole. "In the individualized opened inter-personal relations men are not socially united in a special *temporal* community, but they are nevertheless bound together in the transcendent unity of mankind."[48] Neither man's individuality nor his communal relationships may be depreciated; both find perfect expression in the body of Christ.[49] Thus prof. Dooyeweerd has laid the foundation for a truly Scriptural conception of inter-individual, communal, and inter-communal relationships.

As the result of a process of individualization in the inter-personal societal relations, the separate individual person has gained a "... sphere of private liberty in his temporal life *outside of all institutional communities.*"[50] In our present society "... the inter-individual relations are no longer enclosed within the narrow limits of the tribe or the primitive ethnic community but, in prin-ciple at least, the individual may enter into free relations with other people wherever his new contacts may carry him. And in itself this is not fatal to human society but, on the contrary, it is completely in line with the opening-process of history and the vocation of man."[51] The *religious unity* of mankind *and* the essentially *limited* place and function of all societal structures guarantees the free development of inter-individual relations through which man's freedom to respond to his divine calling can express itself. At the same time this development confronts man

---

[47]   Dooyeweerd, *A New Critique,* III, p. 582.
[48]   *Ibid.,* p. 583.
[49]   *Ibid.,* II, p. 418.
[50]   *Ibid.,* III, p. 580.
[51]   *Ibid.,* p. 581.

with the corporate responsibility to develop and integrate every institution and organization, every communal relationship in such a way that they truly become expressions, each in its own particular way, of the *corpus Christi*.

This Scriptural perspective stands in radical opposition to all individualistic and universalistic, to all disintegrative and depersonalizing tendencies of modern society.[52] The Biblical view of human freedom "... excludes in principle both universalism and individualism, and it enables us to see the structural patterns in the complicated interlacements between inter-individual and communal relationships. The internal sphere-sovereignty of the different temporal structures of societal relationship is the expression of the transcendent destination of mankind. This is the only basis of a harmonious relation of authority and freedom in social development."[53]

Against this general background it is not difficult to understand Dr. Dooyeweerd's conception of the church. The Church "... is found wherever the Christian attitude to life expresses itself in a temporal form," wherever there are people of God, there the Church is to be found.[54] In its central religious sense the Church manifests itself everywhere and "... pervades temporal society in all its structures."[55] All human relationships and societal structures, including the institutional church, must be seen in the light of the *religious* unity of mankind.[56] In Adam mankind in its entirety fell away from God, but in Christ the new humanity is restored to fellowship with God, and it is only this *religious* community in Christ that can embrace the whole of the Christian life. No single institution or organization can or may encompass all communal relationships and exercise absolute control over man's life. Christ alone may demand total obedience; all other authority is delegated to man by Christ and is limited in scope. The identification of the institutional church with the fulness of the body of Christ, therefore, must necessarily lead to a universalistic absolutization or a deification (spiritualization) of the empirical church and the ecclesiastical offices. "The critical point in any Christian

---

[52] *Ibid.*, pp. 169, 193ff., 260.
[53] *Ibid.*, p. 603.
[54] *Ibid.*, p. 525.
[55] *Loc. cit.*
[56] *Ibid.*, I, p. 60: III, pp. 170, 196; cf. also his *Vernieuwing en Bezinning*, pp. 29, 46, 174.

view of this temporal society is the question what position is to be ascribed to the Church as an organized institution." [57]

What is at stake here is not merely some (philosophical) theory concerning the church, but a fundamental conception of human society as a whole, which in turn is based upon a certain religious commitment. One cannot talk about the church as a genuine communal relationship, fully integrated in the order of creation, without saying something (even if it is only by implication) about society in general. Any attempt to deal with the church in and by itself, without considering the structure and interrelation of societal relationships in general, is bound to lead to a "docetic" view of the church and, consequently, to a dualism between the church and the world, or a spiritual realm and a secular realm.

Since the church is fully integrated in the order of creation and functions within all the (modal) aspects of reality, it is not higher or superior to any other societal structure. Looked at from the religious perspective all communal relationships are equivalent to one another, since they have a common basis in the "universal" Church and function, each according to its own typical nature, within the same creation-order. Each societal relationship has its own irreplaceable value and typical structure, but as expressions of the Church (in its central religious sense) in the different spheres of life they are all equal in rank. This does not mean, of course, that the institutional relationships are not more important and more fundamental for human society than the free associations and the inter-personal relationships. But considered from the point of view of the all-embracing religious community in Christ all societal structures are equivalent to one another. [58]

Among the various societal relationships, however, the church does occupy a completely unique and exceptional position, since it is qualified by the function of faith which determines its entire structure. The peculiar nature of the "pistical" aspect, immediately

---

[57] Dooyeweerd, *A New Critique*, III, p. 215.

[58] *Ibid.*, p. 535. To avoid misunderstanding we should add that not every marriage or state as it is actually realized or given positive form can be considered a Christian marriage or a Christian state. "Insofar as the other societal relationships [other than the empirical church], in their actual reality, are *subjectively* withdrawn from the '*Corpus Christi*', they fall outside of the '*ecclesia visibilis*'. Only in this respect do they remain enclosed within the *civitas terrena, viz.* in a *subjective sense*. But the conserving grace in Christ preserves and maintains the structural offices of the institutional organizations and communities, and liberates them, at least in principle, from the *civitas terrena*." (p. 535) Cf. also the pp. 500-508 and his more popular booklet on the state *De Christelijke Staatsidee*, Rotterdam-Utrecht: Libertas Drukkerijen, 1936.

referring beyond itself to divine Revelation and the central sphere of human existence, also characterizes the church. According to its inner nature this community can only embrace the Christian believers and their children. In this respect the church differs from the family or the state, which can be made up of both Christians and non-Christians. The church can only exist as a Christian community of faith pointing directly to the fulness of the body of Christ, the Church in its central religious sense. [59]

Unlike the family, which is a "natural" institution, the church, like the state or the school, is founded in an organization of "historical" power. But again, the typical nature of this power of the faith-community differs radically from that of other "historically" founded institutions and associations. The organization of power upon which the church is based is the power of the Word of God, which immediately points towards Christ's reign in the hearts of His people, to the power of His Spirit. In the institution of the apostolic office and the divine charge to administer the Word and the sacraments, Christ Himself has given this (faith-) power its initial organization.

The various ecclesiastical offices and functions, which by a process of differentiation and individualization already during the New Testament period arose out of the apostolic office, are all characterized by the power of faith, which refers directly to the fulness of power in Jesus Christ, to His absolute authority and universal kingship. These offices, therefore, are to be conceived of as instruments for the working of the Word and the sacraments. [60]

The unique character of the church as a community of faith and the typical nature of its authority (the law-side), however, can only be realized by sinful human action (the subject-side). For its empirical existence and continuation the church depends on the faithful and obedient activity of the fellowship of believers. Invested with the general (ecclesiastical) office of believers, all Christians everywhere are called to co-operate in the formation and maintenance of the special (ecclesiastical) offices for the administration of the Word and the sacraments. As a concrete communal structure the church is an imperfect human organization continually in need of reformation.

---

[59] *Ibid.*, pp. 523, 535. Cf. Vollenhoven, *Isagogè*, p. 79.
[60] Dooyeweerd, *A New Critique*, III, pp. 533, 536.

The difference and relation between the church as an organized community and the Church in its central religious sense as the new covenant people in Christ, can also be illustrated from the distinction and relation between the general office of believers and the specific ecclesiastical offices.

Man, as the image-bearer of God, has received the mandate to rule over and to preserve God's creation. In the Lord's name he is called to administer His love and care for this world. This is the very meaning of his existence, to live in loving fellowship with His Creator and Lord by praising Him through whole-hearted service. All men are called to this general office of living as genuine human beings according to God's ordinances, of maintaining genuine love relationships, of engaging in meaningful creative work, and of playing before the Lord to their hearts' content.

Mankind, however, misusing its delegated power for its own glorification, enslaved itself to the powers of darkness instead, with all the disastrous results for this world. Only the God-appointed Deliverer, Christ Jesus, can free man from this bondage and restore him to his royal status. All those who share in the anointing of the Son of Man, He enables to live as people of God. As a royal priesthood the community of the Messiah, the Church, may testify to Christ's triumphs and administer God's love and care for this world, for such is their reasonable service. Christ Himself endowes His people with the gifts of His Spirit, enabling them to live as a devoted people, renewed in knowledge after the image of their Creator.

This is what we mean by the "office of believers", or as it is commonly called, the "priesthood of all believers". These expressions are somewhat confusing, since they may induce one to think of some general *ecclesiastical* office. But if it is used in this limited sense, then we need another term to indicate the general office of being man. [61] It is better, therefore, to speak of a general

---

[61] Cf. K. J. Popma, *Inleiding in de Wijsbegeerte*, pp. 40ff; C. G. Krom-minga, in his *The Communication of the Gospel*, pp. 108-150, has not entirely escaped the ambiguity of the term "office of believer". Sometimes Dr. Krom-minga uses the term in the sense of the *general calling* of the people of God, and sometimes in a very limited sense as in his one-sided interpretation of and exclusive reference to I Peter 2:9. His presentation is further complicated by the fact that he combines the word "laity" (the people of God) with Kuyper's concept of the church as "organism", without being aware of the ambiguous use Kuyper made of this term. If one uses the phrase "the general office of believer" in the sense of the general *ecclesiastical* office which every member

and a special ecclesiastical office and to reserve the term "office of believer" for the general office of being man. For to be a Christian believer is nothing more or less than to be *genuinely human*, renewed after the image of our Lord and Redeemer. [62]

Through the re-publication of this good news about man's high calling, Christ Himself gathers a new people dedicated to the service of God. His Word is living and active, the very power of God unto salvation, regenerating the heart, and the Lord demands that this Word, together with the administration of the sacraments, be proclaimed everywhere, until He comes. Thus the people of God are bound to institute and maintain a church wherever possible and to let it function through the offices Christ has ordained. For through the administration of His Word He would gather, instruct, admonish, and comfort His people. The special ecclesiastical office-bearers, therefore, have no other task than to build up the body of Christ in His name and through His Word, so that the people of God may be fully equipped to serve their Lord. [63] Like all other office-bearers in the various areas of life, they have a limited authority and a very specific task. [64] But the Word of God which they have been charged to administer is directed to the heart of man and makes a total claim upon his life.

Thus there is an inseparable relation between the people of God in general as they are united in Christ and the institutional church. There can be no question of the ecclesiastical offices lording it over the general office of believers, but neither can there be any depreciation of the unique calling and significance of the institutional church. The church cannot legislate for other areas of life, but it can and must give fundamental directives. How these directives are to be realized and put into practice in every area of life is to be worked out by the community of believers who jointly receive God's mandate and who are to cooperate in giving

---

of the church holds, one would do well to keep van Ruler's warning in mind. "In ieder geval zullen wij ons bij dit spreken moeten hoeden voor een ecclesiologische verenging van het Christen zijn." A. A. van Ruler, *Bijzonder en Algemeen Ambt*, Nijkerk: G. F. Callenbach N.V., 1952, p. 42.

[62] Cf. the *Heidelberg Catechism*, L.D. XII.

[63] Cf. Kuyper, *Encyclopaedie*, III, p. 476; K. Sietsma, *De Ambtsgedachte*, Amsterdam: S. J. P. Bakker, n.d., pp. 84ff; Van Ruler, *Bijzondere en Algemeen Ambt*, pp. 50ff.

[64] Cf. H. Evan Runner, "Sphere-sovereignty," *Christian Perspectives*, Hamilton: Guardian Publ. Co. Ltd., 1961, p. 69.

it positive form. But the church need not do anything else but administer the Word of God and the sacraments and from this administration we may expect a reformation of all of life.

The relation between the special ecclesiastical offices and the general office of believers once more illustrates the unique but limited place and function of the church *and* its great importance. It must be fully acknowledged, and at times it needs to be emphasized, that the empirical church is the veritable expression of the body of Christ. But in all our thinking about the church we shall also have to guard ourselves against the sinful desire to deify (in one way or another) the church and "... to give the temporal authority of the Church dominion over the souls of the believers, and ... over the whole of societal life..."[65]

This then is the central issue: whether or not the church as we commonly refer to it can be identified with the fulness of the body of Christ and whether or not the church as we know it today can embrace the total life and witness of the people of God. The *choice* we make with regard to this issue determines our entire conception of the structure and the function of the church. Ultimately this choice is a *religious* choice, a choice between a view which has not radically rejected the traditional scholastic ground-motive of nature and grace *and* the Scriptural ground-motive. It is our basic commitment which determines this issue, and not our exegetical considerations or ecclesiologies, for the Word of God is not at our disposal and cannot be controlled by our theological studies. On the contrary, the Word dominates us, including our theologizing and requires our surrender. It is only the driving force of the Scriptural ground-motive that can deliver us from the power of all forms of synthesizing. In our thinking about the church, therefore, it will not do merely to dissociate ourselves from the dualism between grace and nature, which for centuries has held sway over the hearts and minds of Christian believers, but it must be counteracted by the power of the Word of God, which must possess us and which demands wholehearted commitment.[66]

---

[65] Dooyeweerd, *A New Critique*, III, p. 511; cf. Popma, *Inleiding*, p. 106f.
[66] Cf. Troost, *Sermo*, X, 9, 13; Dooyeweerd, *Vernieuwing en Bezinning*, pp. 12, 13!

B. THE STRUCTURE AND THE FUNCTIONS OF THE CHURCH

The church, instituted by Christ Himself, functions within all ". . . the modal and radical typical structures of temporal reality given already at creation."[67] The church is not some supra-natural phenomenon, but a communal relationship with an individuality structure of its own, fully integrated in the temporal world-order.[68] It has its own *type* of fellowship, its own *typical* order, music, art, financial policies, gatherings, language, symbols, traditions, education, buildings, and so forth.[69] These moral, juridical, aesthetical, economic, and other aspects in which the church functions as a communal structure cannot be placed over against the "spiritual" essence of the church, its faith-aspect. The church is indeed the veritable expression of the body of Christ, but thereby it is not lifted out of the creation-order and made into a "supra-natural" institution without *internal* connection with the "natural" order.[70] There is nothing in the various (modal) functions as such that is incompatible with the inner nature of the church.

As a concrete communal relationship the church functions in all the aspects of creation, but always as *church,* that is, in its own typical manner. Its exceptional character as a community of belief, therefore, should come to expression in all its activities and not only in the administration of the Word of God and the sacraments. Its buildings must in ever greater measure become *church-*buildings, its music *church*-music, its instruction *catechetical* instruction, its aid and care an expression of the compassion and love of *faith,* its fellowship a fellowship of *believers,* and its counsel and admonition a ministry of the *Word.* The unique character of the church must come to expression in every aspect of its life.[71]

---

[67] Dooyeweerd, *A New Critique*, III, p. 526.

[68] *Ibid.*, p. 536.

[69] Cf. Vollenhoven, *Isagogè.* p. 87: "Het beweegt zich dan ook op het gebied van de taal, heeft eigen sociale omgangsvormen (het ambtelijk bezoek), goederen in eigen beheer, een eigen schoonheid (met roeping tot een eigen kerk-kunst), een eigen recht (kerkrecht), en eigen zeden."

[70] Dooyeweerd, *A New Critique*, III, p. 513.

[71] *Ibid.*, p. 538; cf. Troost, *Sermo*, X, 9, 12f: "Een kerk van Christus zal niet anders willen en kunnen en mogen zijn dan een menselijk samenlevings-verband dat zijn geestelijke aard en verbondenheid aan Christus toont in alle vormen en activiteiten waarin het optreedt: prediking, sacramentsbediening, eenheidsstreven, kerkrecht, belijdenis, liturgie, enz. Niets is hier 'maar relatief'."

This "historically" founded individuality structure of the church has as yet had very little attention. But without an extensive analysis of the church's structure many essential aspects of its life remain (theoretically) unexplained. Prof. Dooyeweerd has extensively demonstrated the need for such an inquiry into the typical manner in which the church functions within the different (modal) law-spheres of reality, and his analysis of the church's law may well serve as an example of his approach.

The church, according to prof. Dooyeweerd, possesses an *internal-juridical* structural aspect. [72] Church-law is not a formal or external facet of the church's life; on the contrary, it belongs to its very nature as a communal structure. The church simply cannot exist without official organization and a church-order. The church's (internal) authority has an original legal aspect to it and the church's rules are of a typical juridical nature. But — and this is decisive — the internal legal sphere of the church is dependent on the exceptional structure of this community. "True *internal* Church-law can only be such law that displays the individuality-structure of the ecclesiastical community. Its material meaning is indissolubly connected with the leading function of the Church as a community of faith and confession in the administration of the Word and the sacraments." [73] The church's law must at all times remain ". . . an instrument of faith for the effectualization of the sole authority of Christ Jesus by His Word and Spirit." [74] At no time may the church-order be applied in a formal manner, so that

---

[72] Dooyeweerd, *A New Critique*, III pp. 551-557. Cf. H. N. Ridderbos, "Kerkelijk gezag en kerkelijk recht in het Nieuwe Testament," *Tweemaandelijks Bulletin der Theologische Radiocolleges*, V, 6 (Sept., 1963), 63: "Wanneer toch het wezen der kerk zich niet volstrekt in de innerlijkheid van het religieus individu, maar zich juist vóór alles openbaart in de concrete, historische ge meenschap van de kerk als volk van God en lichaam van Christus, kan men kerk en kerk-recht, wezen en verschijning niet neven-schikkend, als tot twee 'rijken' behorend, tegenover elkaar stellen. Dan moet juist gevraagd: hoe moet zij zijn ingericht en georganiseerd, zal zij aan haar wezen beantwoorden, welke bevoegdheden en welk gezag zijn haar gegeven en op welke wijze moeten die in haar worden uitgeoefend en bekleed?"

[73] Dooyeweerd, *A New Critique*, III, p. 555.

[74] *Ibid.*, p. 556: cf. D. Nauta, "Actuele opvattingen over de grondslagen van het Protestantse kerkrecht," *Tweemaandelijks Bulletin*, V, 4, 5, (Maart, 1963), 33f., who refers to the views of H. Dombois, which, according to him, should be seriously considered. "Ernstige overweging verdienen de volgende door hem te berde gebrachte opmerkingen: . . . dat aan de kerk het rechtsmoment inhaerent is; . . . het is noodzakelijk een diepere karakterisering te geven van de geaardheid van het recht dat in de kerk functioneert; het is ten diepste recht der genade."

the legal rules begin to dominate the activity of faith and destroy
the bond of love between the "brothers" and "sisters" of the
"household of faith". The church-order is a very sensitive instrument for the working of God's Word and must be completely
bound by the peculiar nature of the church as a community of
faith and a fellowship of believers.

A similar state of affairs exists with regard to the other aspects
of the church's life. [75] This is perhaps most evident when we seek
to give an account of the church's music, art, or architecture. As
long as the "sacred" music of the church, for example, is opposed
to the "secular" music of the world, it is impossible to explain the
characteristic features of church-music as a *unique type of music,*
for then the *internal* coherence between the different types of
music cannot be acknowledged. On the one hand, therefore, we
must maintain that church-music, no matter how unique, remains
music, subject to the general aesthetic norms that hold for all
music. On the other hand it needs to be emphasized that church-
music must be completely bound by the inner nature of the church
if it is to function harmoniously in the worship-services of the
community of believers.

The inner nature of the church, its faith-character, not only
determines the nature of its preaching, confessions, discipline, and
financial policies, but also the *inner boundaries* of its authority and
tasks. The acknowledgment of this state of affairs is of the utmost
significance for establishing the scope of the church's educational
task and the range of its curriculum. Moreover, it provides us with
a criterion to distinguish meaningfully between the instruction in
the Christian faith as carried on in the home, the church, the
school, youth societies, or other organizations. In view of its
importance we shall briefly examine the scope of the church's
authority, of its preaching, and of its confessional statements.

Previously we established that in all its activities the church is
bound to its inner nature as a community of *faith.* Its power is the
power of *faith,* and outside of this sphere the church has no
competence. This sphere-sovereignty of the church based upon its
inner nature as a faith-community does not in itself determine
which tasks the church may legitimately engage in and which not.
The extent of its activities may vary, depending on the historical
situation, the level of cultural development, the subjective faith
of the believers, the cultic influence of other religions upon daily

---

[75]   Cf. Dooyeweerd, *A New Critique,* III, pp. 549-551, 557-561.

life, and so forth. But the normative structure of the church *does* determine the *inner boundaries* of its authority and tasks.[76]

Every service of the church must be seen as an instrument of faith for the effectuation of the absolute authoritiy of the Word of God. Through the administration of the Word and the sacraments Christ would build up His body. The special ecclesiastical offices are the gifts of His Spirit to equip God's people for work in His service. They are to be conceived of, therefore, as *ministries* within the fellowship of believers. Through proclamation and admonition, instruction and guidance, care and assistance, the congregation is to be built up in the faith. In this upbuilding of the faith of the body of Christ the ministry of the church finds its inner boundary.[77]

This does not mean that the church's competence is limited to a specific *area* of life or that in the administration of the Word the office-bearers must restrict themselves to the "spiritual" life of the believers. The church is not merely to be an institution of salvation in the narrow sense of saving souls from perdition unto (future) eternal life. Jesus came to preach the good news of the Kingdom of God, which has reference to all of creation and not only to man's "spiritual" life. The all-encompassing and concrete nature of the Word of God does not allow such a dualistic separation between a spiritual sphere and a natural sphere. The Gospel addresses itself to the center of man's existence and by redirecting the heart and restoring man to the general office of believer God makes a total claim upon his life. God's Word is to

---

[76]   Cf. Troost, *Casuïstiek*, p. 122: "Het is onze overtuiging, dat deze competentie-grens niet kan worden bepaald zonder dat men in rekening brengt karakter en doel van de kerkelijke geloofsgemeenschap, d.w.z. dat deze grens bepaald wordt door de *normatieve structuur* van het kerkelijk instituut." See further Dooyeweerd, "Omvang en aard van de staatstaak," *Mededelingen*, (Sept., 1953), 4-6; Vollenhoven, "De souvereiniteit in eigen kring bij Kuyper en ons," *Mededelingen*, (Dec., 1950), 4-7; Van Riessen, *De Maatschappij der Toekomst*, Franeker: T. Wever, 1953³, pp. 77-99; —————, "De souvereiniteit in eigen kring," *Correspondentiebl.*, XVIII (Juli, 1954), 14-21, XVIII (Dec., 1954), 6-12; Runner, *Christian Perspectives 1961*, pp. 53-87; J. D. Dengerink, *Critisch-Historisch Onderzoek naar de Sociologische Ontwikkeling van het Beginsel der "Souvereiniteit in Eigen Kring" in de 19e en 20e Eeuw*, Kampen: J. H. Kok N.V., 1948; —————, "De grenzen van de staatszaak," *Correspondentiebl.*, XVI, (Mei, 1952), 23-27.

[77]   Cf. Troost, *Casuïstiek*, p. 123: "Maar steeds zal deze ruime competentie *innerlijk begrensd* zijn door het dienstkarakter in de geloofs-gemeenschap. De prediking, ook in haar 'toepassingen', moet blijven een 'prediking des geloofs', dienstbaar aan het in liefde heengroeien naar Christus', door de doorwerkende macht van Gods Woord en Geest."

be a lamp unto our feet in the service of God and it is the task of the church to proclaim this Word in all its fulness, so that the body of Christ may be built up in the faith.

In principle, therefore, the church is authorized to deal with all of life, every area, and every human activity, but it can do so only from the perspective of faith.[78] The church has no other task than to equip Christ's body for service in His Kingdom through the administration of His Word and sacraments. To accomplish this task it may have to engage in many different activities, but whatever the range of its services, its one and only concern remains man's faithful acceptance of the Word of God as the direction for all of life and the norm for his faith. This principle of the church's sphere-sovereignty is not a formal, static rule, but a dynamic principle which is inseparably related to the actual (subjective) faith of the believers and the cultural situation.

Limiting the church's competence to the aspect of faith does not mean that by a roundabout way we confine its functions to a specific *area of* life after all, nor does it mean that we restrict the influence of the Word of God to man's "spiritual" life. The unique character of the "pistical" law-sphere and its exceptional place in the total law-order makes it impossible to conceive of this structural principle in such a manner. As the limiting aspect of the creation-order, the faith-aspect refers immediately beyond itself to God's revelation and to the religious center of our existence. In its ministry the church may (and ought to) relate all of life to the faith of the believers, which is to say, relate every experience to the fundamental relationship of the believers to Christ and place every situation in the light of the Word of God. The church's authority can be none other than the authority of the Word of God *as the divine norm for faith and religion.* The nature of the Word of God correlates with the peculiar character and the exceptional place of the "pistical" function in man's life.[79]

---

[78] Cf. *Ibid.*, p. 125: "Wanneer de vraag gesteld wordt in hoeverre de bediening van Gods Woord competent is met gezag in te gaan op het leven van de kerkleden, dan kan het criterium alleen hierin gelegen zijn, dat prediking, vermaan, onderwijzing en bestraffing zich beperken tot het materiële en directe geloofs-element in het leven. Dat wil zeggen: zij mogen niet meer dan *Gods Woord*, als normwet voor geloof en religie laten ingaan in het leven, kritisch én vertroostend." See also p. 127: "Juist wanneer de prediking en de vermaning zich beperken tot het *geloofs*-element in de volle levenspraktijk, en daarin ook haar *grens* zien, die zij niet mogen overschrijden, dan is hun *dienst* aan het Woord door de werking van de beloofde Geest het meest effectief."

[79] Cf. *Ibid.*, pp. 126-128. See above p. 45f.

Through the aspect of faith our entire life is consciously related to God's revelation in Jesus Christ and to His Kingdom. As the *leading* function, our faith governs and directs all our activities, however they are qualified. Through faith we understand that God has created us and that He has subjected all things to His good and holy law. Through faith we understand something of the radical fall into sin and the equally radical restoration in Jesus Christ and His kingship over all of creation. The inscripturated Word of God addresses man in his totality and confronts him with God's claim upon his life. In this sense the Word of God is the norm for faith and religion, determining the religious direction of our life, and in this sense it is to be a light upon our path as the Direction for our daily activities.

But the Bible does not contain the totality of God's revelation; there is also a revelation of God's will in the order of creation. [80] Limiting the church's competence to the aspect of faith and its authority, to the authority of the inscripturated Word of God, therefore, indeed implies a restriction. At the same time this limitation shows the great importance of the church, for it lies within the domain of the church's ministry to preach the Gospel in its universal significance for all of life. It is only through the guidance of the Word of God as revealed in the Scriptures that the creational ordinances can be concretized and given positive form. It is only under the leading of our faith in subjection to the norms of Scripture that the structural laws can be positivized in keeping with the central love-commandement.

Through the fall into sin we are no longer able, nor do we (want to) see how, we can love God and our fellow men unconditionally in and through His creation. Only the powerful Word of God as revealed in Christ can re-direct our lives and renew us daily to walk in His light and to do His will. Only His Word can cause us to see the creational law-structures as a revelation of God's will, and only the central love-commandment can make us understand how the creational ordinances are to function in our lives. [81] The structural laws have no meaning in themselves, they are only meaningful as Kingdom-laws, as fulfillments of the great commandment, and it is by giving positive form to these divine ordinances in our daily life that God would

---

[80]   Cf. Troost, *Casuïstiek*, pp. 126ff., 354ff., 362ff. Dengerink, *Phil. Ref.*, XX, 3, 4 (1955), 97-122. See below pp. 113-117.
[81]   Cf. Troost, *Casuïstiek*, pp. 44-58, 101-105, 130, 152-154.

have us serve Him wholeheartedly. Only the inscripturated Word can tell us in which manner the structural laws must be concretized and how they are to be fulfilled. This means that the Bible as the inspired and authoritative Word of God cannot be isolated from the revelation of God's will in the law-structures of creation. On the contrary, Scriptural revelation and creational revelation are inseparably related and interwoven. To talk of natural (autouomous) laws, therefore, that can be discovered and known by reason would be to foster a grave misconception, but it would be an equally serious misunderstanding if we were to conceive of the Scriptural ordinances as isolated (autonomous) principles which by way of logical deduction could be applied to a certain situation. It is only in the light of the central love-commandment, divinely positivized and particularized in Scripture, that the creational ordinances can be truly fulfilled.

If the Word of God is truly proclaimed in all its fulness and the congregation is truly built up in the faith, every aspect of creation and every human activity and relationship will be opened up under the guidance of faith and will find its focus and fulfillment in the coming of God's Kingdom. In this sense the church has a limited but nevertheless *leading* function in the life of the believers. [82] From its faithful ministry we may expect a restoration and reformation of every area of life. But this also means that the church has a great responsibility and that if it fails in its task the Christian life in all its aspects suffers and languishes . . . which is often the case.

Even though the church has been charged to proclaim the Word of God in all its fulness, it can do so only in an ecclesiastical manner. The church can and must speak prophetically, but it can do so only in the language of faith and with regard to the "pistical" aspect of concrete circumstances and problems. It cannot specify the meaning of the Gospel for other areas of life, that is, it cannot indicate how the creational laws and norms must be

---

[82] Cf. Mekkes, *Phil. Ref.*, XVIII, 4, 151: "Indien echter de kerk, trouw in haar *verkondiging, dienst aan* het Woord verricht, dan zal de christengemeenschap, ook in haar kennisverwerving op alle gebied, een geestelijke omtuining vormen, waarbinnen haar leden, in de strijd hunner persoonlijke aktvoltrekkingen, telkenmale steun vinden tot het hervinden der richting, die door het geloof wordt gewezen." See also De Graaf, *Het Woord Gods en de Kerk*, p. 52: ". . . ze [the church] roept op tot het buigen voor het Woord des Heeren, en alzoo tot de ontmoeting met Hem. Van dezen wederkeer tot den Heere moet de genezing van het geheele leven uitgaan."

concretized in a particular situation so as to give expression (in its own specific way) to the central love-commandment. This is beyond its competence. Its testimonies, teachings, and admonitions regarding current social situations, political actions, economic conditions, or "moral" relationships are to be genuine *pronouncements of faith,* which *as such* cannot function as social, political, economic, or "moral" principles. The church may only demand that the responsible people in the different institutions and organizations give positive form to the various structural norms *in the light* of its testimony.

Thus the church is limited in its ministry by its inner nature as a community of faith charged to proclaim the Word of God as recorded in the Scriptures. This inner boundary of its authority and competence must come to expression in all its functions, in its preaching as well as in its discipline,[83] in its diaconate[84] as well as in its confessional statements. Particularly the church's confessions are illustrative in this respect.

The fellowship of believers is bound together by its common faith in Jesus Christ as Lord and Savior. The inner unity of this community cannot be imposed from without; it can only be the outcome of a common confession which binds the believers together. By its very nature the community of faith must be a confessional church.[85] In its confessions the church gives *positive form* to the norm for its faith as revealed in the Scriptures.

But in keeping with the nature of the inscripturated Word of God as the norm for faith and religion, to which the inner nature of the church as a faith-community corresponds, ecclesiastical confessions must necessarily be of an all-encompassing, total nature. The church's creeds are general confessions of faith that witness to our fundamental relation to Jesus Christ. They do not and cannot specify the meaning of this relationship for the area of education, labor, or political activities. It is not sufficient, therefore, for Christian political parties, labor unions, or educational institutions to refer to the ecclesiastical creeds as a statement of principles. The office-bearers of these various Christian institutions and associations must formulate their own specific educational

---

[83] Cf. Troost, *Casuïstiek,* pp. 119, 123. See also De Graaf, *Het Woord Gods en de Kerk,* p. 51; Von Meyenfeldt, *Kerkelijk Vooruitzicht,* pp. 129-157.

[84] Cf. Dooyeweerd, *A New Critique, III,* p. 549f; Von Meyenfeldt, *De Diaken als Componist der Gemeenschap,* Den Haag: Van Keulen, 1955; De Graaf, *Het Woord Gods en de Kerk,* p. 50f.

[85] Cf. Dooyeweerd, *A New Critique,* III, pp. 540ff.

creeds, political testimonies, or witness with regard to labor (relations), if there is to be genuine unity and a common aim within their particular area. But again, such differentiated and specific creeds can only be formulated in the light of Scriptural revelation and, therefore, *in harmony with* the confessions of the church. In this sense the ecclesiastical creeds have a *leading* function, since they give expression to our most basic commitment and the fundamental direction of our life, as Lord's Day I of the *Heidelberg Catechism* beautifully formulates it: "That I, with body and soul, both in life and death, am not my own, but belong unto my faithful Savior Jesus Christ; who ... by His Holy Spirit ... makes me heartily willing and ready, ... to live unto Him." All other creeds are limited in scope and are characterized by the communal relationship within which they function. [86]

Prof. Dooyeweerd's analysis of the church's inner structure reminds us strongly of Dr. Kuyper's and prof. Biesterveld's approach to catechetical instruction. [87] In fact, we may conclude that he has provided us with the "tools" to work out the main principles presented by Kuyper and Biesterveld. The inner boundaries of the church's authority and competence as we have briefly sketched them above provide us with a criterion to determine the nature and scope of the church's educational ministry, especially in distinction from the instruction in the Christian faith of the home, the school, and other organizations. If it were not for a number of complications, these principles for the church's education could now be set forth and developed. But the ambiguity and confusion that exists with regard to education in general, makes it impossible to proceed in this manner. Before the main directives that we have discovered thus far can be worked out, the nature and aim of education in general must be clarified. For without a fundamental understanding of the general principles governing all forms of education, it is impossible to gain an insight into the peculiar nature of the church's instruction. It is precisely at this point, as our orientation amply

---

[86] Cf. J. M. Spier, "De puriformiteit van ons belijden," *Bezinning*, II, 7 (Sept., 1947), 209-213; II, 8 (Oct., 1947), 241-249; —————, "Proeve van een schoolbelijdenis," *Bezinning*, III, 2 (Febr., 1948), 53-54; —————, "De eenheid van ons belijden," *Bezinning*, III, 6 (Juni, 1948), 178-182; K. J. Popma, "Eenheid en pluriformiteit van ons belijden," *Phil. Ref.*, XVI, 4 (1951), 178-189; XVII, 1 (1952), 1-15; R. Schippers, "Souvereiniteit en eigen kring en de 'inter-kerkelijkheid' der V.U.," *Correspondentiebl.*, XII, 2 1948), 3-9.

[87] See above pp. 28-31.

illustrates, that many previous studies have fallen short. The following chapter, therefore, will be entirely devoted to an analysis of the normative structure governing all pedagogical activities.

CHAPTER III

THE NATURE OF EDUCATION

In order to describe the peculiar character of the church's education we must first of all seek to gain an understanding of the nature of education in general. No doubt this procedure has certain disadvantages, because it forces us to divide our attention between two different fields of investigation. But the present stage of (under) development of both Christian education and catechetics as systematic disciplines leaves us no other choice. In view of the complexity of the problems, however, we shall strictly limit ourselves to matters of *prolegomena* and to a *provisional* analysis of the structure of education.

What is education? In the course of history many different answers have been given to this fundamental question. Philosophers and educators have seized upon one aspect of human life after another to explain the fundamental characteristics of education. There have been biological, psychological, social, ethical, and many other interpretations, all claiming to have a true insight into the nature of education.[1] The coming and going of various conceptions has kept equal pace with the changes in philosophical theory. Each school of philosophy has given rise to new principles of education. This situation complicates our task considerably, for where shall we turn for an answer? Is one conception to be preferred above another, or can the latest point of view make a better claim to universal validity than some older theories?

In the Netherlands (and in Germany) a number of prominent educators have attempted to solve this basic problem by making use of the phenomenological method. They claim to take their

---

[1] Cf. J. Waterink, *Theorie der Opvoeding*, Kampen: J. H. Kok N.V., 1958[2], pp. 20, 47f; N. Perquin, *Pedagogiek*, Roermond-Maaseik: J. J. Romen & Zonen, 1964[7], p. 7f.

starting-point in the actual pedagogical activities and relationships as they present themselves to *any* careful observer. Before anything else these educational phenomena must be analyzed and described. Later on, if necessary, these phenomena can be placed in a broader perspective, but not until the essential features of the actual pedagogical situation have been discovered and set forth. Since these phenomena as they are found in actual experience are accessible to any interested observer, they can form a common basis for educators committed to different points of view. [2]

This is an intriguing approach to the great diversity of opinions with respect to the nature of education. By returning to the educational phenomena as they are given in actual experience the dogmatism of the contradictory theories could perhaps be overcome and genuine communication, at least on this primary level, could be restored. Regrettably, however, this approach suffers from a fundamental weakness in as much as it *assumes* that everyone can or ought to be able to accept the phenomenological method as a valid and fruitful way of dealing with educational phenomena. But this method is much more than a mere instrument for analyzing the essential characteristics of certain phenomena as they present themselves to us in actual experience. [3] Far from being a neutral

---

[2] Cf. M. J. Langeveld, *Beknopte Theoretische Paedagogiek*, Groningen: J. B. Wolters, 1965[10], p. 27: "Dit verschijnsel willen wij voorlopig alleen *als zodanig* analyseren. Wij willen het niet interpreteren uit een andere bron dan uit zichzelf, al weten wij wel dat de mogelijkheid bestaat dat de uiteindelijke zin ervan pas begrepen kan worden, wanneer wij het opnemen in een omvattende interpretatie van wijsgerige, resp. wereldbeschouwelijke aard. Wij beginnen echter fenomenologisch." "Een fenomenologische werkwijze gebiedt ons — ook waar wij andere, diepere zekerheden hebben — de mede-onderzoeker te ontmoeten in het verschijnsel waarover men het samen wenst te hebben en nergens anders. Wij gaan dus in het geheel niet uit van 'een algemeen begrip' maar van het verschijnsel zelf zoals het in die ervaring wordt aangetroffen, welke wij allen kunnen delen als wij slechts bereid en in staat zijn die ervaring te laten gelden en dus niet reeds in deze fase van ons onderzoek vooruitlopen op de beschikbare inzichten en reeds hun uiteindelijke zin geopenbaard willen zien." See also Perquin, *Pedagogiek*, pp. 14ff; S. Strasser, *Opvoedingsweten-schap en Opvoedingswijsheid*, 's-Hertogenbosch: L. C. G. Malmberg, 1963[2], pp. 63ff; and many other publications by Langeveld, Perquin, de Klerk, *et al.*, (see bibliography).

[3] Cf. the penetrating studies of prof. J. van der Hoeven and Dr. Th. de Boer: J. van der Hoeven, *Kritische Ondervraging van de Fenomenologische Rede*, I, Amsterdam: Buijten & Schipperheijn, 1963; —————, *The Rise and Development of the Phenomenological Movement*, Hamilton: The Association for Reformed Scientific Studies, 1965; ————— "Merleau-Ponty en het anthropologisch dualisme," *Correspondentiebl.*, XXIX (April, 1965), 22-25;

method which can lead to universally valid knowledge, the phenomenological method presupposes a certain view of man and reality. Before we can make use of this method (as leading to universally valid knowledge), therefore, we must first be able to accept the (ultimately religious) presuppositions on which it is founded. Prof. Langeveld's description of nurture, maturity, or parental authority and responsibility, for example, is much more than an analysis of actual phenomena as they present themselves to us in experience.[4] Such a *pure* description of the educational process *in and by itself* must be considered a phantom, since one's total perspective always enters in and since the phenomena cannot be separated from their meaning (creation does not *have* meaning, but creation *is* meaning). The many valuable contributions which Dr. Langeveld and his associates have made to the theory of education merit careful consideration and certainly cannot be dealt with in passing. But even though the publications of this group of educators deserves a great deal of attention, especially as a counterbalance to many Anglo-American writings, their insights cannot serve as a general basis for various educational theories.

The terms themselves, such as education, nurture, training, upbringing, and other synonyms, obscure the issue even more, since most of these terms are equivocal. To nurture, for example, can be used equally well with reference to raising flowers, training animals, or rearing children; yet there is an essential difference between these three types of nurture. When this state of affairs is not acknowledged the child is reduced to a bio-social organism which, in interaction with his environment, can develop into a personality. In that case we can hardly speak of education *(educere)* in the sense of leading someone to a certain goal according to certain norms. The only task left to the educator in this conception is to create such environmental conditions and to

---

Th. de Boer, *De Ontwikkelingsgang in het Denken van Husserl,* Assen: Van Gorcum & Comp. N.V., 1966; —————, "Wat is fenomenologie?" *Correspondentiebl.,* XXIX (April, 1965), 25-28.

[4] Cf. J. Waterink, *Keur uit de Verspreide Geschriften,* Groningen: J. B Wolters, 1961, pp. 31-36, 75-107. Even though in general we can agree with Dr. Waterink's critique of the phenomenological approach to education, yet we are convinced that a more thorough evaluation must be both more critical and more appreciative. Prof. Waterink's own conception of science and nurture considerably weakens his arguments and prevents him from penetrating to the (religious) basis and presuppositions of the phenomenological method as used by Dr. Langeveld and his associates and makes it impossible to do full justice to the structural states of affairs brought to light by these educators.

provide such learning opportunities as will stimulate the growth and development of the organism which must unfold according to its own pre-determined nature. Education, or rather, educational psychology then becomes primarily a matter of describing the various stages of growth the child goes through and the opportunities for learning at each level. [5]

When used with reference to the upbringing of children or the guiding of adults such basic concepts as growth, development, nurture, and maturity will remain ambiguous and will continue to lead us astray unless they are qualified in some manner. But how shall we determine the precise meaning of these terms within the context of education? Since they can easily be distinguished from other human activities, there is obviously something very unique about pedagogical activities. [6] But what is it that characterizes these pedagogical activities and relationships? Or, to put it differently, what criterion shall we use to delimit our field of investigation and to describe the basic categories used in educational theories?

Many educators have attempted to give an answer to these fundamental questions, and it cannot be denied that these different answers have provided us with important insights into the peculiar nature of education and that many theories have greatly enhanced our understanding of the educational process. Each theory, therefore, regardless of its particular emphasis, merits careful

---

[5] Cf. Strasser, *Opvoedingswetenschap,* p. 14f: "Het 'Wachsen' kan als *ontwikkeling in de biologische zin* van dit woord opgevat worden. Ontwikkeling is dan essentieel een 'loswikkeling' van datgene, wat reeds oorspronkelijk als aanleg aanwezig is geweest. Het nieuwe ontstaat ten gevolge van processen dus die aan *immanente wetten* van het organisme gehoorzamen." "Is het 'groeien' of 'wassen' een autonoom proces, dan kan bij het groeien zelf geen hulp geboden worden; hulp kan slechts in het scheppen van gunstige voorwaarden bestaan." See also N. Beets, *De Grote Jongen,* Utrecht: Uitgeverij Erven J. Bijleveld, 1961³, pp. 15-18, 237; A. Kuypers, *Een Paedagogische Beoordeling van het Amerikaanse Persoonlijkheidsbegrip.*

[6] Cf. S. Strasser, *Opvoedingswetenschap,* p. 65: "Immers het feit, dat wij in staat zijn dat, wat zich als opvoeding voordoet, als zodanig te herkennen, te identificeren en te verstaan, is niet voor twijfel vatbaar. Of wij nu bedoeïenen gadeslaan of eskimo's, vrijdenkers of mohammedanen, wij vatten spontaan bepaalde handelingen als opvoedingshandelingen op, bepaalde situaties als pedagogische situaties, bepaalde verhoudingen als pedagogische verhoudingen. De wijze, waarop zich het opvoeden voordoet, verschilt zonder meer van de manier, waarop het economische, seksuele, politieke, of juridische handelen van mensen verschijnt." Moreover, we have immediate knowledge of educational norms. "Een op dwang en dril berustend opvoedend handelen zal op ons een onbevredigende indruk maken. In het kader van een algemene theorie der pedagogiek zal dan ook sprake moeten zijn van goede en van verkeerde opvoeding."

analysis. [7] Nevertheless, however fruitful an investigation of the various educational theories might be, opinions continue to differ and many theories remain mutually exclusive. For that reason we must penetrate to a more fundamental level of understanding, namely to that of the religious starting-point, the presuppositions, or the total perspective of the different theories.

Looked at from that point of view we can only conclude that every theory of education, knowingly or unknowingly, has its starting-point in a pre-scientific religious commitment which is simply presupposed. [8] In view of this state of affairs, it should be clear that any conception that involves an absolutization of one of the aspects of human life, reducing man to a social, moral, rational, or psychical being, cannot serve as a basis for a Scripturally founded and directed theory of education. When accepted or adapted by the Christian educator, such views, which are founded in an unscriptural religious ground-motive, invariably lead to a denial or a compromise of the Christian faith. Since every theory of education presupposes a certain belief with regard to man and life in general, a truly critical theory ought to begin with an acknowledgement of its religious commitment and starting-point.

Thus we are in need of a Scripturally orientated theory of education which does not suffer from inner contradictions but which is clearly based upon and guided by the Word of God. But precisely at this point we encounter a formidable problem, for in spite of centuries of Christian nurture in the home and

---

[7] In spite of the great differences that exist between the various theories, this fact is usually acknowledged and therefore we object to the somewhat rancorous remarks made by Perquin in his *Pedagogiek*, pp. 10,12, which do injustice to the manner in which non-Christian theories have been evaluated by Christian educators. Cf. e.g. Waterink, *Grondslagen der Didactiek*, Kampen: J. H. Kok N.V., 1962, p. 46f., and his *Inleiding*, Deel II, *De Geschiedenis der Paedagogiek*. Being critical of a particular point of view is not yet the same as doing injustice to one's opponent, and the absence of critical evaluations in a study on education is not necessarily a virtue! It seems that Dr. Perquin himself has not been entirely free of prejudice. See Waterink, *Keur*, pp. 75ff.

[8] Waterink, *Theorie der Opvoeding*, p. 48: "Niet daarin ligt het verschil tussen de richtingen, dat de één wel en de ander niet een grondprincipe heeft als uitgangspunt; niet daarin ligt het verschil, dat de één wel en de ander niet poogt *geloof* voor zijn a priori bij zijn lezers te vinden: maar hierin ligt het verschil, dat de één zijn a priori aandient als geloofinhoud, als overtuiging, als belijdenis, als vrucht van openbaring God's, terwijl de ander zijn geloofsbelijdenis *aandient* als een door de wetenschap bewezen waarheid, dus met wetenschappelijk aureool omgeven en ergo niet voor tegenspraak vatbaar." Cf. Dooyeweerd, *A New Critique*, Vol. I, *passim*. See also Waterink, *Inleiding*, Deel I, *De Paedagogiek als Wetenschap*, pp. 371ff.

many decades of instruction in specific Christian day schools, it is still rather difficult to give an adequate *theoretical* account of the nature of Christian education. Many inspiring books and articles have been written about the subject, but "... when we stop to examine critically what we have done, we are embarrassed to find how vague our notion of Christian teaching still is."[9] In many ways our analysis is still in the pioneering stage and much needs to be done before we can meaningfully speak about the principles of Christian education.

This perplexing situation, however, should not make us overlook or count lightly the work that has already been done. Here we think especially of the many publications of Dr. Jan Waterink, professor emeritus of the Free University in Amsterdam.[10] Prof. Waterink has been one of the few to work out a theory of education from a Reformed point of view and if in the following pages we take exception to some of his theories, it should be remembered that this is possible only because he has provided us with a wealth of material to reflect upon. He has given the next generation occasion to re-think and re-formulate the principles of Christian nurture, and if there are things we cannot accept, the foundation remains the same![11] Before we subject the structure of education to a further analysis, therefore, we shall briefly examine a few of the existing theories of Christian nurture.

A. SOME CHRISTIAN THEORIES OF EDUCATION

In his *Inleiding tot de Theoretische Paedagogiek,* Vol. I, *De Paedagogiek als Wetenschap* (1926-1931) Dr. Waterink has given an extensive account of his conception of pedagogy as a science. As prof. Waterink himself indicates, his theory is primarily based on Kuyper's, Woltjer's, and Hepp's idea of science.[12] Thus we find reference to the "organic relation" between the "subject" and

---

[9] C. Jaarsma, *Fundamentals in Christian Education,* Grand Rapids: Wm. B. Eerdmans Publishing Co., 1953, p. 7. See also p. 470.

[10] His *Inleiding tot de Theoretische Paedagogiek,* Deel I, *De Paedagogiek als Wetenschap,* Deel II, *De Geschiedenis der Paedagogiek,* and his *Theorie der Opvoeding,* constitute his major works on education. A number of other publications are listed in the bibliography.

[11] Cf. Waterink, *Theorie der Opvoeding,* pp. 619ff.

[12] Waterink, *Inleiding,* Deel I, *De Paedagogiek als Wetenschap,* pp. 38, 56, 89, 134-167. Cf. also L. van Klinken, "Karakter en betekenis van de paedagogiek van prof. Dr. J. Waterink," in *Feestbundel,* p. 93.

the "object", the different "moments" that can be perceived in the object, the "logical" relation between the moments, the activity of the "Logos" both in the object and in the subject, the idea of "Lehnsätze", the distinction between the "natural" sciences and the "normative" sciences, and the division of the sciences into five faculties. [13] But this entire conception of science and the epistemology that goes with it has long since been subjected to a critical analysis by prof. Dooyeweerd, who has clearly demonstrated its Thomistic-Aristotelian origin. [14] On this basis, which is incompatible with a Scriptural perspective, it is impossible to build an integral Christian theory of education. This can best be demonstrated from Dr. Waterink's conception of nurture itself.

Realizing that the word "nurture" can be used in many different ways, prof. Waterink has attempted to find a delimitation of this concept in the parent-child relationship. [15] He opposes any theory that makes training a life-long process; genuine nurture must be strictly limited to the upbringing of children. All other forms of "nurture" are that only in name, since they lack the peculiar bond that exists between parents and children. This parent-child relation is unique not only because it is founded in the order of creation but above all because it is of a religious nature. The covenantal tie between parents and children is not found anywhere else. The Word of God itself charges the parents to bring up their children in the "nurture and admonition of the Lord". This divine calling is the basis for the unique character of parental authority. All other institutions that are (partly) responsible for the upbringing of children must derive their authority from that of the parents. The school, for example, must be seen as an extension of and an addition to the home. Every genuine pedagogical situation is normed by the covenant relationship and must be seen in the light of the religious bond between God and man. Any form of leading that lacks this relationship cannot be called nurture. Briefly formulated this is Dr. Waterink's main thesis. [16]

---

13 Waterink, *Inleiding,* Deel I, *De Paedagogiek,* pp. 39., 89., 134ff.

14 H. Dooyeweerd, "Kuyper's Wetenschapsleer," *Philosophia Reformata,* IV. 4 (1939), 193-232.

15 Waterink, *Theorie der Opvoeding,* pp. 11-21; *Keur uit de Verspreide Geschriften,* pp. 1-30.

16 Consider the following excerpts from his *Theorie der Opvoeding:* "De verhouding: ouders-kinderen is zonder twijfel specifiek. Deze verhouding omsluit niet alleen het leven in natuurlijke zin, maar ook in religieuze zin." (p. 15) "En het object van de opvoeding is het kind, ..." "De ouders, die het kind ontvingen, hebben voor de opvoeding van het kind *verantwoordelijkheid.* En zij

Several aspects of prof. Waterink's conception must be considered indispensable for a Christian theory of education. This ought to be fully acknowledged and perhaps it needs to be emphasized. Yet it is questionable whether nurture can be adequately defined and delimited and whether the basic structure of education can really be clarified by the parent-child relationship. There are several reasons for this doubt. First of all there is an inconsistency with regard to the description of the covenant between God and man. On the one hand Dr. Waterink seems to limit this relation to the family — a tendency often found in publications dealing with Christian education — but on the other hand all of life and all relationships seem to be encompassed and determined by this religious bond.[17] Would prof. Waterink maintain that of all human relationships only the family is included in God's gracious covenant with man? According to Dr. Waterink life is a unity and in Jesus Christ God restores all of creation.[18] Would this not include *all* institutions and *all* communal relationships? We can readily agree that the bond between parents and children is a unique relationship which has a religious focus, but this can be said of every human relationship.[19]

In a similar manner prof. Waterink argues that the kind of

---

hebben tevens naast de *plicht* omtrent het kind, het recht om dat kind, ... *naar hun overtuiging* te leiden. Hier groeit een geheel eigen paedagogische structuur." "Bovenal ontvangt deze opvoeding een eigen karakter door de *gezagsverhoudingen* die er zijn tussen ouders en kinderen." "Het ouderlijk gezag berust op scheppingsorde en op verbondsverhouding." (p. 16) "Elke andere vorm van zogenaamde opvoeding is in wezen geen opvoeding. Men kan daarvoor het woord opvoeding blijven gebruiken, maar men mist daarbij de feitelijke structuur, die er bij de wezenlijke opvoeding wordt gevonden." (p. 17).

17 Waterink, *Keur*, p. 6: "Evenzeer fout meen ik het te zijn, dat wij de *specifieke verbondsbetrekking*, of wil men, de *bijzondere religieuze betrekking*, die er is in de verhouding ouders-kinderen, uit het oog te verliezen, ..." And p. 25: "Maar gaan we consequent zien de roeping die we hebben, dan kan het niet anders of wij aanvaarden de eenheid des levens als van God gegeven; dit, wijl heel het leven ligt onder de religieuze binding Gods; en dan ook zóó, dat wij dat leven als éénheid — én maatschappelijk, én sociaal, én staatkundig, én politiek, én oeconomisch — ja in ál zijn betrekkingen — zien als eenheid onder het licht van Gods openbaring en onder de tucht van Gods wet." Cf. also p. 12 and his *Theorie*, pp. 20, 21ff.

18 Waterink, *Theorie*, p. 578: "Natuur en genade zijn niet twee elkaar tegengestelde grootheden. 'Genade' is geen nieuwe schepping, maar 'genade' is *her*schepping. Door genade ontvangt de natuur haar gerechtigheid terug." "Veeleer is het zo, dat de genade de schepping zelf wederom omzet en heiligt, zodat de richting, die door de zonde negatief werd, weer positief wordt....." Cf. also pp. 24ff., 433.

19 Cf. the instructive article by E. G. Van Teylingen, "Verbond der genade en gezin," *Bezinning*, XVI, 2 (1961), 61-73.

authority given to parents is not found anywhere else, since it is *directly granted* by God and is *all-inclusive*.[20] But again, it is doubtful whether this thesis as set forth by dr. Waterink can be maintained. The Word of God indeed explicitly charges the parents to bring up their children in the fear of the Lord. But would prof. Waterink deny that the minister, the officer, the teacher, or any other office-bearer that is called upon to instruct and guide receives his authority from God? Is not *all authority* delegated by the Lord and are not *all* office-bearers directly reponsible to Him for the discharge of their duty? Is the minister not under *divine charge* to build up the body of Christ? Is the officer in the army not *responsible to God* for the kind of guidance his soldiers receive while in training?[21] Is there an essential difference between these various *types* of authority simply because Scripture does not explicitly mention and describe the educational task of the many offices and organizations that exist today in our differentiated society? Any reference to Scripture in *this* connection could only be a biblicistic appeal![22]

Every person, including parents, that is called upon to instruct, train, guide, or care for others, whether they be adults or children, may do so only because the Lord has entrusted him with a

---

[20] Waterink, *Theorie*, p. 17: "Maar een gezag van een karakter als wij dat vinden bij de ouders, een gezag dat heel het leven én in nationale én in religieuze zin omsluit, een gezag dat rechtstreeks van God is opgedragen en in zijn opvoedende activiteit op een rechtstreeks door God gesteld doel is gericht, kent men nergens elders."

[21] *Ibid.*, p. 14: "Wanneer een predikant zijn gemeente wil opvoeden en een majoor wil zijn bataljon opvoeden, dan komen wij al dadelijk in aanraking met tweeërlei betrekking van de opvoeder tot zijn objecten. De predikant heeft een geestelijk ambt en staat, als herder der zielen, tot zijn kudde in een verhouding met geheel eigen structuur." "Stellen wij daarnaast de verhouding waarin de majoor staat tot zijn bataljon, het gans andere object, ... dan gevoelen wij, dat aard en wezen van de opvoeding in deze twee onderscheiden verbanden practisch niet onder één noemer zijn te brengen." Recognizing the sphere-sovereignty of different societal relationships ("geheel eigen structuur", "het gans andere object"), prof. Waterink fails to realize that each office-bearer — in keeping with the specific nature of his office — can engage in education and that all such education, although *typically qualified*, has certain common structural features. Cf. K. J. Popma, "Opvoeding, Onderwijs, Schoolverband," *Phil. Ref.*, XII, 1 (1947), 39ff.

[22] Waterink, *Keur*, p. 5: "Wat nu is de doorgaande gedachte der Schrift? Wel, dat er een *zeer speciale* betrekking is tussen ouders en kinderen, een betrekking, die geheel op zichzelf staat, ..." The Heidelberg Catechism, however, when dealing with the parent-child relation interprets the fifth commandment as demanding subjection to *all* lawful exercise of authority. L.D. 39: "That I show all honor, love, and fidelity to my father and mother, and to all in authority over me; ..."

particular and limited responsibility. It cannot be maintained, therefore, that parental authority is all-inclusive in the sense of unrestricted, for it is of the very nature of all human authority to be limited. No one has complete dominion over someone else, not even his own children. This comes to expression in the inseparable relation (correlation) between authority and freedom.[23] Therefore it is misleading to call the child the *object* of nurture. The obvious difference between parental authority and the responsibility of the minister for his catechumens, for example, does not concern the *essential nature* of their authority, but only the *types* of responsibility. In the first instance the reponsibility concerns the initial development of the child which includes every aspect of its life, while in the second instance the concern is limited to certain aspects of the child's faith-life through which the fundamental religious direction of his total life directly expresses itself.[24]

If, as we have maintained, there is no essential difference in the nature of the various types of authority, if other persons as well as parents are under divine obligation to lead and to instruct, and if all such relationships must first of all be looked at in the light of the covenant between God and man, that is, if all such nurture must be seen as religiously directed education, then it is impossible to find the normative structure and the most characteristic features of child-rearing (only) in the direct command of God, the nature of parental authority, and the covenant relation as it comes to expression within the family.

Prof. Waterink does acknowledge that there are many other forms of nurture (which he prefers to call *leading* or *influencing)* beside child-rearing, and he concedes that these different types of education have certain things in common. They can all be described as attempts to achieve certain *goals according* to certain *norms* through certain *means.*[25] But, Dr. Waterink maintains, a

---

[23]   Waterink, *Keur*, p. 8: "Maar evenzeer met het gezagsprincipe verbonden is het principe van *de vrijheid van het kind*. Het kind is *vrij*, d.w.z. het heeft een *eigen bestaan, eigen geaardheid, een eigen karakter* en in dit kind zal zich het schepsel Gods, dat in aanleg in het kind aanwezig is, moeten ontplooien." In this sense, therefore, parental authority cannot be called all-inclusive, nor can the child *as such* be seen as the object of nurture. Cf. also his *Theorie*, pp. 16, 17.

[24]   See below pp. 133ff.

[25]   *Ibid.*, p. 17: "Feitelijk hebben we daar steeds te doen met een doelmatig georganiseerde leiding, die een zeker doel wil bereiken." And p. 14: "... ook is er bij de opvoedende instantie een zekere visie, een zekere opvatting omtrent *aard en wezen van de objecten,* die worden opgevoed, en tevens is er een zeker

("phenomenological") analysis of these common features that characterize all forms of leading cannot tell us anything about the basic structure of nurture.[26] The norm for "true" nurture can only be found in the direct command of God, in the peculiar nature of parental authority, and in the covenant relation between parents and children. Dr. Waterink has made *one* of the unique pedagogical relationships the standard for determining whether or not an activity can be called *genuine* nurture. Per definition all forms of leading which do not manifest the same unique characteristics as child-rearing are ruled out.

At this point it is instructive to examine prof. Waterink's description of nurture in somewhat greater detail, for then the *source* of the ambiguities and difficulties with regard to the covenant, religion, authority, and office will come to light. To educate, according to prof. Waterink, is to pull the child in a certain direction and to guide him toward a particular goal. The child has to be formed; his thoughts must be captivated, so that he may learn to submit himself willingly to God's law. This requires persuasion and at times even force. The aim of all this training should be to prepare the child for a life of service in God's Kingdom. The young person must learn to serve his Lord with all the abilities he has been given and to do His will in whatever circumstances he may find himself in later life.[27] But in order to serve God wholeheartedly with all his abilities for the benefit of mankind, the child must become (be formed into) an independent mature personality.[28] The purpose of education is first of all to

---

inzicht omtrent aard en doelmatigheid van de *middelen* en *methoden,* die tot het doel leiden." In these descriptions Dr. Waterink touches upon the common structure of all forms of nurture, including child-rearing.

[26] *Ibid., p. 14:* "De vraag is nu, of wij langs deze phaenomenologische weg kunnen komen tot de oplossing van de vraag wat eigenlijk opvoeden is, speciaal wat eigenlijk het object is van de zogenaamde opvoedkunde." It is true that the nature of education and the boundaries of the field of inquiry dealing with this "phenomenon" cannot be discovered with the aid of the phenomenological method, but at the same time it should be remembered that our knowledge of the *normative creational structure* that holds for all education can only be gained through our actual and integral experience of pedagogical activities and relationships and by faithfully reflecting upon this experience in the light of the Word of God. See pp. 113ff. of this chapter.

[27] *Ibid.,* pp. 71ff., 85ff., 121ff.

[28] *Ibid.,* p. 121: "... dat wij het doel van de opvoeding definieerden als *de vorming van de mens tot zelfstandige, God naar Zijn Woord dienende persoonlijkheid, geschikt en bereid al de gaven, die hij van God ontving, te besteden tot Gods eer en tot heil van het schepsel, in alle levensverbanden, waarin God hem plaatst."*

develop the child's personality. The first part of this description of
nurture can readily be endorsed, since it deals with essential
aspects of all true nurture but the second part raises some serious
questions.

The forming of the child's personality involves both *integration*
and *regulation*. The various drives, feelings, desires, dispositions,
perceptions, wishes, concepts, in short, the entire content of the
"psychic" life must be properly integrated and balanced. Moreover,
the "I" or the "spirit" must learn to regulate and rule over the
psychic life, so that its content becomes hierarchically ordered
according to the inner values of the various parts.[29] On the one
hand the development of a person's character depends on the
proper integration of his psychic life, while on the other hand
maturity depends on how well a person has learned to submit
himself willingly to the world of values as determined by the
Word of God. Nurture, therefore, is partly a matter of forming
and integrating the psychic life and partly a matter of teaching
the child to obey God's ordinances. These two aspects presuppose
one another, even though the latter aspect is the most important.
Basic to this conception of nurture is Dr. Waterink's view of man.

In anthropology, according to prof. Waterink, one must first of
all distinguish between the "I" or the *immortal soul directly
created* by God *and* the *psycho-somatic human nature* which comes
into existence through *generation*. The inner "I" or the spirit,
which is to be distinguished from the I used in the more general
sense of man as a totality, is *rational* and *moral*, since it is of a
religious nature. The spirit of man expresses itself through the
"self" or the psycho-somatic human nature. Within the hierarchically ordered microcosm of man's individual existence the spirit
must rule over the psychic life.[30] In short this is the anthropology

---

29 *Ibid.*, p. 123: "Onder de integratie verstaan wij de op harmonische wijze
tot stand gekomen organisatie en afgrenzing tegen de buitenwereld van de
verschillende aanleg-structuren en de verschillende psychische inhouden,..."
"Maar daarnaast is het nodig, dat het *ik* van de mens in deze wereld van
psychische inhouden heerst. Niet het psychische is dominant in het menselijk
leven, maar de geest." "Wij hebben het kind op te voeden tot een harmonisch
geintegreerde persoonlijkheid. En dit kind zal dan bovenal leren moeten met
zijn aan Gods orde onderworpen *ik*, de orde in zijn eigen levensbestaan te
handhaven."
30 *Ibid.*, p. 442: "Als wij deze mens nu zien naar de hierarchie van de eigen
persoonlijkheidsstructuur, dan staat boven aan de orde het "ik", naar schriftuurlijke opvatting door God geschapen en heersend in de mikro-kosmos van het
individuele bestaan van deze mens." Cf. pp. 123, 564. See also his *Inleiding,
Deel I*, p. 432f; *Ons Zieleleven*, pp. 11, 15, 228ff; *De Oorsprong en het Wezen*

that serves as the starting-point and basis of Dr. Waterink's theory of education and psychology. It is primarily at this point that our critique of his theory of education concentrates itself, for this anthropology has its origin in Thomistic-Aristotelian philosophy and can in no way be harmonized with the Scriptural view of man as a religious being.[31] When we take our starting-point in this scholastic view of man, it is impossible to arrive at an integrally Christian theory of education.

In an address entitled "Man as Religious Being and Modern Psychology" prof. Waterink *does* stress the centrality of man's religion."[32] There he states: "Man, as God has made him, functioned towards, in the direction of the Father; his whole being, all his activities were borne by his religion . . ." "When sin appears, the tendency of all this changes." "Now, too, his whole being, his activities are borne by religion, but by *religion directed to the wrong object*." " . . . the fact that man is religious, determines his whole being." "Hence religion is not only an aspect of life or of the person. No, man *is* a religious being."[33] But this thoroughly Scriptural conception of religion, as the concentration-point of man's existence in which he is either directed toward God or away from Him, cannot be harmonized with the anthropological framework that serves as the foundation of his theory of education and his psychology. The influence of this scholastic anthropology which finds its source in an un-Scriptural dualism regrettably prevents the truly Scriptural insight into the all-embracing character of religion to permeate his scientific writings.[34]

---

van de Ziel, pass. See further H. R. Wijngaarden, *Hoofdproblemen der Volwassenheid*, Utrecht: Erven J. Bijleveld, 1955[3], pp. 29ff; and J. G. Fernhout, *Psychotherapeutische Zielzorg*, Baarn: Bosch & Keuning N.V., n.d., pp. 12ff.

[31] Cf. Dooyeweerd, *Phil. Ref.* IV, 4, 200, 202; *Phil. Ref.* VIII, 3, 4; IX, 1, 2; X, 4; XI, 1, pass.

[32] J. Waterink, "Man as Religious Being and Modern Psychology," *Free University Quarterly*, VI, 1 (February, 1959), 1-30, (Separate). The same article can be found in his *Keur*, pp. 43-74.

[33] Waterink, F. U. Q., VI, 1, 24, 25. Similar expressions can be found in his *Theorie*, passim.

[34] Although we can appreciate Dr. Berkouwer's interpretation of prof. Waterink's intention in emphasizing the religious nature of the inner "I", we cannot agree with his conclusions. Cf. G. C. Berkouwer, *De Mens het Beeld Gods*, p. 338f: "Duidelijk blijkt hier, dat het niet gaat om een nieuw (toegevoegd) substantie-begrip, maar om wat de ganse mens is als *religieus* wezen, terwijl het diepste wezen van de mens zonder dit essentiele nimmer te peilen is." "Wanneer men echter over het 'wezen' van de mens niet anders dan in *deze* betrokkenheid kan spreken, is het niet meer mogelijk de dualiteit in te dragen in de oorsprong der *ziel* en van het *lichaam* binnen de ene mens." " . . . en wie

The antinomies to which this dualistic ground-motive leads manifest themselves repeatedly. As soon as religious education, for example, is thought of as embracing all aspects of education, one can no longer speak of religious education in distinction from other specific kinds of education. Then "religious" education could not refer to some distinct kind of education (however fundamental and however organically interwoven with moral, social, cultural, or national education), but only to the *religious direction* of the various kinds of training. The very fact that prof. Waterink considers it possible to devote a separate chapter to "religious" education is an indication of an antinomy. [35] It demonstrates that in some sense the dualism between grace and nature, between religion (the "I", the spirit) *and* man's psycho-somatic human nature is maintained. Whenever the centrality of religion is acknowledged, one can no longer speak of "religious" education

---

— gelijk Waterink — het creatianisme in zijn oude 'exclusieve' vorm 'onder geen enkele voorwaarde' meer kan aanvaarden, heeft m.i. principieel het creatianisme losgelaten, omdat dit *naar zijn aard* exclusief is en blijven wil." It seems that in these last words, however, the wish has been the father of the thought, for apparently Dr. Waterink considers it possible to maintain the first (man as a religious being) and not abandon the second (the duality between creation and generation)!

In 1929 Dr. Waterink wrote: "De onsterfelijke ziel, het eeuwige principe in den mensch is den door God in het ogenblik der generatio geschapen menschelijke geest, of het 'ik';..." "Maar het psychische wordt 'gegenereerd', met het somatische." (*Inleiding*, Deel I, p. 433) After 1946 prof. Waterink writes: "Dat de ziel des mensen een eigen substantie heeft en geformeerd is voor de eeuwigheid, leert de Schrift ons duidelijk," (*Ons Zieleleven*, p. 11.) And in 1958 he still maintains: "Ik ben er van overtuigd, dat bij de generatie, of liever in het moment van de conceptie, er een mens ontstaat, omdat twee levende cellen met elkaar contact maken, terwijl God naar Zijn orde aan dit ontstane, nieuw leven, aan deze menselijke individu in aanleg, een 'ik' en daarmede een geest geeft." (*Theorie*, p. 561.) From Dr. Waterink's publications we can only conclude that he has not abandoned creationism *and all that goes with it* (substance, psycho-somatic human nature, rationality, morality, hierarchy of values, the subject-object relation, the working of the Logos, etc., etc.). One cannot do justice to Dr. Waterink's conception of creationism without considering his total anthropology.

[35] Waterink, *Theorie*, p. 53: "Omdat het religieuze het alles omvattende is, bespreken wij dat punt het laatst;..." "Deden wij omgekeerd, dan zou bij de bespreking van de andere, gespecialiseerde aspecten telkens herhaald moeten worden wat onder het religieuze aspect reeds was genoemd vanuit godsdienstig gezichtspunt." But as soon as religion is conceived of as the *direction* of man's heart (for or against God), one can *only* speak of religion in connection with the (direction of the) various aspects of nurture. This would not be a repetition, for religion is not something that can be added, but it is *in* our actual training and guiding, and *in* our description of the different aspects of child-rearing that the religious direction of our activities and our theorizing must come to expression.

(in distinction from moral or social education) but only of Roman Catholic, Reformed, Mohammedan, or Humanistic education!

It is instructive to see how Dr. Waterink seeks to escape the dilemma he faces when dealing with "religious" education.[36] After some introductory remarks, he devotes the major part of the chapter to "religious" education in the *special sense* of instruction in the Scriptures and the confessions, and of introducing the child to the life of the church and the activities and aims of youth societies, while only one section deals with the relation between religion and morality. Thus he immediately focusses the attention upon that aspect of the child's life which *does* allow of a certain formation, namely that aspect through which the religious direction of the child's heart directly expresses itself in belief, worship, confession, and prayer. Understandably so, for religion in the sense of concentration-point (the "I"), as all-embracing, or better yet, as direction or relation is not subject to human formation. The educator cannot re-direct the heart of the child; only Christ's Spirit can turn a person toward God and sanctify his life. But the child's faith-life *does* allow of a certain formation. The child's faith can grow and mature and the educator can guide the child in this development and instruct him in the Christian faith. It is remarkable that when Dr. Waterink discusses the religious nature of man (religion, image of God, office), he concludes his presentation with a description of man's *faith*.[37] Is there perhaps more to the distinction between religion and faith than it would seem at first? Regrettably Dr. Waterink has never explicitly dealt with this issue; had he done so when these matters were first presented (around 1930!) many of the ambiguities and unresolved problems that we now encounter in his writings would undoubtedly have been clarified.

Summarizing our brief presentation of Dr. Waterink's conception of nurture we must maintain that in an integral Christian theory of education which takes its starting-point in the religious nature of man concentrated in the inner "I", we cannot speak of the (personality of the) child as the object of education, nor could we speak of the Logos, of substance, knowledge, morality, hierarchy of values, and the psychic life as prof. Waterink (Hepp, Woltjer, Kuyper) does. Through his many publications Dr. Waterink has indeed given us occasion to re-think and re-form the principles

---

[36] *Ibid.*, pp. 581ff.
[37] *Ibid.*, p. 62f.

of Christian education, and in spite of our fundamental critique it would not be difficult to fill as many pages and more with an account of the valuable insights and perspectives his publications afford. For whenever the anthropological framework with its tenacious religious ground-motive does not interfere, there is a truly Scriptural approach to child-rearing.

Next we briefly turn to a study by Dr. C. Jaarsma entitled *Human Development, Learning and Teaching.*[38] Although this work suffers from a lack of coherence and integration, it contains some valuable insights and many good descriptions. Depending on the writings of J. Waterink, A. Kuypers, H. R. Wijngaarden, and L. van der Horst for his anthropological basis, prof. Jaarsma has attempted to set forth a Christian theory of human development and learning. In view of our present inquiry we shall limit ourselves to a brief analysis of the basic perspective of this study.

Taking over Dr. Waterink's view of man and his conception of the psychic life,[39] prof. Jaarsma defines education as "... the process by which we direct an immature person, a child, in the development of its resources so that he is formed into a mature personality." [40] By personality Dr. Jaarsma means the total person functioning in all his aspects. "Within its scope fall not only what we have called pneuma, psyche, and soma, but also the various dimensions of the person's social expression." [41] Through education the personality of the child is formed.

Even though there are many similarities between Dr. Waterink's description of human development and education, *and* Dr. Jaarsma's account, there nevertheless is a striking difference between these two conceptions. Prof. Waterink has described the development of man's personality in terms of *both* integration *and* regulation; consequently he conceived of education *both* as forming the child's personality *and* teaching the child to submit himself willingly to the Word of God. In Dr. Jaarsma's conception,

---

[38] C. Jaarsma, *Human Development, Learning and Teaching*, Grand Rapids: Wm. B. Eerdmans Publishing Company, 1961.

[39] *Ibid.*, p. 23: "In order to function in this world, the self manifests itself in two distinguishable but not separable ways. It manifests itself *psychically*, in the soul-life, and *physiologically*, in the life of the body." "The person, then, is the single psycho-physical life of the self." And p. 29: The soul life is the area of thinking, feeling, willing, purposing, judging, valuing, etc. of the person. We speak of these as mental functions in distinction from physical functions."

[40] *Ibid.*, p. 29. Cf. also pp. 52, 58, 73, 86, 168.

[41] *Ibid.*, p. 50. Cf. also pp. 80, 155.

however, this two-fold aim has been reduced to the forming of personality. Instead of Dr. Waterink's emphasis on the "I" or the spirit as the *"monarch"* that must *govern* the psychic life, prof. Jaarsma speaks of the spirit as a *source* of *energy,* as the life principle, and as the source of direction and vitality. [42] Endowed with a potential for self-development, the spirit impels the organic whole to maturity. The spirit, therefore, constitutes the third factor (heredity, environment, and spirit) in the forming of personality. [43]

No doubt this change in emphasis is to be attributed to the influence of American psychology. Whatever its origin, this conception of the spirit as the deepest *source* of energy — instead of the "monarch" of Dr. Waterink's concept of man — allows the author to define education entirely in terms of development and the "forming" of the developing personality. His conception of development as ". . . the unfolding of a pattern already implicit in the organism," in turn explains the author's understanding of Christian education. [44] Christian education can be considered "Christian" only if the child that is being educated is in Christ. "If *in* Christ, the personality is being formed by education according to the inner motivation of the new life. If *outside* of Christ, the personality is being formed according to the motivation of the man of sin." [45] Understandably so, for if the spirit as a source of energy endowed with a potential for self-development is regenerated, then the young person must necessarily develop according to the developmental pattern of a son of God. [46] If not in Christ the child can only develop according to the "pattern" of

---

[42] *Ibid.,* p. 23: "The human self . . . is the source of direction and vitality for every aspect of the human being, . . ." And p. 55: "Not only the body and the soul are sources of energy, but the spirit as well." "The soul is a source of energy in its psychic structure, and the spirit is the life principle involved in the psychosomatic. The spirit acts in the self-conscious choices and motivations of life" And p. 79: "The spirit is the very life principle of the psychic or mental functions and of the physical functions."

[43] *Ibid.,* p. 72: "The spirit as life principle impels the organic whole to maturity." Cf. p. 77: "Part of the difficulty originates in the fact that psychologists generally recognize only two factors in human development, heredity and environment. Because Christian psychology recognizes three factors, the controversy takes another turn." See also p. 80: "God endows the I, or spirit, with a potential for self-development according to the call he places upon a person in life. In his inscrutable wisdom he equips the spirit with a psychosomatic structure of corresponding potential."

[44] *Ibid.,* p. 63.

[45] *Ibid.,* p. 57.

[46] *Ibid.,* p. 66.

the man of sin. Thus one can find Samuels and Timothys as well as Esaus and Sauls in the "Christian" school, and perhaps even some Pilates.[47] Genuine Christian education, therefore, depends entirely on whether or not the child is regenerated.

Each child, according to Dr. Jaarsma, has within him some force of growth and development potential which asserts itself from very conception according to a pre-determined pattern. Through interaction with the environment there is a spontaneous process of growth in the organism so that the structure unfolds and matures. As soon as the structure reaches a new stage, the child is ready to learn new things. This is where education comes in, for with each new stage of maturity the child develops new needs which create new tensions. These felt needs must be met by satisfying goals. The chief purpose of education, therefore, is to select and to adopt such goals as are capable of meeting the true needs of a person. Since the child learns spontaneously, he only needs to be directed toward the right goals. This is the task of the teacher; he must activate needs, furnish the child with source materials for his self-activity toward the accepted goal, and support the learner in his task. The school need not do anything else but provide the medium — "the culture and civilization as organized body of knowledge" — through which learning can take place. The recognition of true needs and the selection of right goals depends on whether one sees the child as a spiritual being or merely as a bio-social organism that strives for self-realization. The "Christian" school, therefore, must provide an educational program that is appropriate for the child in Christ.[48]

Considering this fundamental perspective it is not difficult to understand why the largest part (175 pages) of this study is devoted to the development of personality and the process of learning and only a very small part (25 pages) to teaching and the teacher. Nor is it hard to understand why the author expects the greatest contributions to education during the next decades to come from psychology and psychotherapy, for this is really what education is all about.[49]

In view of the preceding analysis our evaluation of the basic structure of Dr. Jaarsma's theory of education can be brief.

---

[47] *Ibid.*, p. 69f.
[48] *Ibid.*, pp. 71, 80, 247, 249, 84, 58.
[49] *Ibid.*, pp. 7, 29, 87, 264.

Regrettably the author has not been able to dissociate himself sufficiently from the generally accepted, naturalistic, American theories of education to escape their influence. The result is a conspicuous synthesis between mutually exclusive anthropologies, which gives rise to numerous contradictions and misconceptions. The reductionistic conception of man as a bio-social organism endowed with a potential for self-development simply cannot be harmonized with the Scriptural view of man as a religious being called to serve God according to His ordinances for the benefit of mankind and responsible to his Maker for the manner in which he fulfills his task. The determinism of the evolutionistic anthropology cannot be overcome by merely adding a third source of energy and a third range of needs and goals. Adding a third dimension to a conception which allows no more than two determinative factors does not change the basic structure of this anthropology, but only gives rise to antinomies. In fairness to the author it must be observed that the general anthropological framework he took as a starting-point (Dr. Waterink's conception of the spirit, man's psycho-somatic nature, and his twofold definition of nurture) left room for this radical adaptation.

Dr. Jaarsma's internally contradictory view of man could not but lead to a fundamental misunderstanding of the nature of Christian education. The determinism of his conception (the unfolding of a pre-determined developmental pattern) really does not leave any room for education in the sense of leading (educere) the child toward a certain goal according to certain norms, teaching him to submit himself willingly to God's ordinances. To overcome this determinism one must completely abandon the notion that human development is a fixed bio-social process and that education is primarily a matter of creating a stimulating environment and of providing suitable learning opportunities. Human development, far from being an automatic, natural process, depends on explicit training and conscious guidance, and education is a responsible task, subject to the divine norms set for this activity. The Christian character of education does not depend on whether or not the child's spirit is regenerated, but solely on whether or not the guidance that is given is in keeping with God's revelation.

From this brief consideration of Dr. Waterink's and Dr. Jaarsma's attempt to formulate a Christian theory of education, we may conclude that an integrally Christian theory of nurture requires first of all an anthropology that is truly based upon and guided by the Scriptural view of man as a religious being.

B. ANTHROPOLOGICAL PRESUPPOSITIONS

Since nurture usually implies a relationship between two or more people, the educator's conception of man is determinative for his theory of education. From our consideration of some of the Christian theories of education it became apparent how much we are in need of an anthropology that is genuinely founded upon the Word of God. Radically rejecting both the traditional theological conception of man as a rational and moral being and the contemporary personalistic and existentialistic view of man, prof. Dooyeweerd has drafted an *outline* for such an integrally Christian anthropology that is based upon the Scriptural view of man as a religious being.[50]

A Scripturally orientated anthropology, according to prof. Dooyeweerd, must take its *starting-point* in 'God's revelation concerning the human I as the religious concentration-point of our existence.[51] For as soon as we try to grasp the human ego in a scientific concept "... it receeds as a phantom and dissolves itself into nothingness. It cannot be determined by any modal aspect of our experience, since it is the central reference-point to which all fundamental modes of our temporal experience are related. A logical I does not exist, neither a psycho-physical I, nor a historical I, nor a moral I. All such philosophical determinations of the ego disregard its central character."[52] The human I is nothing *in itself*, that is, it is nothing as long as we view it apart from the three

---

[50] Cf. Dooyeweerd, *A New Critique*, II, pp. 112-116, 147; III, pp. 88, 115, 781-784; ————, *In the Twilight*, pp. 25-33, 173-195; ————, *Inleiding tot de Encyclopaedie der Rechtswetenschap*, pp. 112-117; ————, "De leer van de mens in de wijsbegeerte der wetsidee," in *Sola Fide*, VII, 2 (Febr., 1954), 8-18; ————, "De idee der individualiteits-structuur en het Thomistisch substantiebegrip," *Phil. Ref.*, XI, 1 (1946), 42-52; ————, "De taak ener wijsgerige anthropologie en de doodlopende wegen tot wijsgerige zelfkennis," *Phil. Ref.*, XXVI, 1, 2, 3 (1961), 35-58; See also K. J. Popma, *Wijsbegeerte en Anthropologie*, Amsterdam: Buijten & Schipperheijn, 1963; A. Troost, *Casuïstiek*, pp. 358ff.

[51] Dooyeweerd, *Sola Fide*, VII, 2, Stelling VI, VII, "De menselijke ziel in haar praegnant religieuze schriftuurlijke zin gaat immers alle wetenschappelijke begrip te boven, omdat zij *vooronderstelde* van alle begrip is. Kennis omtrent haar is *religieuze zelf-kennis* en de *waarachtige zelfkennis* is slechts mogelijk in de weg der *waarachtige Godskennis* uit de Goddelijke Woordopenbaring." "De eigenlijke *wetenschappelijke* kennis omtrent de mens blijft dus principiëel beperkt tot de structuur van het menselijk lichaam in zijn brede zin van *tijdelijke existentievorm van het menselijk leven.*"

[52] Dooyeweerd, *In the Twilight*, p. 25.

central relations which alone give it meaning (our relation to the temporal order of our existence, to the egos of our fellowmen, and to our Creator and Lord). Apart from God's revelation in Jesus Christ and the re-direction of our hearts through the power of His Spirit, there can be no true knowledge of our inner selfhood, and, consequently, no true knowledge of our temporal existence and our communal relationship to others. [53]

Presupposing the Scriptural view of man as a religious being, created in the image of God, called to serve Him with his entire being and to unfold His creation for the benefit of mankind, (philosophical) *anthropology* must restrict itself to an investigation of the structure of the human body ("as the individual whole of man's temporal existence"). In a number of publications prof. Dooyeweerd has presented an initial analysis of this structure. The human body, in the full Scriptural sense of the word, ". . . shows a very complicated interlacement of different typical structures which are combined in a form-totality, qualified by the so-called act-structure. This act-structure is successively founded in an animal, a vegetative and a material structure. It gives the human body its proper character. But this act-structure, though it functions in all of the modal aspects, lacks, as such, a typical qualifying function within a temporal sphere. It is the immediate temporal expression of the human I-ness, which transcends the cosmic temporal order." "The act-structure of this body is neither qualified by a logical, nor by an ethical function. It is not even qualified by the faith-aspect." "It is this very structure which makes the human body the field of free expression for the human spirit, *i.e.* for the religious centre of human existence." [54]

---

[53] *Ibid.*, pp. 181ff.
[54] Dooyeweerd, *A New Critique*, III, p. 87f. Cf. propositions IX, X, and XII in *Sola Fide*, VII, 2, "Aan de anthropologie van de wijsbegeerte der wetsidee ligt ten grondslag de schriftuurlijke idee van de menselijke ziel als *integrale wortel van het gehele tijdelijke menselijke bestaan*. In deze geestelijke wortel is het menselijke leven nog 'ongedeeld' (Kuyper), omdat daarin *alle* tijdelijke functies geconcentreerd zijn in de religieuze grondverhouding tot de Oorsprong aller dingen. Daarom wordt hier ook het menselijk lichaam niet als een *abstract materielichaam* gevat, maar als het *geheel van 's mensen tijdelijke existentie*, dat zijn diepere eenheid slechts aan zijn band aan de 'ziel' dankt. Het lichaam is diensvolgens nimmer als een 'zelfstandigheid' of 'substantie' te vatten, daar het bij de losmaking van zijn integralen band aan de ziel (in de tijdelijke dood) aan de *ontbinding* is prijsgegeven." "Het menselijk lichaam is opgebouwd als een *enkaptisch geheel* in een *viertal individualiteitsstructuren*, waarvan telkens de lagere in de hogere *morphologisch gebonden* zijn. De natuurlijke lichaamsvorm of lichaamsgestelte is dus het knooppunt der *vervlechtingen* tussen de onderscheiden structuren. Deze structuren behouden ook in haar

This fundamental anthropological perspective has important implications for a Christian theory of education, as we hope to demonstrate in the following pages. First of all this conception of man delivers us from many pseudo-problems and false dilemmas. It prevents us from misinterpreting nurture as a bio-social process in which the educator's only task is to create the best possible environment for the growing organism and to provide the right learning opportunities at the various stages of development. Educational progress is indeed *founded upon*, thus, *presupposes* the bio-physical development of the child, but development in an educational sense is a *pedagogical* concept which can only be measured by *educational* norms. Development in this sense does not take place automatically, but depends on *pedagogical* influence and interaction, on the exertion of *formative* power, resulting in a conscious change of conduct.

It also prevents us from accepting the well-known dilemma between nurture and nature, or, in Theodor Litt's terms, between "Führen oder Wachsenlassen".[55] The solution to this dilemma is not to find some kind of balance between two mutually exclusive

---

onderlinge vervlechting haar interne eigenwettelijkheid en souvereiniteit in eigen kring." "Daar de lichaams*vorm* het knooppunt is van alle structuur-vervlechtingen in het menselijk lichaam, is het principiëel onmogelijk, bepaalde organen of delen van het menselijk lichaam in *morphologische zin exclusief* bij een dezer structuren in te delen. *Morphologisch* fungeert het menselijk lichaam met al zijn delen noodzakelijk *in alle vier structuren gelijkelijk*." See also his *Inleiding*, p. 113: "Deze acten *gaan steeds uit* van het *boven-tijdelijke* en dus *integrale centrum* van de menselijke natuur, dat door de Schrift in praegnante (religieuze) zin het *hart*, de *ziel* of de *geest* van de mens wordt genoemd. Maar zij kunnen zich slechts afspelen *binnen het menselijk lichaam* als enkaptisch structuur-geheel, nader binnen de typische act-structuur van dit laatste." "Dit wil dus zeggen, dat zij [de acten] in alle aspecten der werkelijkheid fungeert. Een denk-acte als *werkelijke* acte heeft dus ook haar *intern-physisch-chemisch*, haar *biotische* en *psychisch-emotionele* zijden en mag nimmer worden vereenzelvigd met haar *logisch aspect*." "Dat men de eigenlijke structuur-theorie van het menselijk act-leven bij de psychologie heeft ondergebracht, valt slechts te verklaren uit de doorwerking van de traditioneel metaphysische opvatting van de 'ziel' als een van het stoffelijk 'soma' onafhankelijk 'geheel' van functies. Het doet er daarbij weinig toe of men met deze twee-deling van de tijdelijke menselijke existentie volstaat, dan wel (zoals in de moderne act-psychologie zeer gebruikelijk is) een drie-deling invoert in *soma*, *psyche*, en *geest*, waarbij dan alleen de laatste (als complex van de hogere gevoelsfuncties, de logische denkfunctie en de aesthetische en 'ethische' functies) als in beginsel onafhankelijk van het 'levend lichaam" wordt gevat. De encyclopaedie der wetenschappen kan eerst dan op een bevredigende grondslag worden gebouwd, wanneer met al zulke valse totaliteits-opvattingen principiëel wordt gebroken."

[55] Th. Litt, *Führen oder Wachsenlassen*, Leipzig: B. G. Teubner, 1931³. Cf. Strasser, *Opvoedingswetenschap*, pp. 13ff, 56; Langeveld, *Beknopte Theoretische Pedagogiek*, pp. 24ff., 84-87; Jaarsma, *Human Development*, p. 76f.

categories, but to come to an adequate understanding of the *nature* of leading. If the term nurture is to have any meaning at all, we must maintain that education always implies a *conscious* and *deliberate* attempt on the part of the educator to lead the child or the adult in a particular direction according to certain norms. [56] But as soon as we describe nurture this way, it is of utmost importance how we conceive of the *nature* and the *limits* of this leading or forming.

In the exercise of formative power we are bound to the nature of our "object". This is true when we mould a piece of clay or (technically) shape some other material, and it is also true when we attempt to train an animal. In all such forming, if it is to be successful, we are bound to the peculiar features and possibilities of the material we are dealing with, or, in the case of animals, to their psychical nature. A human being, however, can never be an object in this sense, since he functions as a subject in all the modalities and — most important of all — since all his functions are related to his religious selfhood. To treat a person like an object or to train and drill him like an animal would be a violation of his human nature. Such "mental engineering", of which we see faint (?!) traces in the upbringing of our children and which has become an awful reality in the "brain washing" of political prisoners, constitutes a demonic temptation for all educators.

Education requires a *fundamental respect* for those we seek to nurture, because they are *human beings made in the image of God,* created to respond to His calling. From the very beginning each person is a complete human being. A child does not *develop* into a person, he *is* a person from the start, he is a religious being. Man as such, therefore, as a religious unity, can never be the "object" of our pedagogical moulding. Our nurture can only direct itself to the various *aspects* of a *person's* existence, to the harmonious development and proper integration of the physical, organic, and psychical individuality structure within the act-structure, [57] in order that he may be (the better) prepared for his task in life. And in doing so the educator appeals to the personal responsibility of the one being educated, so that even when he "passively undergoes" a certain pedagogical forming, he is still actively involved in the educational process. Since he is a religious

---

[56] Cf. Waterink, *Theorie,* pp. 108-116; J. Hoogveld, *Keur uit de Werken,* Groningen: J. B. Wolters, 1951², pp. 4ff; Langeveld, *Beknopte,* p. 37.

[57] See above p. 109, note 54.

being, he must necessarily relate the guidance he receives to his inner selfhood and to his God-given calling in life. The exercise of educational power over the individual development of a (certain aspect of a) person's life, therefore, does not exclude the personal cooperation and responsibility of the one being educated. Those who are being nurtured always remain free human subjects. This has far-reaching consequences for the nature, limits and ultimate aim of our education. Man's religious nature in principle determines the character of all pedagogical relationships.

To nurture is something fundamentally different from stimulating the growth of a human organism, from creating suitable surroundings, or from caring for a person's physical comfort. To nurture means to give actual direction to the development of a person's life, to lead him toward a particular goal according to certain norms, in short, to nurture means to exert real formative power. But *in* this leading the educator is *bound* to man's religious nature and calling. The power which he exercises over people in pedagogical forming is not a personal privilege or a particular skill that he may use as he pleases. He may not follow his own whims or wishes, nor is he free to use whatever means he considers suitable to achieve his purposes.

When man's human nature (his freedom and his responsibility) is not respected, nurture invariably turns into a pure demonstration of power and domination, or it becomes mental persecution, manipulation, mechanical training, or it is reduced to overprotection, doting, or a mere laissez-faire attitude. Such antinormative guidance can only result in stubborn rebellion, obstinacy, aggression, fearful submission, immaturity, neurotic tendencies, disharmony, and, in some instances, permanent deformities, or give rise to undisciplined behavior, confusion, and uncertainty. The violation of human nature inevitably leads to pedagogical impotence and failure.

The very fact that man is a religious being with a divinely given charge makes education a *normative* task. The Christian has no other task than to witness to the resurrection of his Lord, who makes all things new. We have no other calling than to testify in all of our activities to the newness of life in Jesus Christ. This is our reasonable service, to offer our very selves, the worship of our minds and hearts to Him, and to demonstrate the triumphs of Him who has called us out of darkness into His marvellous light. We are to become fit instruments for the work of the Lord. The pedagogue is bound to this revelation concerning man's vocation in life. The final aim of all forms of Christian nurture and instruction can be nothing else than the provision of fundamental guidance with regard to this calling. Wherever the child or the adult is placed, whatever his abilities or limitations, he must learn to submit his life to God's will. His one and only task is to serve God according to His ordinances, unfolding and developing His creation for the benefit of mankind to the praise of his Lord and Redeemer. To prepare the child for this service and to give the adult guidance with regard to this calling must be the final aim of Christian education. [58]

This Scriptural view of man excludes every idealistic or humanistic goal for education. Neither the skilled or cultured person nor the integrated or socially adjusted personality, neither the self-reliant or ethical person nor the responsible citizen, neither the converted individual nor the devout and pious Christian can serve as the ultimate goal for education. All such personality-ideals are basically humanistic and incompatible with the Scriptural witness concerning man's religious nature. For as soon as one of the aspects of reality is absolutized, whether this be man's faith-life or his personality, the community or man's basic drives, science or labor, humanity, or art, when one of these aspects becomes the final aim of education, the meaning of human life is falsified and distorted. In that case education becomes an instrument for the self-glorification of man, which can only lead to his destruction. Man has only one calling and that is to serve God with all his heart and to love his neighbor as himself.

C. THE NORMS FOR EDUCATION

In order to determine the basic structure of nurture it is not sufficient, as Dr. Waterink seems to think, [59] to refer to the covenantal bond between parents and children and to the divine charge given to the parents to bring up their children in the fear of the Lord. Scriptural Revelation, to which prof. Waterink refers as the ultimate norm for our understanding of the unique character of education, indeed has much to say about the parent-child relationship and the upbringing of children. In due course we shall

---

[58] Cf. K. J. Popma, "Opvoeding, onderwijs, schoolverband," *Phil. Ref.*, XII, 1 (1947), 38f; Waterink, *Theorie*, pp. 20, 61, 71, 111, 125ff., 576.

[59] See above p. 96.

return to this issue. But, even though the Scriptures mandate us to raise our children in a manner that is in accord with God's will, they do not tell us precisely how we are to go about this activity, nor do they contain a description of the *specific* nature of the parent-child relation, not to mention other pedagogical relationships. They simply tell us that we are responsible for the manner in which we bring up our children and that we are to keep in mind the ultimate aim of our endeavors.

The inscripturated Word of God alone, therefore, is not sufficient to determine the specific structure of educational activities and relationships. This state of affairs should neither surprise nor disturb us, since, as we have noted in the previous chapter, the Word-revelation cannot be separated from the revelation of God's will in creation. We *believe* that all of creation, mankind included, is subject to God's law and that He reveals His will not only in the Scriptures but also in the order of creation. If we are to gain an insight into the peculiar features of child-rearing and other forms of education, we must turn to the educational process itself and seek to discover the *norms* that govern this process. Like any other human activity, education is bound to the structural norms God has put for this activity. These creational norms cannot be derived from the Word-Revelation, nor can they be truthfully described and analyzed by means of the phenomenological method. [60]

Over against all subjectivism, objectivism, and realism [61] we must maintain that there is an inseparable relation (correlation) between the law-side of creation and that which is placed under the law. [62] The structural law-order which holds for all of reality, both subjects

---

[60] See below p. 116 f., and notes 64, 66.

[61] Cf. D. H. Th. Vollenhoven, *Kort Overzicht van de Geschiedenis der Wijsbegeerte*, pp. 2ff., 13ff.

[62] For a further discussion of this conception of law, see: Dooyeweerd, *A New Critique*, I, pp. 92-113, II, 25-36, 237ff; —————, "Van Peursen's critische vragen bij 'A New Critique of Theoretical Thought'," *Phil. Ref.*, XXV, 3, 4 (1960), *passim*; —————, "De Wijsbegeerte der Wetsidee en de 'Barthianen'," *Phil. Ref.*, XVI, 4 (1951), 158ff; Vollenhoven, *Hoofdlijnen der Logica*, pp. 24ff; —————, "Norm en Natuurwet," *Mededelingen*, (Juli, 1951), 3-6; Mekkes, "Beschouwingen naar aanleiding van de discussie rondom het recht van verzet," *Phil. Ref.*, XVIII, 4 (1953), 145-170; —————, "Wet en subject in de Wijsbegeerte der Wetsidee," *Phil. Ref.*, XXVII, 3, 4 (1962), 126-190; —————, *Scheppingsopenbaring en Wijsbegeerte, passim*, —————, "Geloven en kennen," *Mededelingen*, (September, 1952), 9-10; Van Riessen, "Over de betekenis van de wetsidee in de wijsbegeerte," *Phil. Ref.*, XXX, 2, 3, 4 (1965), 159-177; —————, *Op Wijsgerige Wegen*, pp. 50ff; Troost, *Casuïstiek*, pp. 125ff., 354ff., 362ff; Dengerink, "Das Wort Gottes und die zeitlichen socialen Ordnungen," *Phil. Ref.*, XX, 3, 4 (1955), 97-122.

and objects, consists of a rich variety of law-spheres. A number of these structural laws (the pre-logical) are realized in the facts (in things, plants, animals, and to some extent, in man) without human intervention. The so-called "natural" sides of reality simply cannot withdraw from these "fixed" laws. The other laws (the logical and post-logical) also hold for reality, but in a somewhat different manner, since they call for human recognition and concretization. To function as they ought these "norm" laws must be recognized and given positive form by man. This does not mean that their validity depends on man's acknowledgment, but rather that, in order to function properly and to be meaningful and binding (on the subject-side), they must be given specific form in keeping with the cultural situation and historical development. The "norm" laws are only given as directives, which require particularization ("positivization") into positive norms.

Although these positive norms, whether juridical or ethical, economical or social, must be accommodated time and again to the course of historical development, this does not mean that they are therefore historically determined and in that sense relative. The positive norms are founded in the firm and unchangeable structural principles which God put for these aspects of His creation and which He faithfully maintains in Jesus Christ. It is the divine law-order which makes life possible and which gives the positive norms their validity and compelling character. Positive norms, therefore, are not merely pragmatic rules that can be changed at will, but they are specifications of the structural principles to which all human activities are subject. Disregard of the creational ordinances can only result in confusion, deterioration, and ultimately in chaos, if God would not prevent it.

The element of human formation, which is an inherent part of the normative law-spheres, focusses the attention upon the religious task of man. In subjection to God's law man is called upon to exercise his freedom and responsibility and to know the Truth. He must discover and evaluate, judge and choose, develop and give form. Such is his calling: to respond to his Creator, serving Him wholeheartedly in obedience to His divine will for the benefit of mankind. In this religious task man is bound to the creational ordinances which *reveal God's* will. These ordinances can never be separated from the Law-giver, for they are the expression of His will, and they can only be fulfilled in the light of the great commandment to love God above all and our neighbor as ourselves.

We *believe* that God's will as revealed in the order of creation can be known to man.[63] This knowledge, however, is not of a (scientific) rational or moral nature (although it has these aspects), but it is basically of a religious nature.[64] To know the truth about the various aspects of the creation-order, we must first of all stand in the Truth, in Jesus Christ through the Holy Spirit.[65] Only in the light of the Word-Revelation can we truly understand and come to know the revelation of God's will in creation.

When we observe the regularity (regula) of the educational processes in the light of the Word of God and under the guidance of our faith, we can truly gain knowledge of the structural norms that govern all forms of education. For the law-conformity given in experience points and refers to the law and gives us our knowledge of the creational ordinances. This pre-scientific knowledge, which comes over us in intuitive self-reflection and which accompanies all our acts, is always partial and inadequate, and tainted by sin, and therefore always subject to correction.[66]

---

[63] Cf. especially Mekkes, *Phil. Ref.*, XVIII, 4, 145-170; and *Mededelingen*, (Sept., 1952), 9-10; See also Dooyeweerd, *Vernieuwing en Bezinning*, p. 56; Troost, *Casuïstiek*, p. 371.

[64] Cf. Mekkes, *Phil. Ref.*, XVIII, 4, 157: "De in de scheppingsorde gegronde structuurprincipes eisen verwerkelijking door menselijke vormgeving en deze verwerkelijking moet dus haar weg nemen door de zondige subjectiviteit. Alleen via deze verwerkelijking zijn zij voor critisch empirisch onderzoek vatbaar, ..." "Daarbij dienen dus uit de volle empirische werkelijkheid de structuurprincipes in hun constant en bovenwillekeurig karakter te worden geanalyseerd in scherpe onderscheiding van hun concrete vormgeving, die steeds op variabelen historischen grondslag rust." "Slechts in het licht van het Kruis, dat ons onzen afval, maar tevens Christus' volkomen genoegdoening toont, vermogen wij de structuren der goddelijke scheppingsorde door de ervaring harer gebrekkige verwerkelijking heen te ontwaren. Doch dan hebben wij vóór alles te bedenken, dat dit licht ons verstand ook in zijn theoretische bezigheden zeer concreet slechts verlicht *in* het (actueel) geloof." And 166: "Het inzicht in de wet is allereerst (voor-theoretisch) *geloofs*inzicht. De geloofsintuïtie grijpt de stand van zaken in de practische levensverscheidenheid vanuit den religieuzen wortel zonder analysering van het gehele zinsverband en zal tot theoretisch inzicht daarin eerst geleidelijk en in afhankelijkheid van de historische ontplooiing der christelijke wetenschapsbeoefening kunnen geraken." And 165: "Hier staan wij inderdaad aan de grens der zone waar te bewijzen valt. Het begrip immers der kosmische structuren, zowel van de modale als van de structuurtypen der individualiteit, is niet te vatten buiten haar idee. De idee wijst boven zichzelve uit naar de vervulling der structuur en deze valt uiteindelijk niet anders te benaderen dan in eerbiedig toetreden, in geloof, tot de ontmoeting vañ wet en subjectieve wetsvervulling in het offer van Golgotha. Het is door het geloof, dat wij rekenschap geven ook van de idee der staatsstructuur."

[65] Cf. Dooyeweerd, *A New Critique*, II, pp. 571ff.

[66] Cf. Mekkes, *Phil. Ref.*, XVIII, 4, 152f: "Wanneer de geloofsblik is gefixeerd op het Kruis en daarmee op de ware volheid van zin, dan gaan de ogen tegelijkertijd open voor de onderlinge betrekkelijkheid van het tijdelijk ver-

Our subjective knowledge, therefore, and our systematic descriptions of the various structural norms, such as prof. Dooyeweerd's analysis of the modal laws and the structures of individuality, may never be identified with the law-order itself. Our theoretical formulations may be more or less correct, our pre-theoretical, concrete, everyday knowledge, upon which our scientific knowledge is based, may be incomplete of faulty, but the dynamic order of creation remains firm and valid and continues to press upon us. Whatever our knowledge, our *faith* in the *givenness* (Revelation!) of the creational ordinances is first and remains central. Much more could be said about this view of creational revelation and how we have knowledge of the law-order, about possible misconceptions and different implications for our theorizing, but it would carry us too far afield to elaborate upon this conception. For a further exposition we must refer to other publications. [67]

Summarizing we can say that the structural norms that hold for all forms of education can neither be derived from the Scriptures nor can they be truthfully described and analyzed by means of the "scientific" method or the phenomenological method. They are

---

scheidene, d.i. voor de souvereiniteit en universaliteit in eigen kring. Van dit geheel enig centrum uit nu hebben wij in onze onderscheidene aktbelevingen geduldig de zingrenzen af te speuren, in onvoorwaardelijke bereidheid tot onderwerping aan de in Christus behouden wereldorde. Dit speuren vindt plaats in ontmoeting met hetgeen in de ervaren werkelijkheid wordt aangetroffen en in deze ervaring is het, dat de wetsidee de conclusies omtrent de wetmatigheden beheerst. Onze wetsidee ligt apriorisch vast in het geloof; in de conclusie kunnen en zullen wij herhaaldelijk falen. Deze zullen telkenmale, in confrontatie der tegenover ons zich handhavende scheppingsorde met de wetsidee naar het Woord Gods, moeten worden gecorrigeerd. Schrijnend doet in dit kernproces de ontwrichtende werking van de macht der zonde zich gevoelen; de kenharmonie blijft ook practisch slechts in de *idee* bevangen. Nochtans hebben wij de worsteling te voeren op hoop tegen hoop, omdat het *getuigen* van de overwinning des Heren ons is opgelegd, als niet meer dan, maar dan ook als volhardend getuigen. Het is waarlijk geen geringe roeping, getuige te moeten zijn van Christus' overwinning, spontaan en zonder omzien. Zij sluit het wetticisme, ook in de zin van een nieuwe dankbaarheids-'ethiek', volmaakt uit. En toch roept zij tot de wet. Zij roept daarheen om ons tot demonstranten te maken van de waarheid, dat Christus alle dingen nieuw maakt." Cf. also his *Scheppingsopenbaring*, p. 127: "Van menselijk oogpunt uit gezien valt er tegen de overmacht der schuldige scheppingsverstoring niets te 'bereiken'. En dit te minder omdat in alles wat de christen onderneemt, in zijn persoonlijk en gemeenschappelijk organiseren onverwijld diezelfde verstoring binnendringt, aanvangend in de georganiseerde kerk. Het is de Meester, Die het alles doet; het is zijn werk dat blijft." See also Dooyeweerd, *A New Critique*, II, pp. 335-337.

[67] See note 59. With regard to various misconceptions cf. Dooyeweerd, *A New Critique*, I, pp. 92ff., and Mekkes, *Phil. Ref.*, XVIII, 4, 154f.

first of all *given* in our *actual* experience of pedagogical situations and in our concrete knowledge of the educational process. God faithfully maintains His law, so that the creation order impinges upon us at all times, whether we recognize and adhere to His law-order or not. Through systematic reflection upon and theoretical analysis of this concrete experience and practical knowledge of the structural norms we can come to a (always provisional) theoretical formulation of these norms. A *true* insight, however, is possible only if our faith is re-directed toward God's revelation by the power of His Word. In that case we can speak of a Christian theory of education, that is, a theory founded upon and directed by the Word of God.

D. THE STRUCTURE OF EDUCATION

In his analysis of the modal law-spheres and the structures of individuality, prof. Dooyeweerd has given us a *theoretical* account of the divine law-order. With the aid of this theory or "ground plan", as Dr. Troost has called it, [68] we shall engage in a provisional analysis of the normative structure governing the process of education. But since these structural norms can be known only through actual experience of the educational process in which these norms are realized, they cannot be worked out abstractly. They can only be (theoretically) described and analyzed through constant reflection upon concrete pedagogical relationships and situations. Our present inquiry, therefore, must necessarily be limited to "some introductory remarks". Moreover, the significance of a structural analysis can only be demonstrated in continual confrontation with current educational theories and problems — all the more reason to restrict ourselves to the *prolegomena* of education.

From our consideration of the ultimate goal of Christian education it is evident that nurture cannot be limited to child-

---

[68] Troost, "Personalisme en ethiek," *Mededelingen*, (Maart, 1966), 5: "Maar dat neemt niet weg dat er ook een christelijke verantwoordelijkheid is t.a.v. de wetenschappelijke bezinning op de structuur der situaties waarin wij leven en handelen. De wijsbegeerte der wetsidee helpt ons daarbij op weg en geeft ons o.a. in de leer der modaliteiten alvast een voorlopige plattegrond in handen, waar we wat aan hebben. Die plattegrond wordt nog wel eens herzien, en is nog niet veel meer dan een ontwerp, geschetst met stippellijnen en krijtstrepen, voor allerlei correctie vatbaar, maar we kunnen er voorlopig mee vooruit."

rearing. Even when the young person reaches a stage of relative emotional maturity and a measure of social, economic, and political independance, even when he is able to make responsible decisions, to vote, and to support himself and a family, even then he is still in need of guidance with respect to the various aspects of his calling as a Christian. It would be arbitrary to limit this guidance to a person's childhood, for as long as we live we are called to grow in our understanding of God's will for our lives. We continually fall short in the fulfillment of our religious task, also in our understanding of God's ordinances which is an integral part of this task, but in Jesus Christ, who alone has fulfilled the law and in whom there is both forgiveness and restoration, there is ever again a new beginning and genuine development. And in His wisdom God has appointed not only parents but also teachers, ministers, and many others to nurture us in the discipline and instruction of the Lord and to counsel us with regard to our respective tasks.

First of all parents have received this divine charge. [69] They are called to prepare the child for a life of service and to lead him to acknowledge and to do the will of God. But they cannot do this alone, since they themselves are dependent upon others for their understanding of God's law. The concrete pedagogical rules which they must establish for their children can only be formulated in coherence with the whole order of creation and the structure of human life. They too, therefore, must be continually instructed and counseled. In the first place they must be continually built up in the faith and instructed in the central meaning of God's law as revealed in the Scriptures. This is fundamental, for it is only in the light of the inscripturated Word of God that the creational ordinances can be known truthfully and given adequate positive form. But even for their concrete knowledge of the structural laws they must to a large extent rely upon the insights and experiences of others. This is true for teachers as well, in as much as they are called upon to select, explain, interpret, and evaluate, which they cannot do without instruction and guidance from others. Each of us constantly depends on further instruction and on the leading of others for the fulfillment of our calling and the reformation of our lives. Parents fail, teachers fall short, leaders are negligent, counselors lead astray, instructors falsify, but in Christ there is both genuine nurture and real growth.

---

69 See below p. 134.

This "broad" conception of nurture pertaining to all age-groups does not mean that every human relationship is a pedagogical relationship. Not every kind of influence, not all exercise of authority, not all information, and not every activity can be considered educational. All forms of association and communication do have a *pedagogical aspect,* but not all relationships and not every situation is a *typical pedagogical* situation. Only when there is a conscious attempt to guide a person with regard to his calling in life, leading him in a particular direction according to certain norms, can we speak of a typical educational relationship. But if education can and must be distinguished from other human activities, it becomes all the more urgent to find a meaningful criterion to differentiate between these various activities, or, to put it differently, to establish the boundaries of our field of inquiry.

Certainly such a criterion cannot be found in the direct command of God and the covenant relation between parents and children, nor in the *specific* aim of child-rearing, for in both instances nurture is arbitrarily limited to the upbringing of children. In this connection it is instructive to note that Dr. Waterink and prof. Langeveld, who both (although for different reasons) limit nurture to child-rearing, consider the expression "adult education", and similar terms referring to specific types of guidance, as an improper, figurative, and analogical use of the word education.[70] But these terms cannot be explained as mere metaphors, for if that were the case it should be possible to substitute other, less confusing terms. Remarkably, however, Dr. Waterink uses the same concepts to describe both "genuine" nurture and other forms of leading.[71] If, on the other hand, there is a real analogy between the upbringing of children and adult education, as prof. Langeveld maintains, it should be possible to explain the similarities and the differences between these two types of guidance. Dr. Langeveld indeed presents such an explanation. The assistance or instruction given to adults is basically different from nurture, according to him, since adults are personally responsible for the guidance they accept, while children are not, and to the extent that adult education is similar to child-rearing it should be looked upon as an emergency measure.[72] We can readily agree that the matter of personal

---

[70]   Waterink, *Theorie,* pp. 13-18; —————, *Keur,* pp. 3-6; Langeveld, *Beknopte,* pp. 82, 83, 173 note 40.

[71]   Waterink, *Theorie,* pp. 18, 116, 71, 77.

[72]   Langeveld, *Beknopte,* p. 83.

responsibility deserves further analysis as it touches upon a central issue, but it is impossible to explain most forms of adult guidance as interventions necessitated by a lack of "maturity".

Contrary to Dr. Langeveld we must maintain that *as soon as* and *to the extent that* the child begins to respond to his upbringing as an individual person, he also begins to bear a measure of responsibility. Already at a very early stage the child begins to assert himself and to take an active part in the educational process. In as much as the child participates, co-operates, and at times even begins to take the initiative, he is also partly responsible for the *manner* in which he takes part in and reacts to the guidance he receives. The manner in which the child responds to his upbringing (the development of his conscience) is not merely the result of nurture or heredity. From the very beginning he is a human being with a *religious selfhood,* created to live in loving fellowship with his Maker. The child's reactions and activities, therefore, can never be considered *apart* from the fall into sin and the redemption in Jesus Christ. Any "anthropology of the child" which does not take this most basic given into account becomes a distortion, because the religious dimension is not something which can be considered subsequently or separately but is constitutive for one's entire conception of the child's development and the ultimate aim of child-rearing. What is at stake here is not merely a difference in theoretical insight with regard to the (psychic) development of the child and the aim of nurture but a different anthropology, and we can only conclude that Dr. Langeveld's "limited" conception of nurture is dictated more by his conception of man as a self-reliant, responsible, moral being than by his observations and analyses.

Man is not a "moral" being who can and ought to act according to certain "values", and the ultimate goal of education, therefore, cannot be the "ethical" man, because, as Scripture reveals to us, man is a religious being called to serve his Lord in newness of life according to His will. A good upbringing requires first of all self-knowledge (also according to Dr. Langeveld[73]), but true self-

---

[73] *Ibid.,* pp. 30, 38. Langeveld describes the general aim of nurture as "... het kind te helpen, bekwaam te worden tot zedelijke zelfbepaling in een morele orde, die onszelf de verantwoordelijkheid laat." (p. 75) Or, as he also formulates it: "... de opvoedeling bekwaam te maken als sociaal-zedelijk-persoonlijk wezen te handelen." "... de opvoedeling te leren zijn leven te leven als de iemand-die-hij-zelf-is zelfstandig zoals het behoort." (p. 74) "De mens is dus een wezen bij machte een zedelijk besluit te nemen en daarnaar te leven." (p. 75) This, according to Langeveld, is a general, formal description of the ultimate goal of nurture which every educator can intepret in accordance with

knowledge is possible only when we have a true knowledge of
God as our Lord and Redeemer through the working of the Holy
Spirit in our hearts. As parents we often fall short in the upbringing of our children when we fail to practice what we teach. The
"values" we are committed to are at best only partially realized in
our daily activities and family relationships. The same holds true
for our children when they fail to live up to expectations and are
disobedient. This falling short is not just a matter of human
imperfection and moral weakness, ultimately it means to miss the
mark of *God's* ordinances, for both parents and children are
subject to *His* will and not to some hierarchy of "values". These
failures render us guilty before God and apart from Jesus Christ,
in whom alone there is forgiveness and restoration, there can be no
true guidance. We can only nurture in faith and by grace. It is
this perspective which makes Christian nurture a humbling but
at the same time a promising and joyful task. [74]

If the final aim of nurture cannot be found in psychical maturity,
self-reliance, or moral self-determination, and if for *that* reason
nurture cannot be limited to the upbringing of children, then the
need for another approach to the theory of education and for
another criterion to distinguish nurture from other human activities
has once more been established.

Just as catechetics as a theological discipline presupposes actual
catechetical instruction, so our theory of education, if it is not to be
a mere theoretical construction, must be founded in our experience
of concrete pedagogical situations. Our pedagogical relationships
have an (objective) knowable side, which enables us to have
genuine knowledge of them. This practical knowledge of education
as it is immediately *given* in our experience in its concreteness and
integral unity constantly remains our frame of reference. Our
educational theories can never replace this non-scientific (not: un-
scientific!) knowledge; on the contrary, in our theorizing we

---

his own particular conception of morality. Far from being a formal description,
however, this conception is radically opposed to the Scriptural view of man as
a religious being and, consequently, to the ultimate aim of Christian nurture.

[74] Cf. J. W. van Hulst, *Een Fundamenteel Probleem der Pedagogiek*, Groningen: J. B. Wolters, 1963, p. 21: "Dat opvoeder en opvoedeling met de Eiser
verbonden blijven, krijgt zijn diepste zin als erkend wordt, dat het tekort
schieten en het falen van opvoeder en kind ten aanzien van de eis der wet,
verzoend wordt door Hem die de wet heeft volbracht. Het antwoord op de
vraag of het kind opvoedbaar is, kan de opvoeder beluisteren, indien hij naar
het gebod en naar de gebodsvervulling in gehoorzaamheid hóórt."

continually presuppose and depend on this practical knowledge. The actual, on-going, pedagogical activities *as such,* as they are given in our experience and as we have immediate knowledge of them, will always escape our theoretical analysis. But through a process of *abstraction* in which we analyze and synthesize (set apart and place together again), it *is* possible to *deepen* our practical, non-scientific knowledge of education and to *disclose* the law-structures which govern our pedagogical activities. Such a theoretical analysis of the pedagogical situation can indeed help us (no more and no less) to gain a deeper understanding of the educational process. [75]

As soon as we direct our attention to the actual pedagogical situation, however, it becomes apparent that *education as such* does not exist. We are always confronted with *particular types* of education, such as child-rearing within the home or in institutions, instruction within different types of schools, and numerous other kinds of leading within various communities. This is so obvious that one would think it needs no further mention, yet it is seldom taken into account or subjected to a further analysis. Most books on education — understandably so — deal with only one or two specific kinds of leading. But when we examine and compare the various types of nurture that urge themselves upon us, this approach does not satisfy, for it leaves the *basic characteristics* which all types of nurture have in common unexplained. An adequate theory of education, even if it dealt merely with child-rearing, should be able to give an account of the *typical differences* that exist between various forms of education *and* of the *common features* that play a fundamental role in all types of leading, regardless within which communal or inter-individual relationship it takes place. Precisely such an analysis of the fundamental characteristics of all types of nurture could provide us with the criterion necessary for establishing the boundaries of our field of inquiry and for determining the exact meaning of the (equivocal) concepts commonly used in educational theories. In the following pages, therefore, we shall briefly examine the modal structure of the educational process and the typical manner in which this structure is individualized within various societal relationships.

A particular pedagogical activity, as a full and integral human act, functions in *all* the modal law-spheres. In each of these acts, however, *one* irreducible modal aspect seems to play a *fundamental*

---

[75] For the theory of knowledge implicit in this conception, see Dooyeweerd, *A New Critique,* II, pp. 430-598. See above p. 54, note 168.

role. Before we examine this modal aspect it may be good to remind ourselves that a "modality" refers to a basic mode of experiencing reality (the "how" and not the "what"), and that the general modal meaning of a specific aspect may be particularized and individualized in many different ways.

The analogical concepts used in connection with education all point to one particular aspect of reality which gives these terms their specific meaning.[76] The modal law-structure which in our estimation determines the nature of all pedagogical activities, prof. Dooyeweerd[77] (in a somewhat confusing manner) has called the "historical" modality. To nurture always means exercising formative power over the individual development of people's lives. The term power (command, control, or mastery) as used in this connection must not be taken in the sense of physical force or psychical influence. Nurturing is fundamentally different from forcing someone to submit to one's will, from "mental engineering", or from persuading someone by logical argumentation. The central meaning of nurture as exercising formative power or control over people can become plain only when seen in coherence with the retrocipatory and anticipatory moments of the "historical" law-sphere. For the "historical" modality is based upon the analytical, psychical, biotic, and other "earlier" modalities and is followed by the lingual, social, economic, and other "later" aspects. This being fitted into an irreversible law-order expresses itself within the "historical" modality in a number of analogical moments and anticipations. A provisional analysis of these moments will clarify the meaning of the nuclear moment of exercising formative control over people.

As a normative task education is bound to structural norms that are elevated above all subjective arbitrariness. The educator is responsible for the manner in which he acquits himself of his calling. Modally this manifests itself in the analogies that refer back to the analytical modality. Nurturing as a distinct human activity, different from "merely" caring for someone, is *imputed* to both the educator and those that are being guided. The nuclear moment of exercising formative power implies a calling and a task, namely, to shape and mould, to unfold and develop, and to

---

76   See above p. 92f.
77   Dooyeweerd, *A New Critique,* II, pp. 58-79, 190-298. Cf. J. Klapwijk. "Een voorlopige standpuntbepaling t.a.v. de geschiedphilosofie van prof. Dr. H. Dooyeweerd," *Correspondentiebl.,* XXIX (April, 1965), 18-21.

control and guide. The educator is held accountable for the fulfillment of this task. The same holds true, although in a lesser degree, for those who are being nurtured. They are called to seek guidance and they are (partly) responsible for the manner in which they react and submit to the guidance they receive.

This logical analogy of imputation reveals an important state of affairs, since it points to the limits set to the formative control over people. Exercising educational power over a person's life always ought to take place within the context of personal responsibility and co-operation. This means that the child or the adult as such can never be the object of our educational concern. Without this fundamental limitation the term "forming", "shaping", or "moulding" would be rather misleading, implying absolute power and complete control over a person to shape him as one sees fit.

The intrinsically normative character of nurturing does not only reveal itself in the logical analogy of imputation but also in that of *contradiction*. We are not only answerable for our pedagogical activities but we are also bound to the structural principles that hold for this activity. These norms are inescapable, even though they can be violated. We can act contrary to the norm and pursue an unpedagogical line of conduct, but such anti-normative education defeats its own purpose and degenerates to the application of brute physical force, becomes mechanical training, or results in a mere laissez-faire attitude. When the normative character of education is not acknowledged, the educator soon discovers that pedagogically he is powerless and that he has no pedagogical influence, even though he may succeed to overpower his pupils.

These logical retrocipations bring to light another peculiar feature of the structural principles governing education. Since the "historical" modality is founded upon the analytical law-sphere, the educator cannot provide actual guidance without *rational consideration* and *distinction*. Nurturing always presupposes an *insight* into the pedagogical *means* and *ends* as pedagogical correlatives. The general meaning of God's ordinances must be particularized and concretized in such a manner that they can truly function in a specific pedagogical situation. The call to nurture appeals to the will of the educator to take such pedagogical measures and to maintain such rules of conduct that truly enable a person to gain an understanding of God's will for his life. [78]

---

[78] Cf. Waterink, *Theorie,* p. 44f.

The educator's drive and desire to form reveals a psychical analogy. To be effective, education requires intense involvement and pedagogical fervor. Without such pedagogical zeal and enthusiasm, which creates a certain tension, the educator can hardly expect to move and motivate his pupils. Although based upon the psychical law-sphere, this desire and ardor to form is essentially different from emotional striving. Parents who truly wish to educate their children cannot let themselves be guided by their emotions. Taking effective educational measures is always a response to a calling and the fulfillment of a task. Personal psychic motives, although they play an important role in the educational process, are ultimately irrelevant for establishing genuine pedagogical rules. We may wish to be good parents or successful teachers, but this desire does not yet make us effective pedagogues. Our feelings may either hinder our nurturing[79] or stimulate us to put forth greater effort, but the final outcome of our educational efforts depends ultimately on whether or not our guidance has been in harmony with the norms for education. These norms hold regardless of our subjective feelings and psychical motives, and the pedagogical desire to form can only demonstrate itself in the adherence to these structural norms.

The psychical influence of the educator and the feeling of submission on the part of the pupil indeed constitute the psychical substratum of education without which nurture would be impossible. It is beyond dispute that the emotions play a fundamental role in the educational process, but this does not mean that education can be reduced to an interplay of emotional factors or that the theory of education can be reduced to applied psychology.

Likewise we must maintain that nurture is something more and other than caring for the bodily needs and physical well-being of children and adults, even though this kind of care constitutes the very basis for all forms of leading. Nurturing in the sense of exercising formative control over people indeed contains elements which remind us of stimulating organic growth. Education requires liveliness, inspiration, stimulation, care, and genuine concern for a person's development. There are educational needs that must be satisfied and there are certain developments that must be stimulated while others must be curbed. All these terms, however, that remind us of the biotic sphere, need further qualification if we

---

[79] Cf. J. H. van den Berg, *Dubieuze Liefde in de Omgang met het Kind*, Nijkerk: G. F. Callenbach N.V., 1960[3], and J. de Wit, *Problemen Rond de Moeder-kind Relatie*, Amsterdam: Uitg. Jacob van Campen, 1962.

are not to be led astray. The concepts "development" and "maturity" as used in education have a different meaning than when we speak of organic development, emotional maturity, or of a more mature insight. Within the "historical" modality these basic concepts are to be understood as biotic analogies. One of these analogies, development, is of a more complicated nature, since it does not refer to the nuclear moment of the biotic law-sphere but to that of the kinematic aspect, making it an indirectly founded analogy of movement. The foundation of this analogy, therefore, is mediated by all the modal aspects following that of movement and preceding that of forming. Educational development contains elements of a fuller understanding, deepened feelings, greater potentiality, and dynamic interplay, all resulting in a change of attitude and a different course of action. Such a development, however, in which a person has been led to a greater understanding of and a deeper feeling for God's ordinances, resulting in a genuine change in behavior, cannot be explained in terms of physical, biotic, (social-)psychical, or analytic categories. The failure to distinguish between the various modal meanings of development and similar terms leads to endless confusion and misunderstanding.

Education seeks to bring about a real change in behavior, but such changes are not the result of a mechanical process of cause and effect, or of the natural unfolding of the successive stages of organic life, nor are they the outcome of a psychic process of stimulus and response. Nurturing involves dynamic pedagogical interaction between two or more people, in which the exertion of formative power results in a genuine change of action.

The educator's influence may vary in degree, but his one aim is to guide people in a certain direction and to reach a certain level of maturity, confident that each normal person has a potentiality for growth and that he is called to stimulate their development. All these numerical, spatial, kinematic, physical, and analytic analogies belong to the very structure of education, but their specific meaning is entirely determined by the nuclear moment of exercising formative power over a person's life.

So far we have limited ourselves to the retrocipatory moments of the "historical" law-sphere. These analogies, of which it was possible to form a concept, have revealed various basic aspects of the structural norm governing pedagogical activities. But in their unopened state these retrocipatory moments remain rigidly bound to the foundational functions. The closed biotic analogies of growth and maturity, for example, remain strictly bound to organic development in a closed community. In this sense education also takes place in "primitive" societies. In these closed cultural communities education remains rigidly bound to biotic development and tribal life.[80]

Only in an opened-up culture, in which the anticipatory structures of the different law-spheres have been disclosed, can the meaning of the nuclear moment and the analogies of the "historical" modality be *deepened*. The meaning of the "historical" modality in its anticipatory structure, however, can only be approximated in an *Idea* (a transcendental limiting concept) of what it means to form and to be formed. This Idea can never be grasped in a theoretical concept, since in the last law-sphere of faith it no longer appeals to a higher modality but directly to Revelation. All education, therefore, is ultimately guided by the personal faith of the educator and the norms he accepts for his faith.

Before we examine this state of affairs in somewhat greater detail, we shall briefly consider the different anticipatory moments. The educational significance of various situations *symbolizes* and announces itself in the activities and reactions of the people involved. This anticipation of the lingual modality immediately points beyond itself to the aspect of social intercourse, for the educationally significant events and situations must be utilized; something must be communicated. Education requires *pedagogical intercourse* or communion during which a genuine exchange can take place. This social anticipation in turn points ahead to the economic, aesthetic and juridical law-spheres. In any pedagogical exchange full justice must be done to the individuality, responsibility and freedom of those who are being formed. Any overpowering or *excessive* forming destroys its own purpose. The educational process demands a *harmonious* relationship that leaves room for active participation and co-operation. The observance or violation of these structural norms brings about its own kind of *retribution*. The call to exercise formative power over people appeals to the *love* for education and teaching. True pedagogical love, will demonstrate itself in the self-denial and devotion of the educator. As soon as this pedagogical love is isolated from the other structural moments and absolutized, this love turns into idolatry, into self-glorification. This "moral" anticipation, finally,

---

[80] Cf. Erik H. Erikson, *Childhood and Society*, New York: W. W. Norton, 1963.

points forward to the function of faith in which the ultimate meaning of nurturing is disclosed. Not only the Christian but every person who is called upon to exercise formative power over the individual development of people's lives must first of all decide upon the *direction* he is going to take (educere) and choose an *ultimate goal*. The faith of the educator, that which he has *committed* himself to, determines the aim of his education. It should be evident that the Christian pedagogue can accept no other norm for his faith than the Word of God, for it is only the divine Word-revelation that reveals the true meaning of life, and, consequently, the final aim of all nurture. Within the pedagogical act the pistical anticipation manifests itself in the conviction and the inner certainty of the educator with regard to the aim of his leading. Without this pedagogical confidence he could not give real guidance.

Summarizing our findings thus far we may conclude that an analysis of the different moments inherent in the "historical" modality indeed clarifies the *nature* of education. It reveals *how, in which manner,* we *ought* to go about this activity. The examination of this modal aspect qualifying all forms of leading truly enables us to overcome the old dilemma between "nature" and "nurture", for it is precisely the *nature* of nurturing that is disclosed by this analysis. The "formative" law-sphere basically determines the nature of every type of education. This educational norm, which holds for all pedagogical situations, is composed of, or rather, includes all the analogical moments of the "formative" aspect and when seen in the light of this structural norm such terms as "forming", "moulding", "guiding", or "nurturing" simply cannot be misunderstood.

On the one hand it is evident that human life allows of a certain forming, but on the other hand it is equally plain that there are definite limits to our directing. It is particularly the (modal) *subject-object relation* which clarifies both the *possibility* and the *limits* of pedagogical moulding. It is the *"formative" object side* of life which makes education possible and it is this same "cultural" objectivity of all human acts which determines the boundaries of our leading. Our forming can direct itself lawfully only to the "formative" object side of a person's life. With regard to the "natural" sides of human life this is immediately evident. We can teach a person how to walk and how to dress himself, how to drive a car and how to play tennis, or, more complicated, how to give expression to his feelings and how to interpret the emotional expressions of others. It is also plain that we can teach a person how to read and count, or how to memorize and to distinguish properly. To learn these things the child or the adult is dependent upon the example, the possibilities for identification with and the actual guidance of others. Without (human) nurture not even the "natural" sides of a person's life would develop (at least, not beyond the level of animal existence). [81] Through education the "natural"sides of human life and the analytic aspect are opened up in the anticipatory direction and given "cultural" form. The "formative" subject function of the educator realizes (gives form to) the *latent* "cultural" object functions of the one being educated.

So far we have only mentioned the forming of the pre-"historical" functions, but obviously nurture is not restricted to these aspects. Our actual believing, our relationships with others, our observance of traffic laws, our appreciation of music, our spending and saving, our manners and speech, all these concrete activities allow of a certain forming. But if we are to maintain the definition of an object implied in the last paragraph as the repetition of the "lower" functions in the "higher", it is plain that our formative subjective function cannot open up or culturally objectify the post-cultural functions *as such*. The concrete human relationships and activities, however, in which these "higher" aspects are realized and which function in *all* the modalities *do* have objective formative characteristics. These (pistically, ethically, etc. qualified) *concrete acts*, therefore, *do* permit, or rather, *do* demand a measure of pedagogical moulding. [82]

The forming of (the formative object side of) acts qualified by one of the post-cultural aspects can only take place under the *leading* of these "higher" modalities and presupposes that the *anticipatory* moments of *both* the formative subject function *and* object functions are completely unfolded. Ethical relationships or economic activities, for example, cannot be formed without antici-pation of ethical or economic norms and it is only under the leading of these norms that we can give concrete guidance with respect to these acts. Or, to present another example, when we teach our children to pray, we can do so only under the leading of the "pistical" norms with respect to the cultural object side

---

[81]   This does not mean that man can be called an *animal educandum* or a *homo educandus* in any sense of the word. Cf. Langeveld, *Beknopte Theoreti- sche Pedagogiek*, pp. 87f., 153ff., and notes 51, 53. See also Dooyeweerd, *A New Critique*, III, p. 301.

[82]   Cf. Dooyeweerd, *A New Critique*, II, pp. 376ff., 390ff., 406ff.

(especially in its anticipatory direction) of praying. We can *tell* a child how the Lord Himself taught us to pray and how we ought to pray. We can *teach* him the words of a simple prayer and *say* it with him at first. But we *cannot make* the child *pray*, that he has to do himself.

Up to this point of our inquiry it was not possible to distinguish meaningfully between the various descriptions of nurture. For that reason we have purposely used the terms "forming", "guiding", "teaching", "rearing", "leading", "instructing", and "directing" interchangeably. Even the common distinction between nurture (opvoeding) and instruction (onderwijs) is of little help, since the manner in which leading and teaching are distinguished from one another often creates the impression that we are dealing with two (structurally) different activities, while in reality they are similar in structure. As this point of our investigation, however, it is possible to make some preliminary distinctions, not so much among the terms as the different aspects and areas of forming.

First of all our forming can direct itself to (the cultural object side of) differently qualified acts. We can focus our attention, for example, specifically upon the analytic aspect with its psychic substrate. This instruction may be done incidentally and in passing, as often happens in the home, or more regularly and systematically, as in preparation for a particular activity or as happens in the school. In the different types of schools this kind of forming deals primarily (or increasingly so) with theoretical knowledge and not with practical knowledge. In the same manner we can single out a person's psychic and organic life, or his social manners and his habits of speech.

Apart from these primary distinctions which are mainly orientated to the modal aspects, we can also make a distinction that cuts across all kinds of forming. We can differentiate between nurture which deals primarily with the "norm" laws or the "normative" side of reality, and instruction which deals mainly with the "fixed" laws or the "natural" side of reality and human life. In the first instance we have reference to nurture in its anticipatory direction and in the second instance to its retrocipatory direction. This difference in direction reveals the element of truth in the distinction that is commonly made between nurture and instruction.

Since the formative law-sphere refers to a fundamental *mode* of experiencing (the "how" and not the "what"), a *modal* analysis must necessarily be followed by an inquiry into the *individuality-structure* of education. For the modal aspects are only realized in structures of individuality, which (in principle) function in all the modalities.[83] As a full and integral act, nurturing manifests an inner structure, which remains the same irrespective within which community the nurturing takes place. The pedagogical activities which we encounter within different communal and inter-individual relationships, although completely bound by the leading function of these societal relations, are not original within these aspects. Nurturing is not an original social, economic. aesthetic, juridical, ethical, or pistical activity. Education is always founded in the formative aspect.

The individuality-structure of the act of nurturing, however, manifests a peculiarity which we do not meet in other acts (qualified by one of the "higher" aspects). The pedagogical act is not only founded in the formative aspect but also qualified by this function. In this respect nurturing differs, for example, from the forming or the performing of the artist, which is also founded in the formative aspect. The inner structure of the latter activity has a different qualifying function, namely the aesthetic modality. This peculiar character of the individuality-structure of education demands that the pedagogical act receives a further qualification. We never merely form, but we always form *unto;* our forming always has a specific aim. This explains, for example, why the school as a strictly *educational* community is dependent upon the interlacement with other organizations and institutions for the further unfolding of its qualifying function.[84] Since the school is characterized by the act of instructing, the leading function of the different types of schools must be disclosed further by the inner structure of the institution or organization with which it is interlaced. It is through these interlacements that the ultimate aim of the various schools is particularized. The nature of the association or institution which maintains a school determines the more immediate objectives of the school.

---

[83] An individuality structure may be described as the typical groupage of the modal aspects within a structural totality. Cf. Dooyeweerd, *A New Critique*, III, pp. 53-260.

[84] Cf. Popma, *Phil. Ref.*, XII, 1, 2, 3 (1947), 36-41, 86-93, 130-144; Mekkes, "Het Schoolverband," *Correspondentiebl.*, XIII (1949), 30-33. Our explanation is very much like prof. Mekkes' exposition, except that we see no need to take recourse to the idea of "pre-fabrication". The seemingly undifferentiated nature of the school and its instruction, finds its explanation in the *inner structure* of the *pedagogical activity as such*.

Until now we have made mention only of the individuality-structure of the act of nurturing. But *the* pedagogical act is no more than a *genotype*, or a primary type, within the *radical* type of culturally qualified acts. [85] This genotype, in turn, is divided into a great number of sub-types. At the end of our modal analysis, this state of affairs already announced itself. [86] The forming of the analytic function with its psychic substrate must be considered as such a sub-type. But since this type of instruction can be given in many different ways, this particular kind of forming is again subdivided, until we arrive at the final sub-types which appear to permit no further differentiation.

The *interlacement* of these sub-types (of the genotype pedagogical forming) with various inter-individual and communal relations gives rise to a great number of *variability-types*, in which the pedagogical activities are *bound* by the inner structure of the societal relationships. This enkaptic binding, however, does not undo or destroy the individuality-structure of the act of nurturing. An enkaptic relation presupposes that the structures enclosed within a particular interlacement have an internal structural principle of their own, and these maintain their sphere-sovereignty. A typical aesthetic activity like making music, for example, retains its inner structure, irrespective of the community in which it takes place. Whether the music is played in a restaurant, a workshop, a music hall, in a home, or in a church, it remains music, even though the leading function of these societal structures binds and directs the musician's performance and the kind of music he plays. Or, to give another example, regardless of whether a prayer is offered within the family, in a school, in private, or in a church, it remains an activity of faith. In the same manner education, no matter where it takes place, remains a type of leading.

By way of illustration we shall briefly consider the individuality-structure of child-rearing as found within the home. The type of nurture we are confronted with in the home is of a peculiar nature, for in principle it can embrace all other types of forming. The unique character of this guidance finds its explanation in the *immaturity* of the child. [87]

---

[85] For the meaning of these terms, see Dooyeweerd, *A New Critique*, III, 76-98.

[86] See above p. 131.

[87] The *re*-education of seriously injured or suddenly handicapped people, of socially maladjusted people or (juvenile) delinquents, or of old people

In this context the term "immaturity" has reference to the *total development* of the child, that is, to the development of every aspect of his life. *Pedagogical* development as described previously,[88] even if it is to be understood as a categorical concept,[89] cannot be identified with the development of the child in other aspects. For even though the child is dependent upon nurture, his total development is not merely the product of education. If we do not keep the distinction between the different meanings of development (growth, maturity, independence, etc.) in mind, we will be led astray from the very beginning in our reflection upon nurture, especially if we take our starting-point in child-rearing. A harmonious upbringing *does* require that all aspects of the child's life and all his activities receive due attention, in keeping with his stage of development. But this "all-inclusive" character of child-rearing does not imply that education is a general, unqualified activity which is aimed directly at the person's total development. The very fact that we can distinguish, as we have seen, various types of education and that we can direct our attention to one or more specific aspects of the child's life indicates that nurture refers to a *particular kind* of influencing which aims at *pedagogical* development.

Thus the parents are responsible for the initial, all-sided unfolding or disclosing of the child's life. They are under divine charge to bring up their children "in the discipline and instruction of the Lord". This commandment is inseparably related to the creational norms governing the nature of the family and the development of the child. The natural helplessness of the child, his dependence upon nurture and the unique bond of love between parents and their children makes the training in the home irreplaceable. The directives of the Word-revelation with regard to parental authority and discipline and the ultimate aim of child-rearing[90] appeals to this state of affairs. These Scriptural references cannot be considered apart from the structural norms which hold for all forms of nurture, nor can the creational norms be understood apart from the Word-revelation. The structural

---

unexpectedly transferred to a home for the aged, etc. present somewhat similar situations.

[88]   See above p. 126f.

[89]   For the meaning of this term, see Dooyeweerd, *Encyclopaedie der Rechtswetenschap,* II, pp. 96ff.

[90]   For a discussion and a summary of the Scriptural references, see Van Teylingen, *Bezinning,* XVI, 2 (1961), 61-73; Waterink, *Inleiding,* II, pp. 133-157, and his *Theorie,* pp. 70-108, 117-126.

norms to which family life and child-rearing are bound can only be *fulfilled* (in the Scriptural sense of the word) under the guidance of the norms revealed in Scripture.

Just as in the church every activity ought to be determined by the inner structure of the church as a community of faith, so within the family every relationship and activity ought to be a complete expression of the inner structure of the family as a natural community of love. As a natural institutional community the family has a typical biotic foundation and a typical moral qualifing function. [91] All nurturing within the home is qualified by this inner structure of the family as a natural community of love. The foundation in the blood relationship between parents and children, far from detracting from the moral nature of parental love, gives this unique type of love a high degree of moral intensity. It is precisely the tender love and care of the parents and their unconditional acceptance and trust which gives this type of nurture its irreplaceable and fundamental character. "The intimate family sphere is the only natural community able to give the first and foundational cultural moulding to the disposition and character of the infant. Both its biotical foundation, and its typical moral qualification as a bond of love between parents and children, provide the formative power of parental education with a particular intimate character not found in any other communal sphere." [92]

This intimate relationship between parents and children binds every pedagogical activity within the family. It demands a high degree of integrity and sincerity on the part of the parents. [93] The rules they establish in the home and the norms they seek to impart to their children must be exemplified in their own attitudes, activities and conversations. Within the home the children must be able to personally undergo and experience something of the divine norms for the various aspects of life. This means that both the divine norms revealed in Scripture and the creational laws must be specified and concretized in such a manner that the child can grasp something of their meaning and their life-restoring and

---

[91] Cf. Dooyeweerd, *A New Critique*, III, pp. 265-345.

[92] *Ibid.*, p. 286. Here we must call attention to Dr. Waterink's emphasis upon the love of the parents as a primary factor in the upbringing of their children. See his *Theorie, passim,* and many of his other publications.

[93] If time and space permitted, many of the structural state of affairs brought to light by Dr. Langeveld, especially his emphasis upon *genuineness* (of his *Kind en Religie)* could be introduced at this point.

maintaining character, so that by God's grace he may truly begin to submit his life to these divine ordinances. [94]

The parents, for example, must teach their children how to behave in the company of others, whether children or adults. They must establish certain rules for acceptable behavior in the home and teach their children certain forms of courtesy. But these structural norms for social intercourse must be given such a form that the child can understand and experience that they are refractions of the central love-commandment. Moreover, these norms must be exemplified in the parents' own attitudes toward and relationships with other people. The establishment of mere formal rules that do not really function within the family can only serve to create hypocritical situations and pharisaic attitudes. Nurture, especially within the family, requires a high degree of sincerity and humility. This example illustrates once more that we can only nurture in faith and by grace. Since we often fail in this high calling it is evident that Christian nurture demands daily conversion.

The inner structure of the family also determines the nature of parental authority and discipline. The exercise of authority within the home is qualified by the aspect of love and has a pedagogical focus. The same holds true with respect to the disciplinary measures the parents may take. "In keeping with the inner structural law of the family in its narrowest sense, parental discipline has an exclusively pedagogical character bound to the special guidance of parental love. The exercise of this disciplinary competence ought to be accomodated to the stage of development of the children." [95]

The normative structure of the family as a natural community of love not only determines the *typical nature* of parental guidance and authority but also the *inner boundaries* of the parents' competence. The child's natural dependence upon parental love and nurture for its development indicates the extent of the parents' responsibility and the immediate aim of their upbringing. Their duties and rights terminate when the young person approaches the "years of discretion" and when he reaches a stage of relative social, economic, and political independence and a degree of maturity with regard to ethical relationships and faith. This general

---

[94] Cf. Waterink, *Theorie*, p. 44f.
[95] Dooyeweerd, *A New Critique*, III, p. 276. See also Waterink, *Theorie*, pp. 70ff.

independence — in the sense of no longer dependent upon parental care and guidance — must be seen as a specification and further concretization of the ultimate aim of all nurture. Not self-reliance or moral self-determination *as such* is the specific aim of child-rearing but independence with respect to parental training and instruction. It is the responsibility of the parents to prepare the child to take up its own religious task in life, and the terms "independence" and "maturity" as used in this context can be no more than an indication of the young person's readiness to accept his various tasks and responsibilities.

When the divine ordinances revealed in Scripture and creation are disclosed to the child so that he begins to understand their meaning, he also learns to distinguish according to these norms. These various types of distinguishing, in turn, result in different kinds of knowledge. Under the leading of the ethical norms, for example, the child learns to understand and to interpret his relationship to other people and the expressions of love between his parents, his friends, and neighbors. Through personal experience and through instruction, the child gains an understanding of the normative aspects of life, also of the norms for his own believing. It is particularly this last type of knowledge, the knowledge of faith, and the instruction in the faith that now demands our attention.

Although we could only engage in a preliminary inquiry into the nature of education and even though many aspects of this theory need further elaboration and exploration, yet it provides us with the educational perspective necessary to analyze the structure of the church's instruction in the faith.

THE CHURCH'S INSTRUCTION IN THE FAITH

The instruction in the faith and the process of coming to know the faith can take place within the home, the school, youth organizations, the church, through other institutions and personal relationships. Since we cannot possibly deal with all of these characteristic types of faith-instruction within the context of this study, we shall limit ourselves to an analysis of the instruction in the faith as it takes place within the church. But even this particular type of faith-instruction is too broad to deal with in a concluding chapter. The conception of the nature and the boundaries of the church and the structure of education presented in the previous chapters has far reaching implications for the total educational ministry of the church (for the educational aspects of pastoral care, preaching, and evangelism). In this final chapter, therefore, we shall limit ourselves to an analysis of the catechetical instruction of the church's *young members*. This implies that we shall not deal with other aspects of the church's educational ministry to its youth, for even an investigation of such a limited area of the church's nurture would require an extensive study. The following analysis must be seen as an illustration of the general *implications* of the perspective presented in the preceding pages.

A. THE KNOWLEDGE OF FAITH

The unique character of the church's instruction in the faith cannot be understood without considering the structure of faith as such. Such an analysis of the structure of the pistical law-sphere will also reveal the peculiar nature of the knowledge of faith, and consequently the *prerequisites* for any type of instruction in the (knowledge of) faith.

At this point we must recall prof. Dooyeweerd's discription of the nuclear moment of the faith-aspect as "that ultimate mode of certitude within the temporal order of experience which refers to an indubitable revelation of God touching us in the religious center of our existence."[1] According to its modal structure, believing means one's wholehearted self-commitment to Him who has revealed Himself as the Divine Origin of all things. This funda-

---

[1] See above p. 59.

mental meaning of the faith-aspect, however, cannot be understood apart from the analogical moments inherent in this irreducible mode of experiencing. Historically, primarily two analogical moments have been brought to the fore, namely, the elements of trust and of knowledge.[2] Besides these two, many other analogies are equally important for our understanding of the structure of faith. For the pistical modality is founded upon and refers back to *all* the aspects of reality. Faith contains elements which remind us of love, of justice, of harmony, of frugality, of fellowship, of symbolic signification, of formative power, of analytical distinguishing, and so forth.[3] To believe means to *worship* God and to *serve* Him according to His will. As our Creator and Redeemer He may *demand* our *trust*. God has a *right* to our *self-surrender* and the *service* of our lives. To believe in God is to love Him, to worship Him, to obey His Word, to do His will, to offer our lives, to have fellowship with Him, to address Him, to know Him as our heavenly Father as He has revealed Himself in Jesus Christ, and to entrust ourselves to His care.

These analogical moments cannot be separated from one another. To do so would be to distort their meaning. When, for example, the element of knowledge inherent in all faith is isolated from the other analogies, faith invariably becomes a form of intellectualism. The meaning of the analytic retrocipation is mediated by all the "higher" analogies (of love, justice, harmony, etc.) and is essentially determined by the nuclear moment of ultimate certitude. The distinguishing of faith, therefore, implies that we believe in God, that we love and adore Him, that we commune with Him, and that we seek to do His will. Only in this manner do we truly come to know God and do we gain true knowledge of His Word.

From this reference to the modal structure of the pistical aspect it is evident that faith can never be reduced to mere feelings. Faith is not blind suggestion; on the contrary, *according to its inner structure* faith is always a *certain knowledge*. The distinguishing

---

[2] Cf. the *Heidelberg Catchechism,* L.D. VII, "True faith is not only a sure knowledge, whereby I hold for truth all that God has revealed to us in His Word, but also a firm confidence which the Holy Spirit works in my heart by the Gospel,...." Cf. also prof. Ridderbos, *Paulus,* pp. 260-278, who discusses the nature of faith under the two main headings of trust and obedience (knowledge).

[3] For a further analysis of these analogical moments, see Dooyeweerd, *Phil. Ref.,* XXIII, 2 (1958), 49-68.

of faith, however, shares in the peculiar nature of the pistical aspect, which in its kernel moment already points beyond itself to God's self-revelation. Genuine faith, therefore, can also be described as the "the knowledge of the glory of God in the face of Jesus Christ." [4]

In the concrete act of believing, functioning in all the modalities, including the analytic aspect, this interrelation between faith and knowledge is even more apparent. In our actual believing, in our praying, and in our confessing we distinguish in- whom we put our trust, to whom we address ourselves, and what we confess about Him. [5] This aspect of analytical distinguishing is an inherent part of the full and integral act of believing. Faith is not a-logical or irrational. Structurally, faith and knowledge are inseparably related; therefore, they cannot be opposed to one another. [6] To believe is to know, and to know is to believe. Neither rationalism nor irrationalism can account for this interrelation between analytical distinguishing and ultimate certitude within the act of believing. [7] Faith is not "rational", but it does have a logical foundation. If we are to gain a true understanding of the Word of God, we must first of all distinguish correctly. To know the will of God, we must discern His ordinances. This knowing is bound to the norm for analytical distinguishing, but it is not qualified by the logical modality. To discern "the will of God, and to know what is good, acceptable and perfect," is an activity of *faith*. [8] Faith-knowledge cannot be acquired apart from the

---

4 II Cor. 4 : 6. Cf. Ridderbos, *Paulus, p.* 268.

5 Cf. Ridderbos, *Paulus,* p. 266f: "Het geloof kan niet uit de gevoelsfeer worden benaderd, bijv. in de zin van de heidense mystiek; het kan ook niet worden omschreven als een daad van overgave of 'Entscheidung' zonder klaar besef, waaráán het zich overgeeft of waarvóór het beslist, maar het geloof veronderstelt een *weten,* waarop het rust en waaraan het ook altijd opnieuw zijn kracht ontleent."

6 *Ibid.,* p. 266: "Uit dit alles vloeit ook vanzelf voort de belangrijke plaats, die het *kennis-element* in het paulinische geloofsbegrip inneemt." "Daarom is het geloof in Christus, als vrucht van de verkondiging van het evangelie, óók kennis en wijsheid en bepalen de begrippen pistis en gnosis elkander wederkerig in de paulinische opvatting van het geloof." See also p. 268: "Het weten treedt daarbij op als grond en motief of als implicatie van het geloof, het draagt zelf ook het karakter van geloofs-weten, ... het qualificeert het geloof in ieder geval als een bewust, gericht en daarom ook overtuigd en verzekerd geloof." "Telkens treden geloof en kennis hierbij als elkander aanvullende en wederzijds bepalende begrippen op." For this entire section regarding the relation between faith and knowledge, compare Troost, *Casuïstiek,* pp. 175-192.

7 Cf. Troost, *Casuïstiek, p.* 177f.

8 Rom. 12 : 2.

subjective act of believing. It is knowledge gained through our fellowship with God, through faithful listening to His Word, through worship and prayer, in a word, through actual believing.

Since this knowledge is the result of our faith-experience, it is imperfect and partial. In as much as we do not continually persevere in our faith, in our adoration, in our fellowship, and in our obedience, our knowledge becomes distorted. True faith-knowledge can only be acquired by believing in Him who is the Truth. "The fear of the Lord is the beginning of wisdom," says the psalmist,[9] and "a good understanding have all those who practice it." Only by committing ourselves to our Creator and Redeemer, shall we truly come to know His faithfulness and mercy, and only by doing His will, shall we truly come to understand His ordinances. The more we grow in understanding and insight, the more we look for that day when we shall no longer know in part, but when we shall see face to face and understand fully.[10]. Until that time we pray: "Teach me good judgement and knowledge, for I believe in thy commandments," mindful of the words of James: "If any of you lacks wisdom, let him ask God who gives to all men generously and without reproaching, and it will be given him. But let him ask in faith, with no doubting,..".[11] So we shall attain "to the unity of the faith and of the knowledge of the Son of God, to mature manhood, to the measure of the stature of the fulness of Christ."[12]

Once the true nature of the knowledge of faith is clearly before us we can no longer misunderstand the Scriptural injunctions to love God with all our mind and to grow in our knowledge of His Word. For to know God is nothing less than "to have all the riches of assured understanding and the knowledge of God's mystery of Christ, in whom are hid all the treasures of wisdom and knowledge."[13] And if this is what it means to know God, we also understand Paul's prayer that we may be filled with all knowledge and discernment.[14] For to have this knowledge is "to lead a life worthy of the Lord, fully pleasing to Him, bearing fruit in every good work"; it is to be "filled with the fruits of

---

[9] Ps. 111 : 10; Cf. Prov. 9 : 10.
[10] I Cor. 13 : 12.
[11] James 1 : 5.
[12] Eph. 4 : 13.
[13] Col. 2 : 2, 3.
[14] Phil. 1 : 9; Col. 1 : 9.

righteousness which comes through Jesus Christ, to the glory and praise of God." [15]

This practical, non-theoretical, full and integral knowledge, gained through actual believing, is entirely qualified by the nature of faith. It points directly to the fulness of meaning in Jesus Christ, in whom alone our hearts and minds find rest. It is evident that this experiential, practical knowledge, which incites to action, can only function rightly within the self-surrendering acts of faith. It is this living knowledge of faith which is our concern in catechetical instruction.

B. INSTRUCTION IN THE FAITH

The church has been charged to instruct its catechumens in the knowledge of faith. [16] But considering the nature of faith-knowledge, we may well ask how this is possible. Certainly we cannot *teach* someone to *believe*. At the most we can teach a person *what* he *ought* to believe and what this would mean for his daily life. In view of this limitation it is all the more important that we ask ourselves how we must conceive of this instruction.

To answer this question we must once more consider the nature of faith-knowledge. From experience we *know* what it means to believe. But when we stop to reflect upon our faith, we also know that we could never grasp this knowledge in a concept. We encounter the same difficulty when someone asks us to explain the meaning of love. We *know* from experience what it means to love a person, but it is evident that we can never give an adequate account of its meaning. Our explanations always fall short, because our full and integral, experiential knowledge of love can never be reduced to its "knowable" (analytic) side. Ultimately we can only appeal to the questioner's own experience of love relationships.

Similarly, we must maintain that the knowledge of faith cannot be grasped by analytic thought. With our thinking we can only *approach* this full and practical knowledge of believing. But in spite of this analytical incomprehensibility of faith-knowledge, we do know what it means to believe and to have found an ultimate resting-place.

---

[15]   Col. 1 : 10; Phil. 1 : 11.

[16]   For a summary of the Scriptural references, see Ridderbos, *Heilsgeschiedenis*, pp. 134-139.

As a concrete pistically qualified individuality-structure, this knowing functions in all aspects of reality, including the analytic aspect. This full and living knowledge cannot be reduced to its analytic side. We cannot grasp it in a number of logical propositions. But by way of its analytic side we have real access to this knowledge. In our conscious (analytically qualified) acts of thinking we can reflect upon our faith-experience. We can formulate our thoughts and communicate these thoughts to others, and when we do so, we are not talking about abstractions. In our thinking about faith (-knowledge), we are indeed limited to its "knowable" (analytic) side, but this does not make our thoughts unreal. We cannot grasp the full reality of this knowledge in our concepts, but it is possible to think about it and to communicate this limited and partial, but nevertheless genuine "knowledge" to others. [17]

To gain a *true* insight into the nature of faith, our thinking must be completely guided by the norms for our believing in the specific acts of reflecting upon the faith. [18] If it is to have any value, far from grasping, subduing and controlling (the knowledge of) faith with our mind, our thinking must *follow* the lead of the pistical norms and be in *agreement* with these norms. In distinguishing analytically we never master our "object", to think so would be to absolutize the mind, turning it into "Reason". In our distinguishing we "merely" discern, observe, notice, perceive, or take cognizance of what presents itself to us and is immediately *given* in our experience. [19] Moreover, the fact that it is *faith* discernment means that this discerning ought to be engaged in with humility and an attitude of trust. After all, it is the *norms* for our believing that we discern. Thinking about the norms for our believing demands confidence in the trustworthiness of God's revelation. Though the content of the Christian faith manifest an analytic side, allowing us to approach it thoughtfully, we shall never be able to explain it

---

[17] To distinguish between the full and integral, experiential knowledge of faith and the partial and limited "knowledge" of our thinking about our faith experiences, we shall place the latter kind of knowledge between quotation marks.

[18] Compare Dooyeweerd, *A New Critique*, II. p. 330, note 1.

[19] Cf. Vollenhoven, *Hoofdlijnen der Logica*, p. 47: "Deze activiteit is nimmer scheppend, zelfs niet heerschend, maar steeds ontwarend en noteerend. I. Ten opzichte van God kan dit ontwaren en noteeren slechts vertrouwend zijn: de laatste grond voor ons geloof, ook voor onze geloofskennis, is de betrouwbaarheid Gods. II. Ten opzichte van de wet is het ontwaren en noteeren primair activiteit in onderdanigheid. III. Ten opzichte van den kosmos is het ontwaren en noteeren ondervragend."

analytically, nor shall we ever succeed in demonstrating it to someone who does not believe in the Gospel.

Everything that has been said about our reflecting upon the knowledge of faith, must also be said about the specific *instruction* in the faith. As a concrete individuality-structure our faith-knowledge functions not only in the logical aspect but also in the "historical" modality. Our faith (-knowledge) always manifests a specific cultural form; it allows of a certain formation. The integral, living knowledge of faith cannot be reduced to its formative side, but it can and must be formed. Without nurture the child's faith-life would not develop; and without specific instruction the adult's faith-knowledge would not develop beyond the level of the "first principles of God's Word" and "the elementary doctrines of Christ." [20] The young person's thinking about his faith-experiences must be moulded and formed, that is, his analytical distinguishing (with its psychic substrate), as it directs itself to the content of his faith, must be activated, opened up and deepened. Through instruction he must learn to discern more correctly, to orientate himself more fully, and, most important of all, to gain a deeper understanding of the norms for his faith.

This specific *forming* of a person's "knowledge" of the faith must be distinguished from the learning that takes place through his actual faith-experiences. We also grow in the knowledge of faith when we read the Scriptures to gain a deeper understanding of God's will for our lives and when we listen to the proclamation of God's Word. But this total and integral learning cannot be reduced to the partial and limited learning that takes place as a result of specific instruction. The instruction in the faith may be one of the avenues by which a person reaches a greater insight into the total meaning and relevance of the Word of God, but the instruction as such cannot provide him with this full and integral knowledge. The instructor (parent, teacher, minister, etc.) cannot teach a person to believe in God, nor can he furnish him with the knowledge of Jesus Christ. In this particular type of nurture the instructor is limited to the activation, disclosure and deepening of the person's thinking about the faith.

The limited place of this instruction does not imply that it is *formal* instruction, or that the resulting insight is mere *abstract* "knowledge". The growth in understanding that the educator seeks to achieve through his teaching concerns a genuine and fund-

---

[20] Hebrews 5 : 12; 6 : 1.

amental aspect of the knowledge of faith. Moreover, the instructor constantly appeals to the pupil's own experience and knowledge of the faith. The pupil cannot but relate his newly gained insights to his religious selfhood and his experience of faith. Learning is never a formal process, but always involves the human "I-ness'. Likewise the instructor is personally involved. Before he can teach others, he must formulate his own thoughts and engage in an initial interpretation of the Christian faith. And throughout the teaching-process he must be constantly guided by the norms for his faith. In every way, both the teacher and the pupil are totally involved in the educational process, which, in this instance, is completely bound by the content and nature of faith.

Faith-knowledge, refelection upon the faith, and instruction in the faith are inseparably related. Within the pistical modality this state of affairs manifests itself, as we have seen, in the logical and cultural analogies that refer back to the analytic and formative aspects. Without these analogies, inherent in the pistical law-sphere, the structure of faith cannot be understood. Within the act-structure this interrelation shows itself in the unique configuration of all the aspects within the structural totality of the act. The concrete act of believing functions in all the modalities, including the analytic and formative aspects. In view of this inseparable relation between faith and the other aspects of reality, we must radically reject every dualism, every tension, or opposition between faith, thought, and instruction. Such a dualism can only arise when faith is elevated to a "supra-natural" level and education is pulled down to a purely "natural" level. A more or less docetic or spiritualistic conception of the Christian faith must necessarily give rise to a dialectic tension between faith and instruction. Any such conception, in which the *inner* connection between faith and the other aspects of reality has been cut through, makes it impossible to account for the structure of faith-instruction. [21]

God's grace does not add a new dimension to our lives. Through the operation of the Holy Spirit working in our hearts He redirects our lives. But this regeneration of our hearts does not change the structure of faith, only its direction. Our believing is inseparably related to the whole order of creation. The (German) dilemma between "proclamation" and "education", therefore, is a false dilemma. The problem of "religious" education is indeed

---

[21] See our discussion of this point in the orientation.

insoluble as long as faith is thought of as being without *internal* relation with the other aspects of reality; and as long as education is conceived of as a more or less autonomous process, unrelated to the religious direction of our hearts.

So far we have only discussed the *general* nature of faith-instruction, which remains the same wherever it takes place. But *the* instruction in the faith is no more than a sub-type, which realizes itself in many different ways within various typical inter-individual and communal relationships, giving rise to a great number of variability-types. One of these variability-types is catechetical instruction.

In this instance the instruction in the faith is completely bound and directed by the inner nature of the church. As a variability-type, catechetical instruction maintains its fundamental structure as an educational activity. It remains a form of teaching. But within the church this activity is disclosed and guided by the aspect of faith which qualifies the structure of the church. On the one hand, therefore, the church's education is like all other forms of (faith-)instruction, while, on the other hand, it is typically different. Both of these aspects need further elaboration.

The church's educational ministry exhibits the same features that characterize all faith-instruction. Like all types of training in the faith, catechetical instruction deals with something it cannot contain. Its subject matter escapes the minister's instruction. He can approach his subject, but he cannot control it and reduce it to a number of logical statements. The knowledge he seeks to convey refers directly to God's self-revelation in Jesus Christ, and confronts both the minister and his catechumens with God's claim upon their lives. This "existential" nature of cate-chetical instruction is characteristic of all types of faith-in-struction. To instruct someone in the Christian faith, one must first of all stand in the Truth and be guided by the Truth, regardless within which community the teaching takes place. In this respect the various kinds of training are all alike. The church's education is not higher than, or superior to, other types of instruction. The enkaptic interlacements with various communities does not change the fundamental nature of the different kinds of training in the Christian faith.

The enkaptic relation with the church does not change the basic character of faith-instruction, but the inner structure of the church *does* unfold and direct the church's education. Since the church is qualified by the aspect of *faith,* the peculiar nature of *faith*-instruction receives special emphasis. The community of faith can give full attention to this instruction. In this regard the church's education differs from that of the home. In the home this specific instruction in the faith is completely bound and guided by the inner structure of the family. This means — among other things — that it must take place within, and as a part of, the daily activities of the family. In may take place during meal-times, in passing during the child's play, or incidentally during a conversation, or more regularly when the children go to bed, but it must always occur during the ordinary course of events within the family. The *inner structure* of the family binds every aspect of its training.

Within the household of *faith*, however, this instruction has a specific place. Since the church has been particularly charged to build up the Body of Christ and to feed the flock, the minister can give this instruction his undivided attention. The inner structure of the church, as the community of faith called to administer the Word and the sacraments, completely *discloses* the basic character of faith-instruction.

The enkaptic interlacement with the church also accounts for the *official* nature of catechetical instruction. The church has been entrusted with the keys of the Kingdom and the office bearers have been authorized to proclaim the good news of the Kingdom of Heaven and to teach the sound doctrine. [22]

In keeping with this divine charge, catechetical instruction is to be described as the church's *official* instruction of its youth. However, as stated previously, [23] we shall not elaborate upon the normative aspect of the church's education, since a thorough discussion of the issues involved (covenant, infant baptism, making confession of faith, church discipline, etc.), requires separate treatment. At this point we simply wish to draw attention to the official character of the church's teaching, for it is against this background that we must see the church's practice to instruct its young members. The church does not merely, as a service to the parents, or the community, provide general "religious" training for all those interested, but the church has been *charged* to do so. Its office-bearers are under divine obligation to preach the Word, to be urgent in season and out of season, to convince, rebuke, to ex-

---

[22] Cf. Ridderbos, "De apostoliciteit van de kerk volgens het Nieuwe Testament," in *De Apostolische Kerk*, Kampen: Kok, 1954, pp. 39-97; and his *Paulus*, pp. 479-543.

[23] See above p. 55f.

hort, and to be unfailing in patience and in teaching.[24] Through this administration the Kingdom of Heaven is opened to all those that believe and shut to those who refuse to believe and repent.

In view of this calling it is not difficult to understand that the church feels obligated to instruct its young members and that it demands that its young people openly confess their faith before they take up their full responsibilities in the midst of the congregation. Whether or not the admission to the Lord's Supper ought to be directly connected with this requirement is debatable. Learning to confess one's faith and actually making confession of faith, certainly cannot be seen as the link between baptism and communion. In as much as the children of believers are full members of the congregation, the church is (partly) responsible for their growth in the faith. The church, therefore, may legitimately demand that the parents send their children to catechism.

Although catechetical instruction shares in the official character of the church's teaching, it remains instruction. The young people must *learn* to confess their faith, they must be *led* to a deeper understanding of God's Word, and they must be *taught* sound doctrine. The fact that the catechumens are baptized, and thereby become full members of the church, does not change the pedagogical structure of the church's instruction. These two factors, the official nature and the educational structure, must be carefully distinguished, and may not be played off against one another. Catechetical instruction requires a *pedagogical* attitude. The young people must be truly *introduced* to the life of the church.

1. *The Scope of the Curriculum*

The general aim of *all* faith-instruction is to lead a person to a deeper and fuller understanding of God's Word. This general aim receives a further particularization and concretization through the enkaptic relation with the church. The aim of the church's instruction is to lead its (immature) members to a deeper and fuller understanding of the faith. Narrowed down to catechetical instruction, this means that the catechumens must be prepared to take up their responsibilities as mature believers in the midst of the congregation. They must be introduced *(intro-ducere)* to the life of the church, to its confessions, its history, its mission, its care, and its diaconate. Through this instruction they are to gain

---

[24] II Timothy 4 : 2.

a greater knowledge of what it means to call upon and to confess the Name of the Lord. They must learn to participate and share in the church's worship, fellowship, service, and witness. This instruction is to be constantly guided by the Word of God, as the norm for our believing. The Scriptures must be given a central place in every part of the educational program.

At first sight, this description may seem like a drastic reduction of the general aim of faith-instruction. But as soon as we consider this program in somewhat greater detail, it is evident that this is not the case. Here we must recall what we have said previously about the church's authority, preaching, and confessions.[25] The inner boundaries of the church basically determine the scope of its educational program. This means that it is *both* all-inclusive *and* limited. In as much as the minister deals with the Word of God and the confessions, he provides fundamental directives determinative for every area of life and for every human activity. In this sense the educational program of the church is not limited. In his teaching, the minister may relate every experience to the fundamental relationship of the believers to Christ and place every situation in the light of the Word of God. But this all-inclusive scope of the church's education also implies a limitation, for the minister can deal with these various aspects of life only from the perspective of faith. If the program were to include a number of lessons on marriage and the family, for example, the minister could only consider the faith-aspect of these institutions. But this is fundamental, because through the aspect of faith these relationships are consciously related to God's revelation in Jesus Christ and to His Kingdom. The Scriptural norms reveal how the structural norms governing these relationships are to be fulfilled. With regard to these creational ordinances the church has no particular competence or authority, but the church may and ought to place every relationship and every institution in the light of the Word of God. The educational program of the church, therefore, is restricted. But this limitation also reveals the great significance of its teaching, for through its instruction the church may set forth and explain the universal significance of the Gospel for all of life and relate every human activity to the Kingdom of God.

Up till now we have used the terms "catechetical instruction" primarily for the instruction of the church's youth. In the following

---

25 See above pp. 81-88.

pages we shall use the words "catechism" and "catechetical instruction" exclusively for this particular aspect of the church's
education, even though these expressions have a more general and
extensive meaning.

In certain situations the church may judge it necessary to
provide special training for the children, the younger adults, or the
older people as well. But, in that case, the specific aim of the
instruction and the scope of the curriculum should be adjusted to
the age-level of the members and the peculiar problems they face.
In many instances there will be no need to organize such special
study groups for different age groups. If, for example, the children
receive adequate training at home, attend a Christian day school,
belong to a Christian youth organization, etc., there is no reason
for the church to arrange for additional instruction periods (Sunday school). Anything the church would do in this respect, would
already be done by the home, the school, and other organizations.
This does not mean that the church, for example, could not, or
should not, provide special services for the younger children,
geared to their level of understanding and their experiences,
during (a part of) the regular worship services. Such an activity,
and similar ones, would not be a duplication. In other instances,
however, when the children receive very little regular training in
the Christian faith, the church may feel obligated to provide
special instruction.

In many (Christian) Reformed churches the whole congregation
receives special instruction each Sunday through the exposition
of the Heidelberg Catechism in a second worship service. When
the Christian community faces many new and perplexing problems, however, or lives under peculiarly difficult circumstances,
the church may have to organize adult study groups or mid-week
congregational meetings (next to, or in place of, the service in
which the Heidelberg Catechism is explained), to consider these
questions and problems in the light of the Word of God. In each
of these instances the general scope of the curriculum must be
specified in keeping with the needs of a particular group.

As indicated at the beginning of this section, the more immediate
aim of catechesis is to introduce the young members to the life of
the church. Before they take up their tasks in the midst of the
congregation, they must gain a better and fuller understanding of
the Word of God as the norm for faith, especially for belief as it
comes to expression in the worship and confession, and in the
witness and service of the church. They must learn to participate

with understanding in the worship services and activities of the congregation.

The scope of the curriculum for this particular age-group is entirely determined by the church's requirement that the young people openly confess their faith before they take up their responsibilities as members of the community of faith. In this study we are presupposing that this is not an arbitrary requirement, maintained by the force of tradition. This demand of the church appeals to, and is fully in keeping with, the young people's stage of development. When the young person reaches "the years of discretion", when he is no longer dependent upon the guidance of his parents, he becomes fully responsible for all his actions and decisions. The church, therefore, may rightly demand that the young members accept the responsibilities of their church membership at this stage of their life, and that they do so consciously, with discretion. For to declare openly that one wants "to take up his full responsibilities" as a member of the community of faith, means nothing less than to make a public confession of one's faith.

This confession does not *make* the young person a (full) member of the church. For by God's grace and faithfulness, which was signified and sealed in his baptism, he has been a member of the household of God from his birth. His confession is no more and no less than a faithful response to God's promises in Jesus Christ. By making confession of faith, the young member openly commits himself to serve his Lord in the midst of the congregation, to call upon His Name in communion with the fellowship of believers, and to submit himself to the proclamation of the Word, as the direction for his life.

Before a person makes such a public confession of faith, the church may legitimately demand that he knows to what he commits himself. And it is this knowledge that the church seeks to convey through its catechetical instruction. The curriculum for this age-group, therefore, has a very definite focus. The young people are to be introduced to the life of the church.

Since the activities of the congregation find their center in the worship services, it is only natural that catechism begins with this aspect of the church's life. From out of this centrum the other activities of the church can be explored, its mission, its care, and its diaconate. A study of these various ministries will lead to a consideration of the relation between the general (ecclesiastical) office of the believers and the special ecclesiastical offices, and to a reflection upon the church's organization. This reflection upon the practices of the (Christian) Reformed churches inevitably gives rise to questions concerning the differences in organization, belief, and worship between the various denominations, and to questions concerning the innumerable divisions among the churches.

This range of subjects constitutes a unified whole and is eminently suited to serve as a *first* introduction to the life of the church (here we think of the younger — 14, 15 — age group). The introduction to the confessions of the church occupies an important place within this curriculum and can best be treated separately (during the following two years of catechism). The Apostles' Creed, the Lord's prayer, the ten commandments, and the sacraments could form the major divisions within this part of the educational program.

The historical creeds of the Reformed churches present a peculiarly difficult problem, since none of the confessions, including the Heidelberg Catechism [26] can serve as a basis for this part of the curriculum. In some respects they are not extensive enough, while in other respects they are too elaborate. Many of the problems that face the Christian in our time are not dealt with in the creeds, while other questions that receive elaborate treatment (the Lord's supper), could be presented more succinctly. In many instances the existing confessions make use of theological formulations, which, *as such,* cannot function directly in the life of the believers. Moreover, many formulations are outdated and less than correct. Since the Reformation the knowledge of the Word of God has deepened and expanded, but very few of these new insights have been incorporated in creedal statements.

To give a meaningful testimony of their faith in a rapidly changing world and in the face of many perplexing problems, the catechumens are in need of both a more differentiated and a more direct (less theological) creed.

Here we are once more confronted with the fact that the knowledge of faith is practical, experiential knowledge, a knowledge which leads to adoration and which incites to action. It is this knowledge that the minister must disclose through his introduction to the confession of the church.

Especially this part of the curriculum confronts the catechumens with the total claim God makes upon their lives. For a creed

---

[26] Cf. the article "De Heidelbergse Catechismus als leerboekje: Een kritisch overzicht," which I have written earlier for *Homiletica & Biblica,* XXIV, 8 (Sept., 1965), 193-197.

should be no more than a resonance of the Word of God, which is the Directive for all of life. Through the activity of faith every relationship and every situation is placed in the light of God's Revelation in Jesus Christ and His Kingdom. The Word of God is the basis and center of all instruction in the faith, including catechetical instruction.

The curriculum for catechism must allow for differences in the cultural situation and the position of the young people in society. These different situations may demand a very extensive program or a more compact and brief course. The two main parts of this curriculum (ecclesiastical worship and practice and confession) could easily cover a period of four years, (the age groups of approximately 14 through 17). This basic program could be preceeded by an "introductory" year in which the group would exclusively study the Scriptures, and followed by a season in which specific problems could be brought to the fore and during which the approach of the minister could be more pastoral and personal. [27]

Many of the things that have been stated in the previous pages have found an initial realization in the material that is being produced by the *Raad voor de Catechese der Ned. Herv. Kerk* and the *Gereformeerde Catechetische Werkgroep.* [28]

2. Methodological Considerations

Having examined the nature of faith-knowledge at the beginning of this chapter, and, directly related to this, the instruction in the knowledge of faith, we must briefly consider how the proposed interaction can be realized in practice. In the first place we must remark that the methods we use ought to be completely in harmony with and do justice to the unique character of faith-instruction. In the second place it is evident that the actual road we travel to reach the goal is, in certain respects, a secondary and a more or less "technical" matter. By formulating it this way we do not mean to say that the questions related to the method are unimportant. For our actual approach in the classroom ultimately determines whether or not we are truly introducing the young people to the Christian faith as it comes to expression in the life

---

[27] Cf. W. A. Smit, *Pastoraal-Psigologiese Verkenning van die Client-Centered Terapie van Carl R. Rogers*, Kampen: Kok, 1960, pp. 246-302.

[28] For a discussion of this project see J. Thomas, "Een vorm van catechetisch samen-werken," *Homiletica & Biblica*, XXIV, 4 (Mei, 1965), p. 87-94.

of the church. What we mean is that the methods we employ ought to be in complete harmony with the unique character of the catechetical instruction. The methods have a subservient place; they serve a purpose.

The analysis of the nature of faith provides us with a real criterion to distinguish between serviceable and non-serviceable methods. Any method, for example, which *reduces* the knowledge of faith to its analytic aspect, or which *isolates* this element from the other aspects must be radically rejected. Such approaches *distort* the nature of faith. Often the question is raised whether or not the catechumens ought to memorize portions of Scripture, the confession, or other ready-made answers. But such a dilemma rests on a misleading basis. Those who tend to answer this question in the affirmative, often separate the analytic side from the other aspects of the full and integral knowledge of faith. The result is some form of intellectualism. Many catechism booklets, both old and new, testify to this fact. In reaction to this tendency the catechumens are sometimes not required to learn anything at all. But in that case one can hardly speak of catechetical *instruction*. The question, however, is not whether the catechumens ought to memorize something, but whether the things committed to memory are a *meaningful* part of a particular lesson, and whether the memorization is an *integral* aspect of the learning-process.

Another (extreme) example of these tendencies can be found in workbooks which contain programmed materials.[29] By programmed instruction is meant the arrangement of material in a logical sequence moving from the simple to the complex. The material is divided into small sections, each of which gives some information and ask a question. The learner is expected to write down his answer in the textbook, check the next frame to determine whether or not his answer was right, and so on. Through this mechanical instruction bits of information can be effectively imparted to the students, but it is questionable whether it can lead them to a deeper and fuller understanding of the faith. The knowledge of faith can be approached thoughtfully, but it cannot be framed and mastered. We can appreciate the concern that the catechumens remember what has been taught. But no amount of recitation or machine-

---

[29] Cf. *Step by Step in Theology*, published by the Association Press, 1962. See also *Steps in Faith*, published by the Committee on Education of the Chr. Reformed Church, Grand Rapids, 1963. To counterbalance the one-sidedness of the programmed instruction, there is an accompanying manual which provides material for classroom discussion.

taught answers can assure us that the young people have truly understood the meaning of what we have sought to convey to them. We should indeed be concerned that the catechumens understand and assimilate what has been taught, but there are better ways to achieve this goal. [30]

Which criteria ought to play a determinative role in the choosing of a correct approach? Catechism does not deal with theoretical, abstract knowledge, but with practical, integral, experiential knowledge, and therefore we must make use of *various* methods. Sometimes the catechumens may have to *discuss* a particular question, in order to gain a better understanding of a certain Bible passage or article of faith. At other times they may have to *act* out a simple situation to achieve the same purpose. Sometimes it may be advisable to have them *look* at some slides or *listen* to a recording. They may have to *interview* someone (a deacon, a prison-chaplain, a priest, etc.), *visit* another church, *attend* a special meeting, *make* or *do* something together, and so forth. The analytic side of the knowledge of faith is integrally interwoven with the other aspects. The logical activity of distinguishing in faith, therefore, cannot be formed in isolation. To gain a deeper insight into the meaning of faith, we must at times see, hear and do things.

Catechism is a *genuine* form of *instruction*. It is not a form of debate, or a pastoral conversation. It is not a type of proclamation, evangelism, or worship. Through its teaching the church seeks to form the catechumens' "knowledge" of the faith. Its aim is to impart "knowledge", but since it deals with practical faith-knowledge, it can achieve this goal by means of many different methods.

Up till now the approach in catechetical instruction has been largely intellectual. It will take some time and the co-operation of many ministers to discover, explore and test other methods, which can be used along side of, or instead of, methods which approach the subject primarily via the intellect. No doubt there are various forms of instruction used in different kinds of group work that could be adapted for catechetical instruction. Before these methods are used in catechism, however, they must be carefully considered

---

30 Cf. F. H. Kuiper, *Hoe gaan wij bidden?* Den Haag: Studiesecretariaat van de Raad voor de Catechese der Ned. Herv. Kerk, 1965, p. 18f.; J. Thomas, *Homiletica & Biblica*, XXIV, 4 (1965), 90-92. See also *Inleiden in het Leven van de Gemeente*, (proefontwerp), produced and published by the Gereformeerde Werkgroep voor de Catechese, 1966, pp. 21, 23.

and tested to see whether they can really *serve* to reach a deeper insight and a fuller understanding of the knowledge of faith.

Once the intellectualism, which has characterized so much of our catechetical training, has been overcome, room is created for other more fruitful approaches. But before we select a particular method for a certain period, we must first determine the specific aim of the lesson. Next we must consider the group that we will be teaching, how it is constituted, and what reactions we can expect with regard to our topic. It is only in the light of these considerations that we can ask ourselves which procedure will help us the most to achieve the specific goal of this lesson.

At this point, where our theory must change to practice, we may once more refer to the materials produced by the Raad voor de Catechese der Ned. Hervormde Kerk and the Gereformeerde Werkgroep voor de Catechese. In these publications many of the preceding principles have found an initial application. [31]

C. PERSPECTIVE

In this final section we want to return a moment to some of the questions we raised in the last part of the first chapter. There we described Catechetics as a systematic discipline which directs all its attention to the church's instruction as a pistically qualified activity. Much of this description has been clarified during the course of our inquiry. A few remarks, however, must be added at this point.

In his *Encyclopaedie der Heilige Godgeleerdheid,* Dr. A. Kuyper attempted to derive every theological discipline from the Scriptures, as the *principium divisionis* for theology. But if one takes one's starting-point exclusively in Scripture, it is impossible to account for man as the believing subject and the church as the community of believers. The Word of God reveals the norm for our faith, it proclaims to Whom we ought to direct ourselves in our believing, and it tells us how man has responded to this revelation. But the Scriptures relate these things in the language of faith. Nowhere does the Word of God give a theoretical account of these norms, nor does it present an analysis of the structural laws that govern our believing and the church with its offices. The Bible appeals to and is in harmony with these structural norms, but to discover and

---

[31] See the references in note 30.

theoretically describe these norms, we must turn to creational revelation. Dr. Kuyper's attempt to derive theology solely from Scriptural revelation stood in the way of a further development of theology and particularly of the diaconiological subjects. [32]

Against this background it is understandable why Dr. Waterink attempted to make room for the psychology and sociology of religion *within theology*. On the one hand he wanted to maintain Kuyper's conception of Scripture as the *principium* for theology, while on the other hand he was forced to acknowledge the structural laws (which cannot be derived exclusively from Scripture). This dilemma was solved by making the psychology and sociology of religion also sub-divisions of theology, which derive their main principles directly from Scripture. [33] New biblical insight, however, indicates that this conception of psychology (the soul) and sociology can no longer be maintained.

Without reference to the structural norms revealed in creation, theology cannot account for man's faith, nor for the church as the fellowship of believers, nor for the nature of the church's ministries. The basic concepts of which theology avails itself cannot be derived directly from Scripture, since the Bible does not contain scientific theological concepts. The Word of God is not a textbook for theology. Even dogmatic theology, therefore, cannot do without an analysis of the structure of faith. If the theologian limits himself exclusively to Scripture, he is continually in danger of confusing the direction, the content, and the structure of faith, which invariably leads to a docetic conception of faith, giving room to a new dualism between grace and nature. We are convinced that these issues that touch upon the very basis and nature of theology can no longer be avoided.

How shall we account for the structure of the church's ministry, its preaching, evangelism, pastoral care, diaconate, and education? Our answer is, by taking serious the revelation of God's will in the order of creation. How else *could* we account for the structural norms that govern these ministries of the church? Since Scriptural revelation is in harmony with and appeals to creational revelation, and since the meaning of Scripture cannot be grasped without considering the creational ordinances, we have felt free to make use of the "ground plan" of these structural norms that has been provided by the Philosophy of *Law*. As a systematic dicipline,

---

32 Cf. Spier, *Phil. Ref.*, XV, 4 (1950), 174ff.; XVI, 1, 2 (1951), 3ff.
33 See above pp. 32ff.

theology cannot do without such a theoretical account of the order of creation.

This conception of theology has a number of implications for "practical" theology. First of all, this sub-division could better be called *Ecclesiology*. The special eclesiastical offices are ministries of the *church*, and as such they are entirely determined by the nature and the place of the church as a pistically qualified community of faith. In the second place, the present practice of dealing seperately with each of the diaconiological subjects should be abandoned. For it is only after the structure and aim of the church in general has been clarified, that we can consider its various ministries. This would imply, in the third place, that catechetics, as one of the sub-divisions of ecclesiology, would have to be placed in a larger perspective, as in fact we have attempted to do in this chapter. For the church's educational ministry includes more than just catechetical instruction. These other aspects (the exposition of the Heidelberg Catechism, special adult study groups, *gemeente-toerusting*, etc.) must also be dealt with under this general heading of the church's education. It would seem that this new approach to "practical" theology, along the lines we have sketched above, opens up exciting perspectives for the further development of this branch of theology.

BIBLIOGRAPHY

I. PHILOSOPHY

Bakker, R., *De Geschiedenis van het Fenomenologisch Denken*, Utrecht: Het Spectrum, 1964.

Berghuis, W. P., "Het Begrip Ambt," *Philosophia Reformata*, III, 4 (1938), 224-246.

Coetzee, J. Chr., "Die Psigologie as Vak-wetenschap," *Phil. Ref.*, IV, 3 (1939), 129-150.

De Boer, Th., "Wat is Fenomenologie?" *Correspondentie-bladen*, XXIX, (April, 1965), 25-28.

———, *De Ontwikkelingsgang in het Denken van Husserl*, Assen: Van Gorcum, 1966.

Dengerink, J. D., *Critisch-Historisch Onderzoek naar de Sociologische Ontwikkeling van het Beginsel der 'Souvereiniteit in Eigen Kring' in de 19e en 20e Eeuw*, Kampen: J. H. Kok, 1948.

———, "Enkele aspecten van het begrip 'orde' bij Emil Brunner," in *Rechtsgeleerde Opstellen*, Kampen: J. H. Kok, 1951, pp. 203-219.

———, "De Grenzen van de Staatszaak," *Correspondentie-bladen*, XVI, (Mei, 1952), 23-27.

———, "Das Wort Gottes und die zeitlichen sozialen Ordnungen," *Phil. Ref.*, XX, 3, 4 (1955), 97-122.

Dirkzwager, A., "Wereldbeschouwing, Theorievorming, Psychologie," *Phil. Ref.*, XX, 3, 4 (1955), 97-122.

Dooyeweerd, H., "Kuyper's Wetenschapsleer," *Phil. Ref.*, IV, 4 (1939), 193-232.

———, De vier religieuze grondthema's in de ontwikkelingsgang van het wijsgerig denken in het avondland," *Phil. Ref.*, VI, 4 (1941), 161-179.

———, "De leer der analogie in de Thomistische Wijsbegeerte en in de Wetsidee," *Phil. Ref.*, VII, 1, 2 (1942), 45-57.

———, "De idee der individualiteits-structuur en het Thomistisch substantiebegrip," *Phil. Ref.*, VIII, 3, 4 (1943), 65-99; IX, 1, 2 (1944), 1-41; X, 4 (1945), 25-48; XI, 1 (1946), 22-52.

———, "Het wijsgerig tweegesprek tussen de Thomistische philosophie en de Wijsbegeerte der Wetsidee," *Phil. Ref.*, XIII, 1, 2, 3 (1948), 26-31, 49-58.

———, "De Wijsbegeerte der Wetsidee en de 'Barthianen'," *Phil. Ref.*, XVI, 4 (1951), 145-162.

———, "De transcendentale critiek van het theoretisch denken en de theologia naturalis," *Phil. Ref.*, XVII, 4 (1952), 151-184.

———, "De verhouding tussen wijsbegeerte en theologie en de strijd der faculteiten," *Phil. Ref.*, XXIII, 1, 2 (1958), 1-21, 50-84.

———, *A New Critique of Theoretical Thought*, Vols. I, II, III, IV, Amsterdam: H. J. Paris; Philadelphia: The Presbyterian and Reformed Publishing Company, 1953-1957.

———, *Vernieuwing en Bezinning*, Zutphen: J. B. van den Brink and Co., 1959.

———, *In the Twilight of Western Thought*, Philadelphia: The Presbyterian and Rerformed Publishing Co., 1960.

——, *Verkenning in de Wijsbegeerte, de Sociologie en de Rechtsgeschiedenis*, Amsterdam: Buijten & Schipperheijn, 1962.

——, *Inleiding tot de Encyclopaedie der Rechtswetenschap*, Amsterdam: H. J. Paris, n.d.

——, *Encyclopaedie der Rechtswetenschap*, deel II, (College dictaat), Amsterdam: Bureau Studentenraad V.U., 1961.

——, "Omvang en aard van de staatstaak," *Mededelingen van de Vereniging voor Calvinistische Wijsbegeerte*, (September, 1953), 4-6.

——, "Het typisch structuur principe van de staat en de leer der staatsdoeleinden," *Weekblad voor Privaatrecht, Nortaris-ambt en Registratie*, 92ste jg., no. 4701 (9 december, 1961), 507-515.

——, "Van Peursen's critische vragen bij 'A New Critique of Theoretical Thought'," *Phil. Ref.*, XXV, 3, 4 (1960), 97-150.

——, De taak ener wijsgerige anthropologie en de doodlopende wegen tot wijsgerige zelfkennis," *Phil. Ref.*, XXVI, 1, 2, 3 (1961), 35-58.

Hart, H. *Communal Certainty and Authorized Truth; An Examination of John Dewey's Philosophy of Verification*, Amsterdam: Swets & Zeitlinger, 1966.

Klapwijk, J., "Een voorlopige standpuntbepaling t.a.v. de geschiedfilosofie van prof. Dr. H. Dooyeweerd," *Correspondentie-bladen*, XXIX, (April, 1965), 18-21.

Mekkes, J. P. A., "De begrenzing der overheidstaak," *Correspondentiebladen*, XII, 2 (1948), 14-15.

——, "Het recht van verzet," in *Rechtsgeleerde Opstellen*, Kampen: J. H. Kok, 1951, pp. 119-140.

——, "Incarnatie en wijsbegeerte," *Phil. Ref.*, XVI, 4 (1951), 163-177.

——, "Wet en ordinantiën," *Correspondentie-bladen*, XVI, Mei, 1952), 5-7.

——, "Geloven en kennen," *Mededelingen*, (Sept. 1952), 9-10.

——, "Beschouwingen naar aanleiding van de discussie rondom het recht van verzet," *Phil. Ref.*, XVIII, 4 (1953), 145-170.

——, "Risico," *Phil. Ref.*, XX, 3, 4 (1955), 123-146.

——, *Scheppingsopenbaring en Wijsbegeerte*, Kampen: J. H. Kok, 1961.

——, "Wet en subject in de wijsbegeerte der wetsidee," *Phil. Ref.*, XXVIII, 3, 4 (1962), 126-190.

——, *Teken en Motief der Creatuur*, Amsterdam: Buijten & Schipperheijn, 1965.

——, "Boekbespreking: Dr. C. A. van Peursen, *Feiten, waarden, gebeurtenissen; een deiktische ontologie*," *Phil. Ref.*, XXXI, 1, 2 (1966) 89-97.

Pleiter, H. R., "Plaats en Taak der Psychiatrie als Wetenschap," in *Perspectief*, Kampen: J. H. Kok, 1961, pp. 304-309.

Popma, K. J., *Inleiding in de Wijsbegeerte*, Kampen: J. H. Kok 1956.

——, *Wijsbegeerte en Anthropologie*, Amsterdam: Bijten & Schipperheijn, 1963.

Rookmaker, H. R., "Ontwerp ener Aesthetica op Grondslag der Wijsbegeerte der Wetsidee," *Phil. Ref.*, XI, 3, 4 (1946), 141-167; XII, 1 (1947), 1-35.

Runner, H. E., "The Relation of the Bible to Learning," in *Christian Perspectives 1960*, Pella: Pella Publishing, Inc. 1960 pp. 85-159.

——, "Scientific and Pre-Scientific," in *Christian Perspectives 1961*, Hamilton: Guardian Publ. Co. Ltd., 1961 pp. 11-52.

——, "Sphere-Sovereignty," in *Christian Perspectives 1961* Hamilton: Guardian Publ. Co. Ltd., 1961 pp. 53-87.

——, „Scriptural Religion and Political Task," in *Christian Perspectives 1962*, Hamilton: Guardian Publ. Co. Ltd., 1962 pp. 135-257.

Schoep, G. K., "Neurose en Religie," *Phil. Ref.*, XIII, 4 (1948), 145-186.

Seerveld, C., *A Christian Critique of Art*, St. Catharines: The Association for Reformed Scientific Studies, 1963.

————, *A Christian Critique of Literature*, Hamilton: The Association for Reformed Scientific Studies, 1964.

Stoker, H. G., "Die Kosmiese Dimensie van Gebeurtenisse," *Phil. Ref.*, XXIX, 1, 2 (1964), 1-67.

Troost, A., *Casuïstiek en Situatie-ethiek*, Utrecht: Libertas, 1958.

————, *Vermogensaanwasdeling en Sociale Ethiek*, Kampen: J. H. Kok, 1964.

————, "Personalisme en ethiek," *Mededelingen*, (Maart 1966), 3-5.

————, "Veranderend Gezinsontwerp," *Geloof en Wetenschap*, 1966, 1-26.

Van der Hoeven, J., *Kritische Ondervraging van de Fenomenologische Rede*, I, Amsterdam: Buijten & Schipperheijn, 1963.

————, *Heidegger en de Geschiedenis der Wijsbegeerte*, Amsterdam: Buijten & Schipperheijn, 1963.

————, "Merleau-Ponty en het Anthropologisch Dualisme," *Correspondentiebladen*, *XXIX*, (April, 1965), 22-25.

————, "Filosofie op het Spel," *Phil. Ref.*, XXX, 2, 3, 4 (1965), 137-158.

————, *The Rise and Development of the Phenomenologigal Movement*, Hamilton: The Association for Reformed Scientific Studies, 1965.

Van Dijk, W. K., "Neurose en Religie," *Mededelingen*, (Dec. 1962), 2-4.

Van Peursen, C. A., "Enkele critische vragen in margine bij 'A New Critique of Theoretical Thought'," *Phil. Ref.*, XXIV, 3, 4 (1959), 160-168.

————, "*Antwoord aan Dooyeweerd*," *Phil. Ref.*, XXVI, (1961), 189-200.

————, *Lichaam-Ziel-Geest*, Utrecht: Bijleveld, 1961[2].

————, "Antwoord aan Mekkes," *Phil. Ref.*, XXVIII, 1, 2 (1963), 58-61.

————, *Filosofische Oriëntatie*, Kampen: J. H. Kok, 1964[2].

Van Riessen, H., *Filosofie en Techniek*, Kampen: J. H. Kok, 1949.

————, *De Maatschappij der Toekomst*, Franeker, T. Wever, 1953[3].

————, "De souvereiniteit in eigen kring," *Correspondentiebladen*, XVIII, (Juli 1954), 14-21; XVIII, (Dec. 1954), 6-12.

————, "The relation of the Bible to Science," in *Christian Perspectives 1960*, Pella: Pella Publ. Inc., 1960, pp. 3-54.

————, *Mens en Werk*, Amsterdam: Buijten & Schipperheijn, 1962.

————, *Op Wijsgerige Wegen*, Wageningen: N.V. Gebr. Zomer & Keunings, 1963[2].

————, *Knooppunten der Moderne Cultuur*, Delft: Waltman, 1964.

————, "Over de betekenis van de wetsidee in de wijsbegeerte," *Phil. Ref.*, XXX, 2, 3, 4 (1965), 159-177.

Vollenhoven, D. H. Th., *Het Calvinisme en de Reformatie van de Wijsbegeerte*, Amsterdam: H. J. Paris, 1933.

Vollenhoven, D. H. Th., and Schilder, K., *Van "Oorzaken en Redenen"*: Minderheidsnota inzake Algemene genade, Genadeverbond, De onsterfelijkheid der ziel, Pluriformiteit der kerk, Vereniging der twee naturen van Christus, en Zelfonderzoek. Kampen/Amsterdam, (stenciled), 1939.

Vollenhoven, D. H. Th., "Anhypostatos?" *Phil. Ref.*, V, 2 (1940), 65-79.

————, "Christendom en Humanisme van Middeleeuwen tot Reformatie," *Phil. Ref.*, XI, 3, 4 (1946), 101-140.

————, *Hoofdlijnen der Logica*, Kampen: J. H. Kok, 1948.

————, "De souvereiniteit in eigen kring bij Kuyper en ons," *Mededelingen*, (Dec. 1950), 4-7.

————, "Norm en Natuurwet," *Mededelingen*, (Juli 1951), 3-6.

————, "De visie op den Middelaar bij Kuyper en bij ons," *Mededelingen*, (Sept. 1952), 3-9.

————, "Schriftgebruik en Wijsbegeerte," *Mededelingen*, (Sept. 1953), 6-9.

————, *Kort Overzicht van de Geschiedenis der Wijsbegeerte*, (College-dictaat), Amsterdam: Uitgeverij Theja, n.d.

————, *Isgogé Philosophiae*, (College-dictaat), Amsterdam: Theja, n.d.

————, *Inleiding tot de Wijsgerige Anthropologie*, (Collegedictaat), Amsterdam: Theja, 1958.

——, "Plato's Realisme," *Phil. Ref.*, XXVIII, 3, 4 (1963), 97-133.

Zuidema, S. U., "Beginselen in het Christendom," *Correspondentiebladen*, XIII, 1 (1949), 3-8.

——, "Pragmatism," in *Christian Perspectives 1961*, Hamilton: Guardian Publishing Co. Ltd., 1961, pp. 133-157.

II· EDUCATION

Aebli, H., *Psychologische Didaktik*, Stuttgart: Klett, 1963.

Ausubel, D. P., *Theory and Problems of Child Development*, New York: Grune & Stratton, 1958.

——, *Theory and Problems of Adolescent Development*, New York: Grune & Stratton, 1962[5].

Baldwin, A. L., *Behavior and Development in Childhood*, New York: Dryden, 1955.

Bavinck, H., *De Opvoeding der Rijpere Jeugd*, Kampen: Kok, 1916.

——, *De Nieuwe Opvoeding*, Kampen: Kok, 1928[2].

——, *Bijbelse en Religieuze Psychologie*, Kampen: Kok, 1920.

——, *Paedagogische Beginselen*, Kampen: Kok, 1930.

Beets, N., *Over Lichaamsbeleving en Sexualiteit in de Puberteit*, Utrecht: Bijleveld, 1958.

——, *Volwassen Worden*, Utrecht: Bijleveld, 1961[2].

——, *De Grote Jongen*, Utrecht: Bijleveld, 1961[3].

Bijl, J., *Inleiding tot de Algemene Didactiek van het Basisonderwijs*, Groningen: Wolters, 1960.

Blair, G. M., R. S. Jones, R. H. Simpson, *Educational Psychology*, New York: The Macmillan Company, 1956[3].

Boekestijn, C., *Sociale Relatie en Zelfbeeld*, Kampen: Kok, 1963.

Boyd, Wm., *The History of Western Education*, London: Adam and Charles Black, 1961[6].

Brubacher, J. S., *Modern Philosophies of Education*, New York: Mc. Graw-Hill, 1962[3].

Bühler, Ch., *Psychologie der Puberteitsjaren*, Utrecht: Bijleveld, 1950[2].

Bijkerk, R. J., *Psycho-Logica; Een Historisch Arrangement*, Amsterdam: Van Soest, 1962.

Cantor, N., *The Teaching-Learning Process, A Study of Interpersonal Relations*, New York: Dryden, 1953.

Calon, P. J. A., *De Jongen*, Haarlem: De Toorts, 1955[3].

Carmichael, L., ed. *Manual of Child Psychology*, New York: Wiley, 1946.

Cavan, R. S., *The American Family*, New York: Crowell, 1955.

Chorus, A. M. J., *Grondslagen der Sociale Psychologie*, Leiden: Kroese, 1953.

Cole, L., *Psychologie of Adolescence*, New York: Holt, Rinehart and Winston, 1959[5].

Cronbach, L. J., *Educational Psychology*, New York: Harcourt, Brace, 1954.

De Jongste, H., "Een nieuwe basis voor schoolidealen?" *Correspondentiebladen*, XVI, (Nov., 1952), 6-11.

——, "Algemeen vormend onderwijs," *Correspondentie-bladen*, XVIII, (Dec. 1954), 2-5.

——, "Over algemene vorming en onderwijs," *Correspondentiebladen*, VIII, (Juli, 1954), 3-5.

De Klerk, L., *De Grondsituatie der Puberteitsopvoeding*, Groningen: Wolters, 1956[2].

——, *Functionele Theorie*, Den Haag: Boekencentrum, 1959.

Dewey, J., *Democracy and Educaton*, New York: The Macmillan Co., 1961.

De Wit, J. *Problemen Rond de Moeder-kind Relatie*, Amsterdam: Van Campen, 1962.

———, *Ontwikkelingspsychologische Beschouwingen naar Aanleiding van de Identificatie*, Wageningen: Zomer & Keunings, 1962.

Diem, H., Langeveld, M. J., *Untersuchungen zur Anthropologie des Kindes* Heidelberg: Quelle & Meyer, 1960.

Dollard, J., and Miller, N. E., *Personality and Psychotherapy*, New York: McGraw Hill, 1950.

Erikson, Erik H., *Childhood and Society*, New York: Norton, 1963.

Flokstra, L. L., *Christian Education: Tradition or Conviction?* Grand Rapids: Calvin College, 1958.

Fokkema, S., *De Project-methode: Een vorm van activiteitsonderwijs*, Uitgave van het Christelijk Paedagogisch Studiecentrum, 1957².

Fokkema, S. D., *Wetenschappelijk Onderzoek in de Psychologie en in de Paedagogiek*, Groningen: Wolters, 1960.

———, *De Begripsvorming in het Probleem-oplossen in de Hedendaagse Denkpsychologie*, Groningen: Wolters, 1961.

Gesell, A., *Youth, The Years from Ten to Sixteen*, Londen, 1956.

Gilhuis, T. M., *Isolement én Apostolaat*, Wageningen: Veenman, 1948.

Gordijn, C. C. F., *Inleiding tot de Problematiek van het Menselijk zich Bewegen*, Arnhem: Van der Wiel, 1963.

Gunning, J. H., *Verzamelde Paedagogische Opstellen*, Amsterdam: Van Looy, 1908.

Guyer, W., *Wie wir lernen*, Zürich: Reutsch, 1960³.

Hall, C. S., Lindzey, G., *Theories of Personality*, New York: Wiley, 1957.

Hansen, W., *Die Entwicklung des kindlichen Weltbildes*, München: Kösel-Verlag, 1960⁵.

Henry, H. B., ed., *Modern Philosophies and Education*, Chicago: The University of Chicago Press, '55. (The Fifty-fourth Yearbook of the National Society for the Study of Education.)

Herskovits, M. J., *Cultural Anthropology*, New York: Knopf, 1955.

Heyster Sis, *Het Meisje*, Heemstede: de Toorts, 1946.

Hilgard, E. R., *Theories of Learning*, New York: Appleton-Century-Crofts, 1956².

Hillebrand, M. J., *Psychologie des Lernens und des Lehrens*, Bern/Stuttgart, 1958.

Hoekstra, T., *Paedagogische Psychologie*, Kampen: Kok, 1930.

Hoogveld, J., *Keur uit de Werken van Prof. Dr. J. Hoogveld*, Groningen: Wolters, 1951².

Jaarsma, C., *Fundamentals in Christian Education*, Grand Rapids: Eerdmans, 1953.

———, *Human Development, Learning and Teaching*, Grand Rapids: Eerdmans, 1951.

Janse, A. *Het Eigen Karakter der Christelijke School*, Kampen: Kok, 1935.

Janse de Jonge, A. L., *Karakterkunde*, Baarn: Bosch & Keuning, n.d.³.

Jenkins, G. G., H. Shacter, W. W. Bauer, *These Are Your Children*, Chicago: Scott, Foresman, n.d.

Jersild, A. T., *Psychology of Adolesence*, New York: The Macmillan Co., 1957.

———, *Child Psychology*, Englewood Cliffs: Prentice Hall, 1960⁵.

Kohnstamm, Ph., *Keur uit het Didactische Werk van Prof. Dr. Ph. Kohnstamm*, Groningen: Wolters, 1948.

———, "Paedagogiek, Personalisme en Wijsbegeerte der Wetsidee," in *Feestbundel Prof. Dr. J. Waterink*, Amsterdam: Holland, 1951, pp. 96-107. *Persoonlijkheid in Wording*, Haarlem: Willink, 1959³.

Kooistra, R., *Facts and Values, A Christian Approach to Sociology*, St. Catharines: The Association for Reformed Scientific Studies, 1963.

———, *The University and its Abolitions*, Hamilton, The Association for Reformed Scientific Studies, 1965.

Kruyswijk, M., *De Christelijke School en de Doorbraakgedachte*, Groningen: Wolters, 1947.

Kuypers, A., *De Ziel van het Kind*, Wageningen: Zomer & Keunings, 1936.

———, *Het Onbewuste in de Nieuwere Paedagogische Psychologie*, Amsterdam: Paris, 1931.

———, *Een Paedagogische Beoordeling van het Amerikaanse Persoonlijkheidsbegrip*, Amsterdam: Bakker, 1951.

———, *Psychologie en Paedagogiek in de Sowjet Unie*, Groningen: Wolters, 1952.

———, *Inleiding in de Zielkunde*, Kampen: Kok, 1953[3].

Langeveld, M. J., *Inleiding tot de Studie der Paedagogische Psychologie*, Groningen: Wolters, 1950[4].

———, *Verkenning en Verdieping*, Purmerend: Muusses, 1950.

———, *Over het Wezen der Paedagogische Psychologie en de Verhouding der Psychologie tot de Paedagogiek*, Groningen: Wolters, 1951.

———, *Studien zur Anthropologie des Kindes*, Tübingen, 1956.

———, *Kind und Jugendlicher in Anthropologischer Sicht*, Heidelberg: Quelle & Meyer, 1959.

———, *Capita uit de Algemene Methodologie der Paedologie*, Groningen: Wolters, 1959.

———, *Ontwikkelingspsychologie*, Groningen: Wolters, 1960[4].

———, *Beknopte Theoretische Paedagogiek*, Groningen: Wolters, 1965[10].

———, *Die Schule als Weg des Kindes*, Braunschweig: Westermann, 1966[3].

Litt, Th., *Führen oder Wachsenlassen*, Leipzig/Berlin: Teuber, 1931[3].

Los, S. O., *Moderne Paedagogen en Richtingen*, Amsterdam: Standaard, 1933.

Maritain, J., *Education at the Crossroads*, New Haven: Yale University Press, 1960.

Mead, M., and Wolfenstein, M., eds., *Childhood in Contemporary Cultures*, Chicago: The University of Chicago Press, 1955.

Mekkes, J. P. A., "Het Schoolverband," *Correspondentie-bladen*, XIII (1949), 30-33.

Melvin, A. G., *General Methods of Teaching*, New York: McGraw-Hills, 1952.

Meunicke, C. A., *Sociale Psychologie*, Utrecht: Bijleveld, 1948[3].

Muchow, H. H., *Jugendgenerationen im Wandel der Zeit*, Wien: Hollinek, 1964.

Mursell, J. L., *Developmental Teaching*, New York: McGraw-Hills, 1949.

———, *Psychology for Modern Education*, New York: Norton, 1952.

Mowrer, O. H., *Learning Theory and Personality Dynamics*, New York: Ronald, 1950,

Mussen, Paul H., Conger, John J., Kagen, Jerome, eds., *Readings in Child Development and Personality*, New York: Harper & Row, 1965.

Niblett, W. R., *Christian Education in a Secular Society*, London: Oxford University Press, 1960.

Nieuwenhuis, H., *Een Noodzakelijke Verandering in de taak van de School*, Groningen: Wolters, 1954.

Oldendorff, A., *De Psychologie van het Sociale Leven*, Utrecht: Bijleveld, 1962[5].

Perquin, N., *Algemene Didactiek*, Roermond-Maaseik: Romen, 1961.

———, *Pedagogische Psychologie*, Roermond-Maaseik: Romen, 1962.

———, *Pedagogiek*, Roermond-Maaseik: Romen, 1964[7].

———, N., *Verwerkte en Verdrongen Sexualiteit*, Roermond-Maaseik: Romen, 1964.

Popma, K. J., "Opvoeding, Onderwijs, Schoolverband," *Philosophia Reformata*, XII, 1, 2, 3 (1947), 36-41, 86-93, 130-144.

Prins, F. W., *Vernieuwingsvragen Over Onderwijs en Opvoeding*, Groningen: Wolters, 1952[3].

Remplein, H., *Die seelische Entwicklung des Menschen im Kindes und Jugendalter*, München: Reinhardt, 1964[12].

Roth, H., *Leerpsychologie in Pedagogisch Perspectief*, Roosendaal: Koepel, 1959.

Rümke, H. C., *Inleiding in de Karakterkunde*, Haarlem: Bohn, 1956[4].

———, *Levenstijdperken van de Man*, Amsterdam: N.V. de Arbeidspers 1959[6].

Schelsky H., *Soziologie der Sexualität*, Hamburg: Rowohlt, 1955.

———, Die skeptische Generation, Dusseldorf/Köln; Diederichs, 1957.

Schorling, R., *Student Teaching*, New York: McGraw-Hills, 1949.

Seerveld, Calvin, "The Christian School in American Democracy," *Convention Addresses*, 44th Annual Christian School Convention, Grand Rapids: National Union of Christian Schools, 1964.

Stellwag, H. W. F., Van de Griend, P. C., *De Leraarsopleiding: Knelpunt of Raakvlak tussen Universiteit en V.H.M.O.*, Groningen: Wolters, 1959.

———, *Begane Wegen en Onbetreden Paden*, Groningen: Wolters, 1961[5].

———, *Viaticum Didacticum*, Groningen: Wolters, 1964[4].

Strasser, S., *Opvoedingswetenschap en Opvoedingswijsheid*, 's-Hertogenbosch: Malmberg, 1963[2].

Ten Have, T. T., *Sociale Pedagogiek*, Groningen: Wolters, 1961.

Thomas, R. M., *Ways of Teaching*, New York: Longmans, Green, 1955.

Van den Berg, J. H., *Kroniek der Psychologie*, Den Haag: Boekencentrum, 1953.

———, *Dubieuze Liefde in de Omgang met het Kind*, Nijkerk: Callenbach, 1960[3].

Van den Dungen, M., *De Jeugdige Mens en de Machteloosheid der Volwassenen*, Utrecht/Antwerpen: Het Spectrum, 1958.

Van Dijk, R., *Mens en Medemens, Een Inleiding tot de Sociologie*, Wageningen: Zomer & Keunings, n.d.[2]

Van Hulst, J. W., *De Beginselleer van Hoogvelds Pedagogiek*, Groningen: Wolters, 1962.

———, *Een Fundamenteel Probleem der Pedagogiek*, Groningen: Wolters, 1963.

Van Klinken, Lucas, *Wijsgerige Achtergronden van de Paedagogische Verscheidenheid bij het Lager Onderwijs in Nederland in de 20ste Eeuw*, Kampen: Kok, 1946.

———, "De Wijsbegeerte der Wetsidee en de Paedagogiek," in *Wetenschappelijke Bijdragen door Leerlingen van Dr. D. H. Th. Vollenhoven*, Franeker: Wever, 1951, pp. 33-43.

———, *Bavinck's Paedagogische Beginselen*, Meppel: Stenvert, n.d.

Van Parreren, C. F., *Pluralisme in de Leerpsychologie*, Groningen: Wolters, 1958.

———, *Psychologie van het Leren*, I, II, Arnhem: van Loghum Slaterus, Zeist: de Haan, 1963[2], 1962.

———, *Didactiek en Leerpsychologie*, Groningen: Wolters, 1964.

———, *Leren op School*, Groningen: Wolters, 1965[3].

Van Poelje, G. A., ed., *Gesprek der Opvoeders*, Amsterdam: Wereldbibliotheek, 1952.

Van Riessen, H., Firet, J., *Moderne Algemeenheid*, Kampen: Kok, 1963.

———, *The University and its Basis*, Hamilton: The Association for Reformed Scientific Studies, 1963.

Van Stegeren, W. F., *Groei naar de Volwassenheid*, Wageningen: Zomer & Keunings.

Vedder, R., *Kinderen met Leer- en Gedragsmoeilijkheden*, Groningen, Wolters, 1962[3].

Waterink, J., *Inleiding tot de Theoretische Pedagogiek*, Deel I, *De Paedagogiek als Wetenschap*, Zeist: Ruys, 1926-1931. Deel II, *De Geschiedenis der Paedagogiek*, Zutphen: Ruys, 1932.

———, *De Oorsprong en het Wezen van het Ziel*, Wageningen: Zomer & Keunings, 1930.

———, *Ons Zieleleven*, Wageningen: Zomer & Keunings, n.d.[6] (1946[5]).
———, *Puberteit*, Wageningen: Zomer & Keunings, 1955[5].
———, *De Psychologie van het Kind op de Lagere School*, 's-Gravenhage: Boekencentrum, 1956[2].
———, *Theorie der Opvoeding*, Kampen: Kok, 1958[2].
———, "Man as Religious Being and Modern Psychology," *Free University Quarterly*, VI, 1 (Febr. 1959), 1-30.
———, *En Toch: "De Christelijke School,"* Kampen: Kok, 1961.
———, *Keur uit de verspreide Geschriften van Prof. Dr. J. Waterink*, Groningen: Wolters, 1961.
Wielenga, G., "Leren met Inzicht — Onderwijzen tot Inzicht," *Feestbundel Prof. Dr. J. Waterink*, Amsterdam: Holland, 1951, pp. 208-219.
———, *Het Experiment in de Didactiek*, Groningen: Wolters, 1951.
———, *Didactiek en Levensbeschouwing*, Groningen: Wolters, 1953.
———, *Moderne Opvattingen Omtrent het „Leren Denken"*, Uitgave: Christelijk Paedagogisch Studiecentrum, 1957.
Winnefeld, F., *Pädagogischer Kontakt und pädagogischer Feld*, München/Basel, 1957.
Witherington, H. C., *Educational Psychology*, Boston: Ginn & Co., 1952.
Wijngaarden, H. R., "Ouderbinding en Levenshouding," in *Feestbundel Prof. Dr. J. Waterink*, Amsterdam: Holland, 1951, pp. 220-231.
———, *Hoofdproblemen der Volwassenheid*, Utrecht: Bijleveld, 1955[3]
———, *Gesprekken met Uzelf*, Utrecht: Bijleveld, 1956[4].
Yoakim, G. A., and Simpson, R. G., *Modern Methods and Techniques of Teaching*, New York: McMillan, 1948.
Zulliger, H., *Opgeschoten Jeugd*, Amsterdam/Antwerpen: Wereldbibliotheek, 1960.
———, *Het Geweten van Onze Kinderen*, Nijkerk: Callenbach, 1962.

III. THEOLOGY

Bakker, J. T., *Coram Deo, Bijdrage tot het Onderzoek naar de Structuur van Luthers Theologie*, Kampen: Kok, 1956.
———, *Kerugma en Prediking*, Kampen: Kok, 1957.
———, *Eschatologische Prediking bij Luther*, Kampen: Kok, 1964.
Barth, K., *Church Dogmatics*, Vol. I/1. Edinburgh: T. & T. Clark, 1960.
Bavinck, H., *De Katholiciteit van Christendom en Kerk*, Kampen: Zolsman, 1888.
———, *Gereformeerde Dogmatiek*, Vol. IV, Kampen: Kok, 1928[4].
Bavinck, J. H., *Religieus Besef en Christelijk Geloof*, Kampen: Kok, 1949.
———, *Inleiding in de Zendingswetenschap*, Kampen: Kok, 1954.
———, "Apostoliciteit en Katholiciteit," in *De Apostolische Kerk*, Kampen: Kok, 1954, pp. 218-242.
———, *Alzo Wies het Woord*, Baarn: Bosch & Keunings, 1960[2].
Berkhof, H., "De Apostolociteit der Kerk," *Nederlands Theologisch Tijdschrift*, II, 3, 4 (1948).
———, *God Voorwerp van Wetenschap?* Nijkerk: Callenbach, 1960.
———, *De Katholiciteit der Kerk*, Nijkerk: Callenbach, 1962.
———, "Tweeërlei ekklesiologie," *Kerk en Theologie*, XIII (1962), 145-158.
Berkouwer, G. C., *Karl Barth en de Kinderdoop*, Kampen: Kok, 1947.
———, *De Voorzienigheid Gods*, Kampen: Kok, 1950.
———, *De Algemene Openbaring*, Kampen: Kok, 1951.
———, *Het Werk van Christus*, Kampen: Kok, 1953.
———, *De Sacramenten*, Kampen: Kok, 1954.
———, *De Mens het Beeld Gods*, Kampen: Kok, 1957.
———, *De Zonde*, II, *Wezen en Verbreiding der Zonde*, Kampen: Kok, 1960.
———, *De Heilige Schrift*, I, Kampen: Kok, 1966.

———, *Conflict met Rome*, Kampen: Kok, 1953[3].

———, "Identiteit of conflict," *Philosophia Reformata*, XXI, 1, 2 (1956), 1-44.

———, "Calvin and the Church," *Free University Quarterly*, VI, 4 (Dec., 1959), 1-6.

Best, E., *One Body in Christ*, London: S.P.C.K., 1955.

Biesterveld, P., *Het Object der Ambtelijke Vakken*, Wageningen: Drukkerij "Vada", 1902.

Blauw, J., *Religie en Inter-Religie*, Kampen: Kok, 1962.

Bohetec, J., "Autorität und Freiheit in der Gedankenwelt Calvins," in *Phil. Ref.*, V, 1, 2, 3, 4 (1940), 1-28, 80-100, 129-159, 235-249; VI, 1, 2, 3, 4 (1941), 41-56, 87-104, 180-192; VII, 1, 2 (1942), 1-8.

Bolkestein, M. H., *Het Gemeentelid, Zijn Plaats en Roeping Volgens het Nieuwe Testament*, (*Horstcahiers*, nummer 14), Driebergen: Kerk en Wereld, 1962.

De Graaf, S. G., *Het Woord Gods en de Kerk*, Zutphen: Van den Brink, 1935.

———, "De genade Gods en de structuur der ganse schepping," *Phil. Ref.*, XVII, 1 (1936), 17-29.

———, *Christus en de Wereld*, Kampen: Kok, 1939.

———, "Christus en de geschiedenis," *Correspondentie-bladen*, VIII, 1 (Dec. 1945), 2-3.

De Zwaan, J., "The idea of the ecclesia in the N.T.," *Nederlands Theologisch Tijdschrift* I, 1 (1946/47).

Diem, H., *Theologie als kirchliche Wissenschaft*, Vols. I-III, München: Kaiser, 1951-1963.

Dijk, K., *De Eenheid der Ambten*, Utrecht: Centraal Bureau van de Diaconieën der Gereformeerde Kerken, 1949.

———, *De Dienst der Kerk*, Kampen: Kok, 1952.

Dodd, C. H., *The Apostolic Preaching and its Developments*, Londen: Hodder & Stoughton, 1963.

Duvenage, S. C. W., *Kerk, Volg en Jeug*, Vol. I, *De Verhouding van Kerk tot Volk*, Zaandijk: Heijnis, 1962.

Flew, R. Newton, *Jesus and His Church*, London: The Epworth Press, 1943[2].

Goumaz, L., *Het Ambt bij Calvijn*, Franeker: T. Wever, 1964.

Haendler, O., *Grundriss der praktische Theologie*, Berlin: Töpelmann, 1957.

Hiltner, S., *Preface to Pastoral Theology*, New York/Nashville: Abingdon Press, 1958.

Hoekstra, T., *Ds Psychologie der Religie en de Ambtelijke Vakken*, Kampen: Kok, 1913.

Hugen, M. D., *The Church's Ministry to the Older Unmarried*, Grand Rapids: Eerdmans, 1959[2].

Kooiman, W. J., "Het algemeen priesterschap der gelovigen volgens Luther," *Rondom het Woord, Tweemaandelijks Bulletin der Theologische Radio-colleges*, VI, 2 (1964), 74-79.

Koole, J. L., *Liturgie en Ambt in de Apostolische Kerk*, Kampen: Kok, 1949.

Kraemer, H., *A Theology of the Laity*, London: Lutterworth, 1958.

Kromminga, C. G. *The Communication of the Gospel Through Neighbouring*, Franeker: T. Wever, 1964.

Kuitert, H. M., *De Mensvormigheid Gods*, Kampen: Kok, 1962.

Küng, H., *Strukturen der Kirche*, Freiburg: Herder, 1962.

Kuyper, A., *Encyclopaedie der Heilige Godgeleerdheid*, Vols. I-III, Kampen: Kok, 1909[2].

———, *Pro Rege of het Koningschap van Christus*, Vols. I-III, Kampen: Kok, 1911-1912.

———, *De Gemeene Gratie*, Vols. I-III, Kampen: Kok, 1934[4].

———, *Het Calvinisme*, Kampen: Kok, n.d.

———, *E voto Dordraceno*, Vols. I-IV, Kampen: Kok, n.d.

Langman, H. J., *Kuyper en de Volkskerk,* Kampen: Kok, 1950.

Lindijer, C. H., *Kerk en Koninkrijk,* Amsterdam: Ten Have, 1962.

Matter, H. M., *De Kerk als Lichaam van Christus,* Den Haag: Willem de Zwijgerstichting, 1962.

Mekkes, J. P. A., "Boekbespreking: J. M. Spier, *Tijd en Eeuwigheid," Phil. Ref.* XXIV, 3, 4 (1959), 183-186.

——, "Boekbespreking: Dr. H. Berkhof, *God Voorwerp van Wetenschap?" Phil. Ref.,* 4 (1961), 219-223.

——, "Boekbespreking: Dr. G. Th. Rothuizen, *Tweeërlei Ethiek bij Calvijn?" Antirevolutionaire Staatkunde,* XXXIV, 10 (Oktober, 1964), 257-262.

Minear, P. S., *Images of the Church in the New Testament,* Philadelphia: The Westminster Press, 1960.

Müller, A. D., *Grundriss der Praktischen Theologie,* Gütersloh: Bertellsmann, 1950.

Polman, A. D. R., *Onze Nederlandse Geloofsbelijdenis,* Vols. I-IV, Franeker: T. Wever, n.d.

Popma, K. J., *De Vrijheid der Exegese,* Goes: Oosterbaan & Le Cointre, 1944.

——, "Eenheid en pluriformiteit van ons belijden," *Phil. Ref.,* XVI, 4 (1951), 178-189.

——, "Inleiding tot Paulus," *Correspondentiebladen,* XVII, (Dec. 1953), 4-8.

——, *Levensbeschouwing,* Vols. I-VII, Amsterdam: Buijten & Schipperheijn, 1958-1965.

——, "Het systematisch karakter van de theologische dogmatiek," *Phil. Ref.,* XXV, 1, 2 (1960), 1-35.

Ridderbos, H. N., *De Komst van het Koninkrijk,* Kampen: Kok, 1950.

——, *Paulus en Jesus,* Kampen: Kok, 1952.

——, "De apostoliciteit van de kerk volgens het Nieuwe Testament," in *De Apostolische Kerk,* Kampen: Kok, 1954, pp. 39-97.

——, *Heilsgeschiedenis en Heilige Schrift van het Nieuwe Testament,* Kampen: Kok, 1955.

——, "Christelijke Vrijheid en Politieke Partijkeuze," in *Antirevolutionaire Staatkunde,* XXV, II (Nov., 1935), 321-333.

——, "De eenheid van de kerk," *Internationaal Reformatorisch Bulletin,* VIII, 20, 21, 22 (Jan., April, Juli, 1965), 39-54.

——, *Paulus: Ontwerp van zijn Theologie,* Kampen: Kok, 1966.

Roels, E. D., *God's Mission: The Epistle to the Ephesians in Mission Perspective,* Franeker: T. Wever, 1962.

Rossouw, H. W., *Klaarheid en Interpretatie,* Amsterdam: Van Campen, 1963.

Rothuizen, G. Th., *Primus Usus Legis, Studie over het Burgerlijk Gebruik van de Wet,* Kampen: Kok, 1962.

——, *Tweeërlei Ethiek bij Calvijn?* Kampen: Kok, 1964.

Schilder, K., *De Kerk,* (College-dictaat, 1942), Kampen: Van den Berg, 3de druk.

Schippers, R., "De weg van de Christelijke organisaties," *Wending,* XVI, 10 (Dec., 1961), 583-594.

——, *De Geschiedenis van Jezus en de Apocalyptiek,* Kampen: Kok, 1964.

Schmidt, K. L., *The Church,* London: Black, 1957.

Schrotenboer, P. G., *The Nature of Religion,* Hamilton: The Association for Reformed Scientific Studies, 1964.

Schnackenburg, R., *Die Kirche im Neuen Testament,* Freiburg: Herder, 1961.

Schweizer, E., *Gemeinde und Gemeindeordnung im Neuen Testament,* Zurich, 1959.

Sevenster, G., "De wijding van Paulus en Barnabas," in *Studia Paulina in Honorem J. De Zwaan,* Haarlem: Bohn, 1953.

——, "De ambten in het Nieuwe Testament," *Vox Theologica,* XVII (Maart, 1957), 97-111.

——, "Het koning- en piesterschap der gelovigen in het Nieuwe Testament," *Nederlands Theologisch Tijdschrift*, XIII, (1958, 1959), 401-417.

——, "Het karakter der nieuwtestamentische gemeente," in *Woord en Wereld, opgedragen aan Prof. Dr. K. H. Miskotte*, Amsterdam: Arbeidspers, 1961, pp. 115-126.

——, "Problemen betreffende het ambt in het Nieuwe Testament," *Tweemaandelijks Bulletin der Theologische Radiocolleges*, V, 1, 2, 3 (Jan., 1963), 21-26.

Sietsma, K., *De Ambtsgedachte*, Amsterdam: Bakker, n.d.

Sillivis Smitt, P. A. E., *De Betekenis van het Gereformeerde Beginsel voor de Ambtelijke Vakken*, Amsterdam: Van Bottenburg, 1912.

Smedes, L. B., *The Nature of the Church and Some Problems in Evangelism*, Grand Rapids: Christian Reformed Publ. House, 1958.

Spier, J. M., "De pluriformiteit van ons belijden," *Bezinning*, II, 7, 8 (Sept., Okt., 1947) 209-213, 241-249.

——, "Het veld van onderzoek voor de theologie," *Phil. Ref.*, XVI, 1, 2 (1951), 1-15.

——, "De norm voor ons geloven," in *Wetenschappelijke Bijdragen door leerlingen van Dr. D. H. Th. Vollenhoven*, Franeker: T. Wever, 1951, pp. 72-89.

Stauffer, E., *New Testament Theology*, New York: Macmillan, 1951[2].

Torrance, T. F., *Kingdom and Church; A Study in the Theology of the Reformation*, Edinburgh: Oliver & Boyd, 1956.

Troost, A., "De sociologie en het geheim van de Kerk," *Sermo*, X, 9 (1953).

Van den Berg, J., *Twee Regimenten, Een Heer*, Kampen: Kok, 1961.

Van Leeuwen, P. A., *Het Kerkbegrip in de Theologie van Abraham Kuyper*, Franeker: T. Wever, 1946.

Van Ruler, A. A., *Religie en Politiek*, Nijkerk: Callenbach, 1945.

——, *Bijzonder en Algemeen Ambt*, Nijkerk: Callenbach, 1952.

Van Teylingen, E. G., "Over de wijsgerige achtergrond der dialectische theologie," *Phil. Ref.*, X, 4 (1945), 2-24.

——, "Dr. H. Berkhof, Crisis der middenorthodoxie," *Correspondentiebladen*, XVII, (Juli, 1953), 1-4.

——, "Over terminologie in de theologie," *Gereformeerd Theologisch Tijdschrift*, LXI, 4, 5 (1961), 117-130.

——, "Verbond der genade en gezin," *Bezinning*, XVI, 2 (1961).

——, "Futurum en Futurisme," *Gereformeerd Theologisch Tijdschrift*, LXIV, 2 (Mei, 1964).

Velema, W. H., *De Leer van de Heilige Geest bij Abraham Kuyper*, 's-Gravenhage: Van Keulen, 1957.

Veranderend Getij, Vol. III, Amsterdam: Stichting Gereformeerd Sociologisch Instituut, 1962.

Volbeda, S., *The Pastoral Genius of Preaching*, Grand Rapids: Zondervan Publishing House, 1960.

Von Meyenfeldt, F. H., "Enige algemeene beschouwingen gegrond op de betekenis van het hart in het Oude Testament," in *Wetenschappelijke Bijdragen door leerlingen van Dr. D. H. Th. Vollenhoven*, Franeker: Wever, 1951.

——, *De Diaken als Componist der Gemeenschap*, Den Haag, Van Keulen, 1955.

——, "Boekbespreking: W. H. Velema, *De Leer van de Heilige Geest bij Abraham Kuyper*," *Phil. Ref.*, XXIII, 4 (1958), 183-184.

——, *The Meaning of Ethos*, Hamilton: The Association for Reformed Scientific Studies, 1964.

——, *Christelijke Levenswandel*, Wageningen: Zomer en Keunings, n.d.

——, *Kerkelijk Vooruitzicht*, Wageningen: Zomer & Keunings, n.d.

Waterink, J., *Plaats en Methode van de Ambtelijke Vakken*, Zutphen: Nauta 1923.

Westerink, H. J., *Het Koninkrijk Gods bij Paulus*, Hilversum: Schipper, 1937.

——, "Enkele opmerkingen naar aanleiding van Judas 9," *Correspondentiebladen*, XIII, 2 (1949), 1-6.

Zuidema, S. U., "Gemene gratie en Pro Rege bij Dr. Abraham Kuyper," *Anti-Revolutionaire Staatkunde*, XXIV, 1, 2 (Jan., Febr., 1954), 1-19, 49-73.

——, *Konfrontatie met Karl Barth*, Amsterdam: Buijten & Schipperheijn, 1963.

——, "Openbaringsinhoud en existentie in de theologische hermeneutiek van R. Bultmann," *Mededelingen van de Vereniging voor Calvinistische Wijsbegeerte*, (Dec. 1964), 2-7.

——, *Van Bultmann naar Fuchs*, Franeker: Wever, n.d.

Angermeyer, H., *Die Evangelische Unterweisung an höheren Schulen*, München: Chr. Kaiser Verlag, 1957.

Asheim, Ivar, *Glaube und Erziehung bei Luther*, Heidelberg: Quelle & Meyer, 1961.

Avery, M., *Teaching Scripture*, Wallington, Surrey: The Religious Education Press, Ltd., 1960³.

Augustinus, *De Catechizandis Rudibus*, Edited and translated by the Paters Augustijnen te Nijmegen. 's-Hertogenbosch: Geert Grote Genootschap, 1955.

Baldermann, I., *Biblische Didaktik*, Hamburg: Furche-Verlag, 1964².

Banning, W., *Over religieuze Opvoeding in het Gezin*, Amsterdam: Arbeidspers, 1936.

Berkelbach van der Sprenkel, S. F. H. J., *Huwelijkscatechisatie*, Nijkerk: Callenbach, 1946.

——, *Catechetiek*, Nijkerk: Callenbach, 1956.

Biesterveld, P., *Het Karakter der Catechese*, Kampen: Kok, 1900.

Bijlsma, R., *Kleine Catechetiek*, Nijkerk: Callenbach, 1962.

Bless, H., *De Pastorale Psychologie*, Roermond-Maaseik: Romen & Zonen, 1958.

Bochinger, E., *Anschaulicher Religionsunterricht*, Stuttgart: Calwer Verlag, 1964.

Bolkestein, M. H., *De Catechese in de Kerkorde*, 's-Gravenhage: Boekencentrum, 1960.

Booy, T., *Kerk en Jeugd*, Amsterdam: Ten Have, n.d.².

Brentjens, H. J. H., a.o., *Jonge Mensen en Kerk*, Hilversum: Paul Brand, 1961.

Burgardmeier, A., *Religiöse Erziehung, in psychologischer Sicht*, Düsseldorf: Patmos-Verlag, 1955².

De Graaf, S. G., "Het vertellen van de Bijbelsche geschiedenis," *Bezinning*, II, 8 (Oct., 1947), 253-257.

——, *Verbondsgeschiedenis*, Vols., I, II, Kampen: Kok, 1952.

Diem, H., Loch, W.,*Erziehung durch Verkündigung*, Heidelberg: Quelle & Meyer, 1959.

Dijk, K., *De Dienst aan de Kerkjeugd*, Kampen: Kok, 1954.

Dross, R., *Religionsunterricht und Verkündigung*, Hamburg: Furche-Verlag, 1964.

Eberhard, Otto., *Evangelischer Unterricht und Reformpädagogiek*, München: Evang. Presseverband für Bayern, 1961.

Faber, H., *De Godsdienstige Ontwikkeling van onze Kinderen*, Amsterdam: Uitgeverij Ploegsma, 1952.

——, *Pastoraal Psychologische Opstellen*, 's-Gravenhage: Boekencentrum 1961.

Fahs, S. L., *Das Erwachen der Beziehung zum Göttlichen im Kinde*, Zürich: Rascher Verlag, 1962.

Fallow, W., *Church Education for Tomorrow*, Philadelphia: Westminster Press, 1965.

Fendt, L., *Katechetik*, Berlin: Verlag A. Töpelmann, 1951[2].

Frör, K., *Was ist evangelische Erziehung?*, München: Chr. Kaiser Verlag, 1933.

——, *Erziehung und Kerugma*, München: Chr. Kaiser Verlag, 1952.

——, *Das Zeichenen im kirchlichen Unterricht*, München: Chr. Kaiser Verlag, 1958[3].

Grässmann, F., *Religionsunterricht zwischen Kirche und Schule*, München: Chr. Kaiser Verlag, 1961.

Goldbrunner, J. ed., *Katechetisch Methoden Heute*, München, Kösel-Verlag, 1962.

Goldman, R., *Religious Thinking from Childhood to Adolescence*, London: Routledge, 1964.

Hagenbeek, D. S. A., *De Moderne Leerkerk*, Kampen: Kok, 1947.

Hahn, F., *Moderne Literatur im kirchlichen Unterricht*, München: Evangelischer Pressverband, 1963.

Hammelsbeck, O., *Der kirchliche Unterricht*, München: Chr. Kaiser Verlag, 1947[2].

Heyns, W., *Handboek voor de Catechetiek*, Grand Rapids: Eerdmans-Sevensma Co., n.d.

Hoekstra, T., *Psychologie en Catechese*, Nijverdal: E. J. Bosch Jbzn., 1916

Hoekstra, F. E., *Evangelisatie en Rijpere Jeugd*, Kampen, 1947.

Hulsebosch, J., *De Groep en het Groepsgesprek*, 's-Gravenhage: Boekencentrum, 1952.

Hummel, G., *Religionsunterricht und Schule*, München: Chr. Kaiser Verlag, 1964.

Jahn, E., *Religionsunterricht und Jugendseelsorge in Psychologischer Sicht*, Heidelberg: Quelle & Meyer, 1955.

Janse, A., *Leven in het Verbond*, Kampen: Kok, 1937.

Jentsch, W., *Urchristliches Erziehungsdenken*, Gütersloh: C. Bertelsmann Verlag, 1951.

Joost, L., *Das Unterrichtsgespräch*, Braunschweig: Georg Westermann Verlag, 1954[3].

Keja, F., *Bijbel en Groep*, Driebergen: De Horst, 1962.

Kittel, H. *Vom Religionsunterricht zur Evangelischen Unterweisung*, Hannover: Schroedel, 1957[3].

Kohnstamm, Ph., *Bijbel en Jeugd*, Haarlem: De Erven F. Bohn, 1923.

Langeveld, M. J., *Kind en Religie*, Utrecht: Erven J. Bijleveld, 1956.

Lotz, P. H., ed., *Orientation in Religious Education*, Nashville: Abingdon Press, 1950.

Loukes, H., *Teenage Religion*, London: SCM Press Ltd., 1964[6].

——, *New Ground in Christian Education*, London: SCM Press Ltd., 1965.

Media-Informatie over boeken en hulpmiddelen voor catechese, godsdienstonderwijs en vormingswerk, Voorburg: Prot. Stichting tot Bevordering van het Bibliotheekwezen en de Lectuurvoorlichting in Nederland, 1963.

Meulenbelt, H. H., *Onze Katechese*, Nijmegen: H. ten Hoet, 1913[2].

Miskotte, K. H., *In de Gecroonde Allemansgading*, Nijkerk: Callenbach 1946.

Müller, E., *Methodik der Evangelischen Unterweisung in der Berufsschule*, München: Chr. Kaiser Verlag, 1955.

Neidhart, W., *Psychologie des kirchlichen Unterrichts*, Zürich: Zwingli-Verlag, 1960.

——, *Disziplinschwierigkeiten im kirchlichen Unterricht*, Zürich: Zwingli Verlag, 1964[2].

Otto, G., *Verkündigung und Erziehung*, Göttingen: Vandenhoeck & Ruprecht, 1957.

——, H. Scheuerl, I. Röbelen, *Neue Beiträge zum Thema Erziehung und Verkündigung*, Heidelberg: Quelle & Meyer, 1960.

——, *Schule, Religionsunterricht, Kirche*, Göttingen: Vandenhoeck & Ruprecht, 1961.

——, *Handbuch des Religionsunterrichts*, Hamburg: Furche-Verlag, 1964.

Price, J. M., et al., *A Survey of Religious Education*, New York: Ronald Press, 1959²

Rinderknecht, H. J., Zeller, K., *Methodik christlicher Unterweisung*, Zürich: Zwingli Verlag, 1960⁴.

Schaller, K., *Die Krise der humanistischen Pädagogik und der kirchliche Unterricht*, Heidelberg: Quelle & Meyer, 1961.

Schamhardt, H., *Handboekje voor het Jeugdwerk*, 's-Gravenhage: Boekencentrum N.V., 1955.

Schieder, J., *Katechismusunterricht*, München: Chr. Kaiser Verlag, 1951⁶

Schmid, L., *Religiöses Erleben unserer Jugend*, Zollikon: Evangelischer Verlag, 1960.

Schmidt, G., *Das Alte Testament im kirchlichen Unterricht*, München: Chr. Kaiser Verlag, 1953.

——, *Katechetische Anleitung*, München: Chr. Kaiser Verlag, 1958²

Schreiner, H., *Evangelische Pädagogik und Katechetik*, Gütersloh: Bertelsmann Verlag, 1959.

Smart, J. D., *The Teaching Ministry of the Church*, Philadelphia: Westminster, 1954.

Smit, W. A., *Pastoraal-psigologiese Verkenning van die Client-centered Terapie van Carl R. Rogers*, Kampen: Kok, 1960.

Stallmann, M., *Christentum und Schule*, Stuttgart: Schwab, 1958.

——, *Die biblische Geschichte im Unterricht*, Göttingen: Vandenhoeck & Ruprecht, 1963.

Stock, H., *Studien zur Auslegung der synoptischen Evangelien im Unterricht*, Gütersloh: Bertelsmann Verlag, 1963³.

Stückelberger, A., *Die religiöse Entwicklung des Schulkindes*, Zürich: Gotthelf-Verlag, 1958.

Taylor, M. J., ed., *Religious Education: A Comprehensive Survey*, Nashville: Abingdon Press, 1960.

Ten Have, P., *Een Methode van Bijbelse Catechese*, Groningen: Wolters, 1946.

——, *Een Vreugdevol Bedrijf*, 's-Gravenhage: Boekencentrum, 1947.

Ter Haar, B., *Catechetische Moeilijkheden en Mogelijkheden*, Assen: Van Gorcum & Co., 1934.

The Covenant Life Curriculum: Basic Paper, Foundation Papers, Curriculum Principles Papers, Presbyterian Church in the U.S., Reformed Church in America, Moravian Church in America, 1960.

The Objectives of Christian Education; The Functional Objectives for Christian Education, The Boards of Parish Education of The American Evangelical Lutheran Church, The Augustana Lutheran Church, The Suomi Synod, The United Lutheran Church in America, 1957, 1959.

Thun, T., *Die Religion des Kindes*, Stuttgart: Ernst Klett-Verlag, 1959.

——, *Die religiöse Entscheidung der Jugend*, Stuttgart: Ernst Klett Verlag, 1963.

Tigchelaar, J., *Godsdienstige Opvoeding in de Puberteit*, Groningen, Wolters 1955².

Uhsadel, W., *Evangelische Erziehungs- und Unterrichtslehre*, Heidelberg: Quelle & Meyer, 1961².

Van Coster, M., *Structuren van de Catechese*, Brugge: Desdie de Brouwer, 1965.

Van de Hulst, W. G., *Het Vertellen*, Nijkerk: Callenbach, n.d.

Van Dijk-Balk, E., *Het Spelen van Bijbelverhalen met Ouderen*, Amsterdam: Hervormde Jeugdraad, n.d.

Van Doornik, N. G. M., *Jeugd tussen God en Chaos*, 's-Gravenhage: Martinus Nijhoff, 1948.

Van Haaren, J., *Jeugdzielzorg*, Hilversum: Paul Brand, 1963.

———, *Jonge Mensen Geloven....*, 's-Gravenhage: Uitgeversmaatschappij Pax, 1963.

Van Nie, J. A., *De Catechisatie*, Amsterdam: Uitgeversmaatschappij Holland, n.d.

Van Niftrik, G. C., *Het Geloof der Kinderjaren*, Den Haag: Voorhoeve, n.d.

———, *Het Kind in het Licht van Christus*, Amsterdam: Uitgave Ned. Zondaschool Vereeniging, n.d.

Van Riessen, H., Firet, J., *Een Dozijn is meer dan Twaalf*, Kampen: Kok, 1960.

Van Riessen, H., *Kerk en Jeugdwerk*, Kampen, Kok, 1960.

Van 't Veer, M. B., *Catechese en Catechetische Stof bij Calvijn*, Kampen: Kok, 1942.

Van Uchelen, A. C., *Het Heilig Onderricht der Kerk*, Amsterdam: 1945.

Waterink, J., *Aan Moeders Hand tot Jezus*, Wageningen: Zomer & Keunings n.d.[15].

———, *Met Moeder bij Jezus*, Wageningen: Zomer & Keunings, n.d.

Wildschut, A. A., *De Godsdienstige Beïnvloeding van de Massajeugd*, Amsterdam: Hervormde Jeugdraad, n.d.

Witt, K., *Konfirmandenunterricht*, Göttingen: Vandenhoeck & Ruprecht, 1959[2].

Wölber, H. O., *Religion ohne Entscheidung*. Göttingen: Vandenhoeck & Ruprecht, 1960[2].

Wolf, S., *Evangelische Unterweisung und Innere Schulreform*, München: Chr. Kaiser Verlag, 1959.

Zimmerman, W., Hafa, H., *Zur Erneuerung der christlichen Unterweisung*, Berlin: Luth. Verlaghaus, 1957.

INDEX

Angermeyer, H., 17, 18, 20, 23.
Baily, A. E., 12.
Baldermann, I., 21, 22, 23.
Barth, K., 12, 16, 40, 65.
Beets, N., 92.
Berkhof, H., 11, 48.
Berkouwer, G. C., 39, 44, 45, 101.
Biesterveld, P., 30-32, 35, 38, 87.
Brunner, E., 26, 65.
Bultmann, R., 22, 49.
Burkert, A., 17, 20.
Bijkerk, R. J., 12.
Bijlsma, R., 56.
Clark, W. H., 8.
Cox, H., 65.
De Boer, T. H., 91.
De Graaf, S. G., 57, 58, 61, 85, 86.
De Graaff, A. H., 152.
Dengerink, J. D., 82, 84, 114.
De Wit, J., 126.
Diem, H., 17, 20, 39, 40.
Dijk, K., 56.
Dirkzwager, A., 33.
Dooyeweerd, H., 26, 28, 33, 36, 38, 39, 40-54, 62, 65, 69, 70, 71-75, 78, 79-82, 86, 87, 93, 95, 101, 108-110, 114, 116, 117, 118, 123, 124, 130, 132, 133, 134, 135, 136, 138, 139, 143.
Dross, R., 16, 17, 20, 21, 22.
Duvenage, S. C. W., 23, 63, 64, 67.
Ebeling, G., 22.
Erikson, E. H., 128.
Fernhout, J. G., 38, 101.
Frör, K., 17, 20.
Fuchs, E., 22.
Gilhuis, C., 38.
Grässmann, F., 17, 20, 21, 23, 24.
Haan, G., 6.
Hepp, V., 103.
Heyns, W., 31.
Hiltner, S., 39, 40.
Hoekstra, T., 31, 32.
Hummel, G., 21.
Hugen, M., 33, 34, 35, 38.
Jaarsma, C., 12, 94, 104-107, 110.
Jentsch, W., 37.

Johnson, P. E., 8.
Käsemann, E., 49, 50.
Kittel, H., 17.
Klapwijk, J., 124.
Kohnstamm, Ph., 27.
Kromminga, C. G., 38, 40, 76.
Kuiper, F. H., 155.
Kuitert, H. M., 51, 52, 71.
Kuyper, A., 28-30, 32, 33, 35, 36, 38, 39, 43, 47, 58, 66-71, 77, 87, 94, 103, 109, 156.
Kuypers, A., 11, 92, 104.
Langeveld, M. J., 90, 91, 110, 111, 120, 121, 130, 135.
Litt, Th., 110.
Lotz, P. H., 3.
Mekkes, J. P. A., 41, 45, 46, 85, 114, 116, 117, 132.
Müller, E., 17, 39.
Olthuis, J. H., 65.
Otto, G., 21, 23.
Perquin, N., 89, 93.
Popma, K. J., 43, 47, 76, 78, 87, 97, 108, 113, 132.
Price, J. M., 3.
Ridderbos, H. N., 44, 58, 59, 63, 68, 71, 80, 140, 142, 147.
Runner, H. E., 77.
Schaller, K., 23.
Schilder, K., 41.
Schippers, R., 49, 50, 69, 70, 71, 87.
Schrotenboer, P. G., 44.
Sillevis Smitt, P. A. E., 31.
Smedes, L. B., 57, 58, 63.
Smit, W. A. 153.
Spier, J. M., 41, 54, 70, 87, 157.
Stellingwerff, J., 39, 41.
Stock, H., 21, 23.
Strasser, S., 92, 110.
Taylor, M. J., 3, 8.
Ten Have, P., 2, 24, 25, 26, 27, 28, 37.
Thomas, J., 153, 155.
Tillich, P. 65.
Troost, A., 45, 62, 64, 65, 71, 78, 79, 82, 84, 86, 114, 116, 118, 140.
Van Buren, P., 65.
Van den Berg, J. H., 126.

Van der Plas, D., 56.
Van der Horst, L., 104.
Van Hulst, J. W., 122.
Van Klinken, L., 94.
Van Peursen, C. A., 43, 114.
Van Riessen, H., 45, 65, 82, 114.
Van Ruler, A. A., 77.
Van Teylingen, E. G., 39, 47, 48, 51, 96, 134.
Velema, W. H., 39.
Vollenhoven, D. H. Th., 32, 33, 36, 39, 41, 66, 75, 79, 82, 114, 143.
Von Meyenfeldt, F. H., 39, 41, 44, 47, 48, 60, 61, 64, 86.
Waterink, J., 32, 33, 34, 36, 38, 89, 91, 93, 94-105, 107, 111, 113, 120, 125, 134, 136, 157.
Wijngaarden, H. R., 101, 104, 105.
Woltjer, J., 103.
Ziegler, J. H., 8, 12.
Zuidema, S. U., 22, 40, 48.